HARVARD HISTORICAL STUDIES

Published under the direction
of the Department of History
from the income of the
Henry Warren Torrey Fund

Volume XCVI

The Diehards

Aristocratic Society and Politics in Edwardian England

Gregory D. Phillips

Harvard University Press
Cambridge, Massachusetts
and London, England
1979

Copyright © 1979 by the President and Fellows of Harvard College
All rights reserved
Printed in the United States of America

Library of Congress Cataloging in Publication Data

Phillips, Gregory D   1949-
  The diehards.
  (Harvard historical studies; 96)
  Bibliography: p.
  Includes index.
  1. Great Britain—Politics and government—1901-1936.
2. England—Nobility.   3. England—Social life and
customs—19th century.   4. England—Social life and
customs—20th century.   5. Great Britain. Parliament.
House of Lords.   I. Title.   II. Series.
DA570.P48   301.44'92'0941   78-16949
ISBN 0-674-20555-3

To my parents

Acknowledgments

This study grew out of two wishes—to learn as much as possible about a way of life that has largely vanished and to avoid condemning myself to research in the basements of anonymous office blocks. The diehards offered a way to approach the broader subjects of the British aristocracy and the relationship between economic status, social influence and political power. My belief that work in this area would be a congenial and rewarding experience was amply justified.

I would particularly like to thank for their kindness and hospitality the Earl Bathurst, the Earl of Scarbrough, Lord Clifford of Chudleigh, and Lord Kilmaine. For permission to cite and consult manuscripts and for help in my research I am grateful to the following: the Earl Cathcart; Lord Dynevor; the Earl of Egremont; the Earl Fitzwilliam and the Agent to his Malton Estate; the Earl of Harewood; the Marquess of Londonderry; Mrs. D. Maxse; the Earl of Morley; the Countess of Onslow; the Earl of Plymouth; the Marquess of Salisbury and Mr. R. H. Harcourt Williams, Archivist, Hatfield House; Lord Saltoun; Viscount Scarsdale; Lord Willoughby de Broke; the Trustees of the Bedford Estates and Mrs. M. P. G. Draper, Archivist, the Bedford Office; the Administrative Trustees of the Chevening Estate; the Trustees of the late Lord Mowbray, Stourton and Segrave; the Executors of the Estate of Lord Stanmore; the Bedford Record Office; the Bodleian Library; the British Library; the Carmarthen Record Office; the Devon Record Office; the Durham Record Office; the Gloucestershire Record Office; the Guildford Muniment Room, the Surrey Record Office; the House of Lords Record Office; the India Office Library and Records; the Kent County Council; the Lambeth Palace Library; the National Army Museum, Chelsea; the National Maritime Museum; the National Trust; the North Yorkshire County Record Office; the Public Record Office; the Sheepscar Library (Leeds City Council); the Shakespeare Birthplace Trust; the Suffolk Record Office; the West Sussex Record Office; and the University of Birmingham. I want to thank Mrs. Sidney Gleason, editor of the Harvard Historical Studies, for her valuable help in the preparation of the manuscript. Mrs. Hilda L. Cooper of Lafayette College has labored over the typescript of the bibliography and appendix. I should note that a modified version of the first chapter appeared as an article in the Spring 1977 issue of the *Journal of British Studies.*

I am particularly grateful to Professor John L. Clive of Harvard University, who directed the doctoral dissertation out of which this book has developed. Both he and Professor Franklin L. Ford provided valuable advice and encouragement. My special thanks to Professor Peter Stansky of Stanford University. His example, assistance and enthusiasm have been invaluable.

My family has provided me with support, encouragement and editorial advice. My wife, Marcela Gonzales Phillips, has cheerfully typed several versions of the manuscript and has helped enormously with revisions and with editing. Any errors which this study contains are, of course, my own.

Contents

1. The Diehards and the Myth of the "Backwoodsmen"   1
2. The "Lordliest Life on Earth"   13
3. Land and Wealth   25
4. Local Government and Politics   57
5. The Armed Forces and the Empire   82
6. The Politics of Unionist Discontent   111
7. The Diehards and the Tory Revolt   142
   Appendix: List of Diehards   161
   Notes   175
   Bibliography   203
   Index   223

Tables

1.1 Attendance at House of Lords, 1902, 1906, 1909   4

1.2. Attendance of diehards and other peers, 1902, 1904, 1906, 1908 (by percentage)   5

1.3. Proportion of interventions by debate, 1911-1913 (by percentage)   6

2.1. Creation dates   21

3.1. Size of estates (in 1882) of peers eligible to sit in the 1911 House of Lords   27

3.2. Geographical distribution in 1882 of lands owned by members of the 1911 House of Lords (by percentage)   29

3.3. Location and acreage of lands owned in 1882 by members
     of the 1911 House of Lords   30

3.4. Marriage patterns   37

4.1. Local office-holding   61

5.1. Birth dates (by decades)   84

5.2. Secondary education of members of the 1911 House of
     Lords   85

5.3. University education of members of the 1911 House of
     Lords   86

5.4. Military service of members of the 1911 House of Lords in
     the regular army or navy   87

5.5. Military service of members of the 1911 House of Lords in
     reserve organizations   88

The Diehards

1 / The Diehards and the Myth of the "Backwoodsmen"

In January 1906 the Liberal party, along with its Labour and Irish Nationalist allies, won an overwhelming victory at the polls and ended two decades of virtually unbroken Tory dominance. The enormous Unionist majority in the House of Lords, politically quiescent during the years of Tory governments, quickly awoke to the dangers presented by a Liberal government determined to carry out social and political reforms. Under the leadership of the Marquess of Lansdowne, the Unionist peers vetoed or maimed much cherished Liberal legislation during the next few years. In 1909 the increasingly frustrated Liberals faced the necessity of raising enough money to meet the expenses of their social legislation and of the armed forces, especially the growing navy. To meet these financial demands David Lloyd George, the fiery chancellor of the Exchequer, presented a budget which included innovative taxes on land. This "People's Budget" so enraged the Unionist peers that they vetoed it in November 1909, thus breaking a long-established tradition of financial control by the House of Commons. After two general elections in 1910, the Liberal ministers, intent on ending the partisan interference of the House of Lords, introduced the Parliament Bill. This measure abolished the power of the peers over money bills and allowed them to delay other legislation for only three years. The Liberal government secured the promise of the new king, George V, to create enough Liberal peers, perhaps five hundred, to swamp the Upper Chamber if the Unionists rejected the Parliament Bill in 1911. Faced with this threat, the Unionist leadership capitulated in July and counselled abstention on the issue. One hundred twelve temporal peers and two bishops rejected this advice. These diehards, or "ditchers" —men who were willing to "die in the last ditch" rather than surrender —defied the Unionist leaders and voted against the Parliament Bill, which was carried on August 10, 1911, by a combination of Liberals and of Unionists who feared a flood of new peers more than the immediate end to the prerogatives of their House.

There has never been a satisfactory explanation of the diehard peers' decision to revolt against their own political leadership and to launch unusually violent attacks on their political opponents. Several hundred Unionist peers regarded the Parliament Bill with loathing. One hundred twelve temporal peers chose to defy all odds and make a futile stand against it. This study of the activities and attitudes of the diehard peers during the three decades prior to 1911 seeks to understand the motivation for their actions on the Parliament Bill; to examine the landed aristocracy of the late nineteenth and early twentieth centuries, to which the vast majority of the diehards belonged; and to determine in what ways the diehards were unique and in what ways representative of the landed aristocracy as a whole.

The last years of the nineteenth century were a period of challenge for the British aristocracy and thus for the diehards. Agricultural depression beginning in the mid-1870s reduced many landed incomes. The extension of the franchise and the democratization of local government, previously dominated by appointed magistrates, threatened the hold of the upper class on political power. The diehards were increasingly concerned about competition with other nations for markets and colonies. They were serious and active participants in the political, military and imperial controversies of their day.

This view of the diehards has not been the one generally accepted. From the time of their campaign against the Parliament Bill in 1911, the diehards have been characterized both by their contemporaries and by later historians as "backwoodsmen." The term had originated in the rhetoric of an embattled Liberal government intent on discrediting an overwhelmingly Unionist House of Lords during the struggle over the "People's Budget" of 1909. The description applied to those peers, supposedly the great majority of the Upper Chamber, who spent most of their time on their country estates, cared little for national politics and participated less, almost never appeared in the House of Lords, but could be relied upon to come to Westminster in vast numbers to veto seriously threatening Liberal legislation. The identification of the diehards with that section of the peerage least experienced in politics stems in part from a case of mistaken identity. Contemporary commentators and later historians assumed that the smaller group of 112 peers who voted against the Parliament Bill mostly belonged to the more obscure section of the much larger group of 350 Unionist lords, labelled "backwoodsmen," who had rejected Lloyd George's budget of 1909.*

---

*The size of the "backwoods" contingent in the 1909 division has been much exaggerated. Of the 350 peers in the Unionist lobby, 107 qualified as "backwoodsmen" if the standard of less than

The long-accepted identification of the diehards with the stereo-typed "backwoodsmen" who had nothing to do with national politics is incorrect.[1] The majority of the diehards were both politically aware and actively involved in national affairs. Analysis of House of Lords' attendance lists, interventions in debate, committee membership, office-holding, and participation in political organizations reveals that the diehards, as a group, were more active politically than the rest of the House of Lords, taken as a group. This is not to say that all die-hards were prominent politicians, but rather that a stereotype does not coincide with the facts. Lord St. Levan, one of their number, sug-gested something close to this when he remarked in 1911, during the debate on House of Lords reform, that "it is as a Back Bench Peer, which I think your Lordships will agree is a totally different thing from a 'backwoodsman,' that I venture to address your Lordships to-night."[2] An examination of diehard participation in the various forms of na-tional political activity reinforces the distinction.

The diehards are often said to have attended the House of Lords only rarely, if at all. Indeed, it has been suggested that many peers could hardly find their way to the Upper Chamber during the consti-tutional crisis. In 1910 the House of Lords, under the direction of the Earl of Onslow, compiled a return which recorded, in addition to other statistics, the number of temporal peers who did not attend or attended less than ten times during the sessions of 1901, 1906, and 1909, when 566, 590, and 589 peers respectively were eligible. The re-sults, which did not include peers of royal blood, but did include those who were minors, away due to official or military duties or because of illness, revealed that 58 percent in 1902, 37 percent in 1906, and 42 percent in 1909 attended less than ten times or not at all.[3]

If this yardstick of non-attendance or attendance of less than ten times is accepted as a major test of "backwoodsman" status, as it seems to have been by contemporaries, the diehards should have included a very large proportion of peers who rarely attended the House of Lords. In fact, this was not the case. In each of the three years included in the House of Lords return, the percentage of diehards who were in the category of "backwoodsmen," as defined by these statistics, was

---

ten attendances per session is accepted as the test of backwoods status, as it was in a contemporary document. Only 22 of these "backwoodsmen" later became diehards. Ninety-four diehard peers took part in the budget division.

smaller than the percentage either of the whole House or of the whole House minus the diehards. For 1902 the difference is not dramatic, but for 1906 and 1909 it is striking[4] (see Table 1.1).

The question of attendance can also be examined by investigating the average number of times each peer came to the House of Lords over a span of years. This method avoids the somewhat artificial standard of ten attendances adopted by the Onslow report. If the diehards were primarily "backwoodsmen," their average annual attendance should have been less or at least no greater than that of the rest of the peerage. To determine whether this was the case, the average annual attendance figures for 1902, 1904, 1906, and 1908 of the 112 diehard peers were compared to those of a random sample of 100 peers chosen from the rest of the membership of the Lords who were eligible to vote on the Parliament Bill. This analysis also reveals that the characterization of the majority of the diehards as "backwoodsmen" is false. On average for the peers studied, the diehard peers attended sessions of the House of Lords nearly half again as often as did members of the sample group (see Table 1.2). The percentage of the diehards attending thirty or more times each year was twice as large as that of the sample. While approximately 40 percent of each group was present eleven to thirty days per annum, only one-third of the diehard peers, as opposed to almost one-half of the sample, attended fewer than eleven sessions. The majority of the diehards were hardly inactive

Table 1.1.   Attendance at House of Lords, 1902, 1906, 1909

	Number of peers eligible to attend	Number attending less than ten times or never
Session 1902		
Diehards	77	43 (56%)
Other peers	489	286 (59%)
Session 1906		
Diehards	95	24 (25%)
Other peers	495	194 (39%)
Session 1909		
Diehards	106	24 (23%)
Other peers	483	225 (47%)

Source: L.J., 1902, 1906, 1909.

Table 1.2.   Attendance of diehards and other peers, 1902, 1904, 1906, 1908 (by percentage)

	Diehards	Other peers: sample of 100
More than 30 times per annum	27%	13%
11-30 times per annum	40%	37%
10 times or less per annum	33%	48%

Sources: Attendance lists in *L.J.*, 1902, 1904, 1906, 1908.

Note: The four years examined were deliberately chosen to remove the possibility of bias in the statistics in favor of the "backwoodsmen" supposedly drawn to Westminster only by the constitutional crisis beginning in 1909. The random sample includes every fourth peer listed in *Burke's Peerage* for 1911, excluding diehards and those ineligible to sit. If a peer selected for the study was unavoidably absent or ineligible to sit in any or all of the years included in the study, those years were excluded from the computation of his personal average annual attendance. Ten of the peers in the random sample were unable to sit during the years studied. The mean was calculated by totalling the personal average annual attendance figures for the peers in the sample group and in the diehard group and then dividing each total by the number of peers in each group eligible to sit during at least one of the four years studied. Percentage figures have been rounded off to the nearest whole digit.

members of the Upper Chamber. The assertion that many peers took the oath only to vote against the Parliament Bill obviously could not apply to any important extent to the diehards.[5] By 1908, ninety-seven of them had appeared in the House of Lords, and most of those diehards who took the oath between 1909 and 1911 had just become eligible to sit.* Lord Dynevor, an M.P. until he succeeded to the title in June 1911, had the distinction of being the only man to vote against the Parliament Bill in both Houses of Parliament.[6]

Attendance in the House of Lords is not necessarily the only standard for determining whether the diehards were primarily "backwoodsmen." Participation in the chamber's functions and in its debates are other legitimate criteria. Work on committees for the consideration of public and private bills composed much of the routine activity of the House. Actually, the proportion of the diehards who participated on these committees was greater than that of the rest of the peerage taken

*Amherst, Brabourne, Dynevor, Hardwicke and Monkswell succeeded to their titles between 1909 and 1911. Farnham, Kilmaine and Sempill became representative peers during these years. Merthyr was granted a title in 1911.

as a whole. For comparative purposes, the hundred-member sample group and the diehards were studied for their work on committees during 1902, 1904, 1906, and 1908. Of the 102 diehards eligible to sit in the House by 1908, thirty (49 percent) took part in committee work, as compared with twenty (39 percent) of the sample group.[7] P. A. Bromhead examined the participation in debate by the peerage during the period 1911-1913 and calculated that 37 percent of the total membership of the House of Lords spoke during these years. The diehards included a slightly higher proportion (45 percent) of speakers than did the house as a whole. Bromhead subdivided the peerage into three groups according to frequency of intervention in debate: "active" (25 or more interventions in three years); "moderately active" (10-24 interventions); and "occasional" (1-9 interventions).[8] While the diehard group contained a somewhat smaller proportion of "active" peers than did the whole House of Lords, a larger percentage of the diehards than of the total membership was included in Bromhead's other categories (see Table 1.3).[9] By this standard, as well as by the others examined above, the image of the diehards as largely "backwoodsmen" obviously does not provide a true picture of their participation in government.

In fact, diehards figured prominently in most spheres of national politics and public affairs in late Victorian and Edwardian Britain. They filled public offices, both at home and abroad, were active in party organizations, and held important posts with pressure groups. Some contributed frequently to periodicals, especially to the *Nine-*

Table 1.3.   Proportion of interventions in debate, 1911-1913

	Diehards	Total membership of House of Lords
"Active" members		
(25 or more interventions)	4% (4 peers)	7% (38 peers)
"Moderately active"		
(10-24 interventions)	12% (13 peers)	7% (33 peers)
"Occasional"		
(1-9 interventions)	29% (33 peers)	23% (128 peers)
Total number of speakers	45% (50 peers)	37% (199 peers)

Sources: 5 *Hansard* (Lords); Bromhead, *House of Lords,* pp. 34-35, 37.
Note: Percentages, rounded off to the nearest whole digit, are figured on the basis of 112 diehards. For the total membership of the House of Lords, Bromhead says only that for 1911-1913 it numbered "about 600."

teenth Century and the *National Review*. Several were leading spokesmen in the Lords, chiefly on those specialized topics in which they had become expert; for instance, Lord Raglan commented during the debate on the Reconstitution of the Lords Bill in May 1911: "My Lords, I do not know whether I am a 'backwoodsman' or not; the *Daily Mail* says I am. But although I have been for a long time a member of your Lordships' House I think this is the very first occasion on which I have ventured to address your Lordships on other than a military subject."[10] Similarly, merchant seamen found their chief spokesman in Lord Muskerry, an Irish yachting enthusiast.[11]

Some of the most important figures in British public affairs were diehards. Among the 131 peers who were privy councillors in 1912, twenty were diehards.* Several former cabinet members were found in their ranks, including the Earl of Halsbury, three times Lord Chancellor; the Earl of Selborne, first lord of the Admiralty, 1900-1905; Viscount Llandaff, home secretary as Henry Matthews, 1886-1892; the fourth Marquess of Salisbury, Lord Privy Seal and president of the Board of Trade, 1903-1905; the Duke of Norfolk, postmaster-general, 1895-1900; and the Earl of Plymouth, first commissioner of works, 1902-1905.

Lords Milner and Roberts, two of the great imperial heroes of the era, were diehards. Milner had been high commissioner for South Africa from 1897 to 1905, when he was succeeded by Lord Selborne, who served until 1910. Roberts was the former commander-in-chief of the army and victor in South Africa. Other men in the diehard lobby had occupied important positions in the empire. Lord Ampthill, who began his career as private secretary to Joseph Chamberlain at the Colonial Office, had served as governor of Madras and acting viceroy of India. Lord Stanmore, a political and personal friend of Gladstone until the Home Rule crisis of 1893, filled at various times the governorships of New Brunswick, Trinidad, Mauritius, Fiji, New Zealand, and Ceylon, and had been the first high commissioner for the western Pacific. Lord Northcote, while carrying out the duties of governor of Bombay and then of Governor-General of Australia, corresponded regularly with Joseph Chamberlain and advised him on the colonists'

*Diehard privy councillors included Atkinson, Clarendon, Clonbrock, Coventry, Erne, Fingall, Halsbury, Llandaff, Marlborough, Meath, Milner, Norfolk, Northumberland, Plymouth, Ranfurly, Rayleigh, Roberts, Salisbury, Selborne, and Waldegrave (*Debrett's Peerage, Baronetage, Knightage and Companionage* [London, 1912], pp. 973-974).

reaction to the tariff reform campaign. Lord Ranfurly served as governor of New Zealand from 1897 to 1904. Though sometimes relatively
isolated from Westminster politics, these peers remained actively concerned with them. As Northcote wrote to Selborne from Bombay in
1902, "Of course home politics are what I am really most interested
in."[12]

Diehards had held other appointive and parliamentary offices below
cabinet rank. Both Unionist whips in the House of Lords in 1911, the
Earl Waldegrave (since 1896 chief whip) and Viscount Churchill,
voted with the diehards. The Earl of Portsmouth served as under-secretary for War in the Liberal government from 1905 to 1908 and as
ecclesiastical commissioner from 1909. Lord Raglan, lieutenant governor of the Isle of Man for nearly two decades after 1902, had been
under-secretary for War from 1900 to 1902. The Duke of Marlborough, paymaster-general from 1899 to 1902, was also under-secretary of state for Colonies, 1903-1905. The Earl of Plymouth worked as
paymaster-general in 1891. Lord Colchester was a charity commissioner in the early 1880s. Viscount Halifax had been an ecclesiastical
commissioner since 1886.

As important members of interest and pressure groups, diehards
occupied positions of influence and became well accustomed to dealing with national political issues and figures. Three important lay
religious leaders were diehard peers and spoke frequently in the Lords
on behalf of their coreligionists on church-related questions. Lord
Halifax led Anglo-Catholics as president of the English Church Union,
1868-1919 and 1927-1934. He ceaselessly promoted reunion of the
Anglican Church with Rome. Joining Halifax in the vote against the
Parliament Bill were the Duke of Norfolk, president of the Catholic
Union of Great Britain and chief lay spokesman for English Catholics,
and the Earl of Denbigh, president of the Catholic Association of England from 1892. In 1889 the prime minister, the third Marquess of
Salisbury, "directed that all matters relating to questions connected
with the Holy See should pass through . . . [Norfolk's] hands."[13]

Britain's military preparedness interested many of the diehards, several of whom were officers of the military pressure groups which became important in the years before the Great War. Lord Raglan
served as first president of the National Service League and was succeeded in that post by Lord Roberts. "Bobs" became the league's chief
spokesman and symbol. The Duke of Somerset presided over the Navy

League for several years, and Lord Willoughby de Broke headed the Imperial Maritime League. Both organizations strenuously advocated increased naval power. Lord Meath worked to strengthen the empire through the foundation of the annual Empire Day and the promotion of innumerable schemes for the improvement of physical fitness. During the Boer War, Lord Lovat founded and led Lovat's Scouts, a volunteer force, and subsequently became a close ally of Lord Roberts in the fight for national service.[14] The Duke of Bedford led the unsuccessful attack in the House of Lords on Haldane's army reforms, especially his plan to eliminate the militia.

As young men, many of the future diehards secured their entrance into national politics in traditional aristocratic ways. Before coming to the House of Lords, twenty-three of them had been members of the House of Commons.[15] Erne and Selborne had both been whips in the Lower House. Early in their careers, several diehard peers had served as private secretaries to important government officials, posts which customarily went to youthful aristocrats.[16] Lord Dynevor later recalled that "Lord George Hamilton, secretary of state for India, in 1899, most kindly made me his Assistant Private Secretary (unpaid), which I know was wholly due to my mother-in-law, Lady Jersey."[17] Diehards had held positions at court, some of which involved more than ceremonial duties.[18] As lords-in-waiting, for instance, Lords Denbigh and Ranfurly acted as spokesmen for the Salisbury government's Irish policy in the House of Lords.

Irish peers played a prominent, though not overwhelming, part in the diehard ranks. Of the twenty-eight representative peers of Ireland, seven voted against the Parliament Bill.[19] According to John Bateman, sixteen of the diehards held nearly all their land in Ireland.[20] Several of these Irish diehards played a leading role in the opposition to Home Rule before 1911 in Ireland and at Westminster. They were not simply ordinary "backwoods" landowners. In fact, they shared a common characteristic of being relatively well known, for various reasons, in political circles. For some of the Irish diehards, notoriety and participation in public affairs derived not from their love of politics but from their position as important Irish landlords in an age of agrarian unrest. Two of the most publicized land battles occurred on diehard estates. Lord DeFreyne's Roscommon estate was the scene in 1902 of a test struggle between the United Irish League and landlord organizations, and was the subject of angry debate in the House of Commons.[21]

One of the primary targets of the first Plan of Campaign effort in 1886, Lord Clanricarde became the symbol of the evils of absentee landlordism. Financially independent of his Irish rents, he successfully frustrated all efforts to ease the situation on his Galway estate until the Land Court forced him to sell in 1915.[22]

Irish diehards took an important part in political action against Home Rule. From the mid-1880s, the Earl of Erne worked as Imperial Orange Grand Master and, with Lord Ranfurly, as a member of the Ulster Unionist party's standing committee. Ranfurly founded and became the president of the Ulster Loyalist Anti-Repeal Union in 1886. Viscount Templetown, chairman of this body, organized the Unionist Clubs Council in 1893, in order to coordinate the activities of groups opposed to Home Rule. Another diehard, Lord Ashtown, operated a fund for the free circulation of a monthly anti-Home Rule publication, *Grievances from Ireland*. In 1907 he was the target of a well-publicized bombing attempt at his shooting lodge. Irish M.P.'s charged that this supposed outrage was actually an effort by Ashtown to discredit Irish nationalism. Lord Clonbrock, a prominent parliamentary spokesman for Irish landlords, worked as chairman of the Irish Landowners' Convention. Lord Meath, more conciliatory than most Irish landlords, helped to arrange the land conference in November 1902 between the landlords and the Irish Parliamentary party at which the seeds of the 1903 land purchase plan were sown. Perhaps it is indicative of the large role of the diehards in the political opposition to Home Rule that, when Lord Ranfurly expressed the wish in 1893 to unite Protestant and Catholic Ulster Unionists, it was to Lord Fingall, a Catholic diehard active in the Irish Unionist Alliance, that he proposed to turn. Fingall was related to Horace Plunkett and made heavy financial contributions to the latter's schemes for Irish agricultural "Cooperation." The diehards also included a former Irish attorney general, Lord Atkinson, who had, prior to that appointment, represented the *Times* in 1888 before the Parnell Commission. Two diehards, Lords Farnham and Leitrim, were actively involved in gunrunning for the Ulster Volunteers during the post-1911 Irish crisis— Leitrim, whose great uncle had been murdered in an agrarian outrage in 1878, even providing a ship and his chauffeur for this purpose.[23]

For many years diehard peers had been active and prominent figures in Unionist party organizations. Diehard ranks included five past presidents of Conservative party conferences (the Dukes of Norfolk and

Northumberland, the Earls of Scarbrough and Plymouth, and Lord Colchester). For five years Northumberland had been chairman of the National Union of Conservative Associations, a post which Plymouth and Northcote each filled for one year. Other diehards were frequent participants at conferences and in their local organizations, although it is difficult to determine the extent of their contribution to party activities. Diehards were well represented at the National Union Conference in 1911. On the central council were Norfolk and Plymouth (trustees), Clifford, Salisbury, Churchill, and Londesborough. Presidents of provincial divisions included Westminster (Cheshire), Digby (Dorset), Winchester (Hampshire), Salisbury (Hertfordshire), Churchill (Leicestershire), Norfolk (Midland and Yorkshire), Leconfield (Sussex), Dynevor (West Wales), and Plymouth (Glamorgan). Lord Selborne was chairman of the Hampshire Division, and twenty-four diehards, including those named above, were vice-presidents of the National Union.[24] Earlier in his career, Lord Selborne, as Viscount Wolmer, had been instrumental in forming the Liberal Unionist Association as its chief whip. In 1903-1904 Selborne helped Joseph Chamberlain capture the Liberal Unionist Association for the tariff-reformers and had become one of the vice-presidents in 1904. The diehard Earl Fitzwilliam later joined him on the executive board of the association as its treasurer.[25]

Thus the diehards included a relatively high proportion of politically active peers. In comparison with the remainder of the House of Lords, they were as a group frequent attenders and speakers. Prominent parliamentarians and imperialists, leading members of pressure groups, and lesser officeholders marched together into the diehard lobby. The "backwoodsmen" did not swell the diehard ranks to an unusually large extent. In fact, the peerage as a whole contained a much larger proportion of "backwoodsmen" than did the diehard segment of it. On the issue of the Parliament Bill of 1911, most of the "backwoodsmen" stayed as far from Westminster as usual. Most of the diehards were found not among those who habitually ignored national affairs, but among those peers, prominent or not, who were accustomed to thinking about and dealing with important and controversial issues.[26]

The diehards saw politics as a normal aspect of aristocratic life which could be indulged in more or less fully, as individual circumstances allowed. The careful conduct of the business of a landed estate did not preclude a serious interest in national affairs. Of course, not all diehards were landowners. Men such as Lords Roberts, Milner, and Halsbury might be described as professionals in public service. They had a wider knowledge of political affairs and more frequent contact with national leaders than did most of the diehard peers. However, the gap between them and the landed aristocrats among the diehards should not be exaggerated. Many noblemen not commonly thought of as politicians shared the attitudes and interests, if not the experience, of those who were.

The fate of the landed proprietor was not the only question in the minds of the diehards when they decided to make a dramatic stand in August 1911. The motivation for their opposition to the Parliament Bill and their willingness to revolt against the Unionist leadership must also be sought in the other national political issues of the day with which the diehards were particularly concerned. These included the spread of democracy at the local level which threatened the landed aristocrats' traditional base of political power in the regions surrounding their estates. In addition, the entrance of Britain's working-class population into the political arena undermined the position of the upper classes in national affairs. The diehards were unusually active and interested in matters involving the military and the empire. They were uneasy about the maintenance of British power in the face of increasing world competition for markets and colonies, and they did not approve of the defense and imperial policies of either the Liberal government or the Unionist leadership. Frustrated for years over policies on such national issues as tariff reform, the Irish problem, and the quest for "national efficiency," many of the diehard peers had become impatient with the traditional usages of parliamentary politics and alienated from their own party leaders. The historical cliché of the "backwoodsmen" which has obscured considerations of motivation has prevented a fuller understanding of the diehards and their society.

2 / The "Lordliest Life on Earth"

The diehards were an important segment of the aristocratic society of late nineteenth and early twentieth-century England. Contemporary writers ascribed many qualities to the aristocracy, including eccentricity, anti-intellectualism, and a sense of duty; but perhaps the attribute most frequently commented upon was a combination of calmness and assurance. An American observer wrote in 1886 that "the high English almost always possess complete ease of manner . . . as a rule, they are remarkable for repose of bearing." Hilaire Belloc and John Galsworthy noted the "superb ease" and "majestic leisureliness" characteristic of members of the best clubs, while Henry James portrayed a young lord as "ever so habitually assured . . . His right figure was that of life in irreflective joy and at the highest thinkable level of prepared security and unconscious insolence."

The aristocrats themselves were aware of this quality of ease and assurance; the eldest son of the diehard Viscount Churchill spoke of the "careful modesty, good manners, and a kind of aristocratic humbleness, but innate superiority was the underlying assumption." The Earl of Warwick prefaced his memoirs with the remark that, "Looking back, I see that I have been able throughout my life to choose my duties as I chose my pleasures, and that I have always taken those I liked best." Lady Ottoline Morrell, sister of the sixth Duke of Portland, was uncomfortable with the men who came to Welbeck Abbey, partially because the "unquestioning, unimaginative arrogance of it all had a power of impressing itself on me as 'The Thing,' that it was 'the supreme life' and that all other existences were simply insignificant and unimportant." An aura of luxury accompanied this feeling of assurance and freedom. Lord Willoughby de Broke believed that those landed aristocrats who lived in the Edwardian era experienced "the high-water mark of creature comforts . . . Whatever was happening to the Empire, comfort and convenience, and everything that makes for luxury, steadily increased until the outbreak of the War." He noted humorously that Liberal criticism of the good life of the aristocracy was justified to some extent. "In reading a Limehouse speech about ourselves, do not let us forget how Joseph Surface reminded Lady

Teazle that if one is to be the centre of a scandal there is no consolation like having done something to deserve it."[1]

There is no doubt, however, that the aristocracy's sense of ease and assurance and their satisfaction with the material standards of their life was tempered by a perception of social movement or flux. The aristocrats were unsure not of their own natural superiority but of the changing conditions of their society. Lord Willoughby de Broke devoted the first pages of his autobiography to the question of the relative material and psychological comfort of three generations of landed aristocrats, born respectively in 1810, 1840, and 1870. He believed that the man born in 1810 would have been the most comfortable because he would have died before the agricultural depression and "the untoward manifestations of the thing called democracy that were destined to disturb the peace of mind of his son and his grandson, and to react so hideously upon the nation at large."[2]

These worries about social and political changes contributed to the extremely serious attitude which distinguishes in both psychological and behavioral terms the late nineteenth-century aristocracy from that of a century or more earlier described so vividly in the prelude to Lord David Cecil's biography of Lord Melbourne. Cecil pictures the Whig aristocracy of the late eighteenth century as a governing class which formed a society of "splendid naturalness," not spiritual, and notable for gambling, drinking, free speech, and a free sexual life. These noblemen were unafraid to show their feelings, valued eccentricity highly, and lived a life of "earthy exuberance."[3] By the end of the nineteenth century that earthy exuberance seems to have been gravely diminished. It had been largely replaced by a fundamentally serious approach (not always adhered to in practice) which emphasized the dangers of idleness, of irreligion, and of a disregard for social norms. Aware of Liberal criticisms and of threats to their position, aristocrats also stressed the necessity of fulfilling one's duties. Frances, Countess of Warwick, a prominent member of the Marlborough House set, recalled that "outwardly it was a life of idle pleasure . . . This was true only in part, for duty was a big word in those days. We took a personal interest in our tenants . . . we obeyed our parents, respected our elders, and kept our promises, even our marriage vows." Even the Earl of Rosslyn, who lost his family fortune at the racetrack and the casino, learned from his errors and later warned: "Without occupation we are dead, are pawns in the great drama of life, have no special reason for encumbering the earth."[4]

Members of the landed elite were imbued with an earnest desire to do the right thing in all their endeavors. This spirit was inculcated early in life. Lord Eustace Percy, a younger son of the diehard Duke of Northumberland, noted that he grew up in "a disciplined home . . . The motive of the parental strictness of those days, which underlay so essentially free and happy a family life, was usually a shrewder fear of the infectious idleness that haunts a leisured society . . . In those houses, Kipling's 'lordliest life on earth' was far from being 'effortless.' " Lawrence Jones, heir to a Norfolkshire baronetcy, remembered similar experiences in his childhood. His parents were ever watchful for personal failings: "I am sure that the hair-trigger liveliness of our own consciences owed much to our up-bringing."[5]

The emphasis on high moral standards, conscientiousness, and a serious approach to life was also instilled in the young aristocrat by his public school. At Eton, the most popular school of the conservative aristocracy, Edmond Warre stressed a sense of duty and a militantly ethical religiosity during his headmastership from 1884 to 1905. His last sermon to boys leaving Eton pictured for them a life of difficult decisions, fraught with moral dangers: "Shoulder your pack and trudge onwards up the hill of life . . . You have learned the contrast between the short space of human life and the infinite breadth of God's commandment . . . You have learned to distinguish between true and false liberty . . . Our dear Mother Eton is justified of those of her children who have walked by that law: they will have added their names to her long and glorious roll of duty keepers."[6]

The diehard second Earl of Selborne received a steady stream of pedagogical letters while he was at school from his father, a distinguished jurist and lord chancellor. The first earl emphasized independent thinking, religious doctrine, and the fulfillment of God's will in everyday affairs. He constantly stressed the future implications of any action or decision. After hearing that his son had done well in school, Selborne wrote him that this success was "a great proof of God's goodness" and "of what we care for still more, — that our dear Willie is trying conscientiously to do right." In 1880, after Wolmer had matriculated at University College, Oxford, Selborne began a series of twenty-two long letters to his son, dealing explicitly with religion. A prefatory

letter urged him to remember "that the happiness, honour, and usefulness of our lives must depend on two things; first, on our being
masters of ourselves. . . and secondly, in endeavouring to fulfill the
purposes for which we were brought into the world, and placed there
in the particular station to which we are called, with a right sense of
responsibility towards God, and goodwill . . . to men."[7]

Religion was an important factor in the lives of many peers, not least
among the diehards. Twelve diehards were among the forty-four Roman Catholic lords listed by *Debrett's* for 1912. Denbigh's father, a
Roman Catholic, "lived as intense a life of prayer as is compatible with
being 'in the world.' " Lady Monkswell visited Lord Clifford of Chudleigh's seat of Ugbrooke Park, Devon, and was "reminded at every
turn" that the family was Roman Catholic. She found "R.C. almanacs
full of saints I never even heard of," Catholic paintings and busts of
prominent clerics, and a priest who celebrated mass each morning in
the private chapel. Other diehards, such as Viscount Halifax and the
Duke of Newcastle, were prominent High-Churchmen.[8]

Most noblemen did not usually discuss religion directly but frequently alluded to it or used terms associated with it in a way which
suggests that religious forms were deeply ingrained in their conscious-
ness. This was another aspect of the serious approach to their role in
life which characterizes most of the diehard peers and their contemporaries. The seventh Earl Stanhope wrote to his mother shortly after
his father's death in 1905, remarking that the event "had brought
home to us the great lessons of Life & Death & Man's final Destiny,
which alas one is so apt to lose sight of."[9] The Earl of Shrewsbury, one
of the very few diehards whose life had been marked by scandal (he
had eloped at the age of twenty with another man's wife), slowly came
to regard religious observance, self-discipline, and self-examination as
habits which deserved emulation. In 1905 he wrote his sister, Lady
Castlereagh (later Marchioness of Londonderry), to thank her for her
hospitality during the Christmas holidays: "Your chapel & its services,
the way you study all your employments and all that you both do . . . is
an example which stirs one up to try and follow."[10]

The Earl and Countess of Meath were among the most insistent and
active apostles of a responsible way of life. They devoted themselves to
philanthropic and patriotic organizations. Self-sacrifice, piety, and
hard work were their solutions to social problems. Lady Meath wrote
to the *Morning Post* in 1906 deploring the "self-indulgent luxurious"

life of the Edwardian upper classes, and the fact that it was "not the fashion nowadays to teach the young lessons of self-denial, on the contrary the one point insisted upon is that they should have a very good time."[11]

Lord Willoughby de Broke, along with Lord Selborne the real leader of the opposition to the Parliament Bill, had a serious, sensitive side which might have surprised those political opponents who were regularly subjected to the harsh language of his partisan oratory. Lord Rosslyn, who considered Willoughby de Broke one of his "greatest friends," testified that he was "always serious minded . . . He preferred to pose as light-hearted . . . He had the softness of his mother and couldn't bear to pain a human being."[12] Although he had firm political opinions, Willoughby de Broke had doubts about his personal goals. In 1914, he wrote a friend that he was attempting "to arrange my own ideas about myself. And I don't quite know what I do want, beyond the many things that have to be arranged sooner or later with the Higher Power."[13] He was acutely conscious of his duty toward other men and toward a Supreme Being. Addressing an audience at Stratford-upon-Avon at the height of the Ulster controversy in July 1914, Willoughby de Broke stated that men had to act in everything "with a recognition of responsibility towards the Divine Providence," and that "there was no real happiness or peace of mind except that which was based upon the knowledge that they must make the most of their opportunities, strive to do their duty, and make themselves efficient."[14]

The Edwardian aristocracy indulged in published self-revelation to an unprecedented degree. The great flood of memoirs and autobiographies was a reflection of the aristocrats' self-conscious and rather exalted conception of their role in a society which they recognized had experienced great and interesting changes. While some memoirs are more sensitive and penetrating than others, their most notable characteristic is their essential similarity. They relate the same types of experiences: childhood in a great country house, early friendships with governesses and gamekeepers, education at private schools and then at public schools and universities, the first fox-hunt and endless sporting events thereafter, and political and social activities with the same set of people. Most memoirs reveal an intense family pride. The same anecdotes and jokes are told. The writing style is generally relaxed and informal, with Latin tags familiar to every public schoolboy. Very little which might be considered even faintly scandalous is touched upon. Paternalistic conservatism emerges as the usual political philosophy.

The phenomenon of Edwardian memoirs may be a literary extension of the highly public life of the landed aristocracy. All the important events of a peer's life were celebrated publicly. Birth, christening, coming of age, marriage, the arrival at a country seat after a long absence, were marked by dinners, tenants' gatherings, illuminated letters of congratulation from tenants, laborers and townspeople, and dances. The coming-of-age celebrations at Chevening for the seventh Earl Stanhope in 1901 stretched over a week and included communion service at the parish church, presentations from tenants and friends, two balls (one for the servants), lunch for the tenants and neighbors, a dinner for employees, and festivities for the children. When Lord Rayleigh resigned his Cambridge professorship and returned to his country estate of Terling Place, he was greeted with the ringing of church bells, a display of fireworks, and a large crowd at his house.[15] Great occasions were not the only times that the aristocrat and his family were in the public eye. The simple process of moving from place to place was a matter of public display. Willoughby de Broke remarked during the 1920s on "Victorian country life, when ladies and gentlemen drove in their carriages, and could be seen by all the world, instead of whirling through the villages, hidden away in the recesses of a motor-car which might belong to any one or to no one." Max Beerbohm recalled the scene in Piccadilly before the Great War as

a constant procession of the best-built vehicles in the world, drawn by very beautifully-bred and beautifully-groomed and beautifully-harnessed horses, and containing very ornate people. Vehicles of the most diverse kinds . . . And their occupants were very visible and were looking their best. The occupants of those low-roofed machines which are so pitifully blocked nowadays all along Piccadilly may, for aught one knows, be looking their best. But they aren't on view.[16]

Life in the public eye also involved a constant round of local activities and duties. Almost every estate and village or town event was marked by the gracious appearance of the leading landowner and his wife. The American wife of the diehard Duke of Marlborough, Consuelo Vanderbilt, quickly learned the importance of visiting neighbors and tenants, and of appearing at agricultural and horticultural shows, school treats, cricket matches, and women's organizations. She realized that her "dress and appearance were more important than any

words I could utter. The cinema star had not yet eclipsed the duchess."[17]

The public quality of aristocratic life contributed to a prevalent
concern with outward form and propriety. Nowhere was the "star"
quality of the aristocracy so apparent as in the ubiquitous press reports
on London society. Publications as diverse as the Radical Henry La-
bouchere's *Truth* and the ultraconservative *Morning Post* avidly reported the perambulations of the upper classes during the "Season,"
which began in April with court presentations and lasted through
countless balls, race meetings and cricket matches to Cowes yachting
in August. There was also a Dublin season, revolving around the vice-
regal court, from Christmas to St. Patrick's Day. Most of the aristocracy participated to some extent in "Society," and the condition and
changes of that society, and the degree of public attention it attracted,
were important both for their view of themselves and their world, and
for their continued significance in national life. A hostile critic from
their own circle, Arthur Ponsonby, noted that the landed aristocracy
dominated the social world and warned that there could be "no
greater error than to dismiss the fact of their social dominance as neg-
ligible. In some ways social supremacy is a stronger force than the positive and ostensible powers of legislation and administration." Or, as
the Duke of Plaza-Toro states in *The Gondoliers,* "Although I am un-
happily in straitened circumstances at present, my social influence is
something enormous."[18]

Comments about society at the turn of the century focused on the
supposed rapid invasion of new wealth into the highest social circles.
This impression stemmed in part from the especially dramatic alteration in the social milieu of the court which followed the death of
Queen Victoria and the accession of Edward VII. Millionaires such as
Sir Ernest Cassell and Sir Thomas Lipton were close friends of the new
king. The so-called "smart set" became prominent in high society and
attracted more attention, because of its novelty, than did the traditional aristocracy. Jews entered court circles for the first time. George
Russell, a Liberal cousin of the diehard Duke of Bedford, wrote two
articles in the first decade of the twentieth century contrasting "Society
as it is" with "Society as it was" in 1880. He noted a decreased number
of balls, an increased number of country house-parties, a more con-
tinuous, year-round season due to the fact that many landowners
could no longer afford to maintain country estates, a growing love of

titles, and more ostentation: "Here again the rushing flood of ill-gotten gold has overflowed its banks, and polluted the 'crystal river of unreproved enjoyment.' " Lady Dorothy Nevill was particularly vehement about the changes wrought in society by "plutocracy" and preoccupation with money. In 1910 she asserted regretfully that anyone willing to spend enough money could enter the highest social circles: "Birth to-day is of small account, whilst wealth wields an unquestioned sway."[19]

There was some truth to these reports of the entrance of new wealth into high society. The first Salisbury ministry of 1885-1886 marked the point when significant numbers of persons with commercial and industrial connections began to enter the peerage.[20] This change, however, was neither sudden nor complete (see Table 2.1). Alterations in the social composition of London society had occurred gradually over many years and were not unique to the late Victorian and Edwardian era. Even Lady Dorothy Nevill, who complained about the transformation of society to accommodate the "vulgar rich" in Edwardian times, recognized that this phenomenon had occurred as early as the 1850s. The Earl of Meath recalled in his memoirs that millionaires had invaded formerly exclusive society in the early 1860s and that efforts had been made by members of the old aristocracy to "erect new barriers within the stronghold against those who had broken through the outer defences." He and a group of friends met in Grosvenor Street in 1864 to plan their resistance:

> I found that it was proposed to form an "Imperium in imperio" — a sort of inner circle of the defenders of the social citadel, composed of the young of both sexes . . . This inner circle was to be called "The Jolly Dogs." It was to be more or less a secret society . . . the members of both sexes undertook to give preference . . . to all who could prove their membership of this club.[21]

Fashionable society in the Edwardian period was too large to have had a uniform experience. Boundaries between different social groups were far from rigid, especially for those members of the titled aristocracy who wished to partake of several varieties of social life. In August 1910, Lord Selborne stayed for a time with members of the "smart set" at Crag Hall, near Macclesfield. Except for one couple, it was "exclusively a party of wives without husbands & husbands without wives, most characteristic of the set." Selborne confessed that, although he liked individuals among the group, "the atmosphere of the set has a

Table 2.1. Creation dates

	Diehards		Other peers	
	Number	% of 112	Number	% of 479
1886-1911	11	9.8	129	26.9
1851-1885	15	13.4	67	13.9
1801-1850	11	9.8	100	20.9
1751-1800	25	22.3	68	14.2
1701-1750	9	8.0	36	7.5
1700 and pre-1700	41	36.6	79	16.5

Sources: Burke's, Debrett's, Complete Peerage.
Note: Creation date for the purpose of this table refers to the date of title currently used in 1911. Thus the table is somewhat skewed toward the more recent dates.

decidedly nasty taste to me." Later in August, after travelling north to Scotland and a new group of people, this time of the more traditional landed circles, he wrote with relief to his wife that he "like[d] this lot immensely better than the smarties."[22]

The diehards and other members of the landed aristocracy were still able to find congenial social circles and were by no means compelled to ignore totally those which included new wealth and power. Titled aristocrats possessed great social prestige. Their symbolic importance in society perhaps even grew at the same time that their economic predominance was matched and then overtaken by newer wealth. George Russell noted a "growing love of titles. In the old days people thought a great deal, perhaps too much of Family . . . No one dreamed of babbling about 'peers' as a separate order of creation, still less of enumerating the peers to whom they were related."[23] The presence of an aristocrat at a ball or house-party lent immediate prestige to the affair, unless he was notably disreputable. The diehards, the vast majority of whom were from older aristocratic families, mixed in their familiar, comfortable social circles and often also, if they chose, in the faster circles of the new reign.[24]

The public character of aristocratic life was also apparent in the counties, where there was only one important social circle rather than, as in London, a variety of different groups and styles of life. For the region around a country seat, "there was but one set of people, one pack of hounds, one everything."[25] Although county society underwent changes after the onset of the agricultural depression and the arrival of new wealth, the landed aristocracy remained at its head. County amusements, such as balls, fox-hunting, point-to-point races, and visits by neighboring landowners, remained the activities to which the traditional elite had been long accustomed.[26] While some of the old county families, especially among the less wealthy gentry, may have slowly fallen away under the pressure of diminishing rents, new names appeared and the traditional round of activities continued.

New members of county society were subjected to a thorough scrutiny before they were accepted. Local society had always been ready to admit new members after a suitable lapse of time: men of wealth who had adapted to the country gentleman's way of life. The change in the late nineteenth century was that newcomers were admitted more rapidly to county social circles, if not to the most intimate aristocratic circle. The criteria of acceptance remained substantially the same over time: a degree of wealth, the desire to participate in traditional county activities, and the recognition of certain public standards of propriety. Yet these criteria were flexible, and fixed caste barriers did not exist. Beatrice Webb noted a common qualification for admission to both county and London society: "the possession of some form of power over other people."[27] Besides the power of wealth, there was the social power given by a title, by an old family name and landownership, by local political and governmental activity, and by the hereditary guardianship of county and sporting traditions. Landed aristocrats were not displaced from their leadership of county society. Rather, they were joined by the parvenus, relative newcomers who adopted as far as possible, sometimes on a more lavish scale, the old social forms and habits.

The fox was one of the principal reasons for the continued social predominance of the landed aristocracy. Fox-hunting, as often as six days per week, was the chief preoccupation, after estate management, of a large number of the peers, and provided them with a strong social bond of common interest and experience.[28] Landed society was extremely serious about both the technical and social aspects of the sport. It "was a devout faith . . . To deny the cult of the horse and the ceremonial slaying of the fox was a . . . serious matter."[29] Landowners regarded fox-hunting as a vital element in local society and as an instrument with which to bind together the governing classes and to ease tensions between different classes in rural Britain. Lord Willoughby de Broke even characterized a hunt he had recently witnessed as a "fine exhibition of the Tory Party."[30] Aspiring members of county society recognized the social importance of fox-hunting for the gentry and aristocracy and participated in the sport as much as possible. Landed aristocrats occupied a position of power and influence as leaders of this crucial social activity.

The master of fox hounds, labelled by one authority the "Sporting Prime Minister" of the county, occupied a social position second only to the lord lieutenant, and it was not unknown for one individual to hold both posts.[31] His responsibilities were great, extending beyond sport to those of local governor, "being ultimately responsible for the welfare of the country over which he presides."[32] The masters of fox hounds, like other aristocrats who were important figures in their local hunting communities, had much experience in handling controversial issues. Occasionally the desire to protect the farmers in the hunt country from serious disturbances resulted in friction between the masters of different packs. A serious dispute between the Beaufort and the Vale of White Horse hunts of Gloucestershire arose in March 1897, when the two masters quarrelled over whether the Beaufort had gone too far into the V. W. H. country while hunting. Bathurst, master of the V. W. H., and others accused Randolph Wemyss, temporary master of the Beaufort, of damaging farmers' land. Bathurst protested that the farmers were "frantic at your having unnecessarily dragged the whole of your enormous field . . . right across the deep grass fields for about two miles . . . That sort of thing . . . does the greatest harm to fox hunting." When Wemyss refused to apologize, Bathurst informed him that "it is my duty to protect the farmers in my hunt, and see that the usual rules of foxhunting between the two counties are observed."[33]

Fox-hunting dominated the lives of many peers for a good part of each year. The diehards' passionate devotion to the sport was reflected in their frequent use of hunting metaphors in political debates. None of the diehards was a more enthusiastic fox-hunter than Lord Willoughby de Broke. When reproached in August 1911 for his opposition to Lansdowne, the Unionist leader, in the division on the Parliament Bill, Willoughby de Broke reportedly said, " 'As master of hounds, I don't like killing a fox without my huntsmen, but it is better than losing my hounds.' "[34] He took great joy in fox-hunting and the sport was never far from his mind:

To take out a pack of Foxhounds, every one of whom you have bred and entered yourself; to know that they will conform to the movements of your horse . . . and will, in fact, do everything that you ask them to do . . . to take them to a covert and hear them open on their Fox; to see them fling themselves of their own accord to recover the scent when they have overrun it; to help them out of one or two difficulties . . . and to enjoy all this from the back of a thoroughbred horse, are things that make life worth living. [35]

Landed aristocrats of the late nineteenth and early twentieth centuries approached the problems of everyday life and politics in a serious manner, conscious of the possible repercussions of their decisions on themselves and on those around them. They were accustomed to responsibility, whether on their estates, in local affairs, in the realm of rural sports, or in national political life. They were also accustomed to command, to social deference, and to the ability to choose their options and make their own decisions within the bounds of social convention.

For the most part the diehards were not professional politicians. They earned their soubriquet because they were the temporal peers, 112 in number, who voted against the Parliament Bill. They fought both the Liberal government and their own Unionist leadership. There were many other Unionist noblemen who were vehemently opposed to the Parliament Bill, yet these peers chose to follow the advice of their leadership and abstain from the division. Was there anything in the experience and attitudes of the diehard peers to separate them as a group from the remainder of the enormous Unionist majority in the House of Lords? In order to understand the reasons for the action of the diehard peers, it is necessary to study these noblemen in relation to the various conditions and issues which confronted the entire aristocracy during the three decades prior to the battle over the Parliament Bill. An examination of the social and political background of this action reveals a great deal about both the group of men who opposed the Parliament Bill and the society in which they lived and for which they fought.

3 / Land and Wealth

More than 100 of the 112 diehard peers were proprietors of large landed estates. The British landed aristocracy faced a severe economic crisis in the agricultural depression of the late nineteenth and early twentieth centuries. Though many landowners had diversified their sources of income, the sharp decline in the price of agricultural products and the rent of agricultural land which began in the mid-1870s affected them all. The depression led to profound changes in the structure of rural society, altering its economic basis and reducing the social and political influence of the aristocracy.

Contemporary comment about the economic condition of the aristocracy during the years of agricultural depression must be approached with caution. The *Quarterly Review* noted in 1906 that landlords and farmers alike had a vested interest in convincing both the government and each other that times were extremely bad:

> Landlords are prone to declare that they do not know where to look for a sovereign, though they probably had a shrewd suspicion where they can find nineteen shillings and sixpence; farmers, on the other hand, aver that they are losing capital with both hands and such rapidity that we are fairly staggered by their continued self-sacrifice. But such statements are well understood on both sides . . . the professional pessimism of both classes must be liberally discounted. [1]

Statements about the economic disasters supposedly suffered by the diehards and their fellow landowners must be carefully investigated before they are accepted as accurate. On the other hand, the ability to continue to live in grand style was not always positive proof of financial solvency. Appearances could deceive, as Anthony Trollope observed in *The Duke's Children*. The struggling Earl Grex and his daughter "dined out together, — of course with all the luxury that wealth can give. There was a well-appointed carriage to take them backwards and forwards to the next square, such as an earl should have. She was splendidly dressed, as became an earl's daughter, and he was brilliant with some star . . . No one looking at them could have imagined that such a father could have told such a daughter that she must marry herself out of the way, because as an unmarried girl she was a burden." [2]

The diehard Earl of Rosslyn was an aristocrat in straitened circumstances who continued to enjoy a cosmopolitan existence and the association of the rich and famous. In 1897, due in part to compulsive gambling, he found himself in bankruptcy court. The Duke of Sutherland, his brother-in-law, granted him an allowance and Rosslyn took up the life of an actor for several years. He remained in the midst of the best society at the most fashionable places. The Prince of Wales and the Marquis de Soveral were his friends and dinner companions, and he maintained close political contacts.[3] Nor was Rosslyn's an isolated case. Other men with like connections did not necessarily rusticate when serious financial problems occurred.

In order to obtain a broad picture of the economic status of the diehards, it is necessary to look beyond the few estate papers which have survived. Bateman's *Great Landowners of Great Britain and Ireland* is an additional source of information, compiled, with many corrections, from the so-called "Modern Domesday Book," the parliamentary *Return of Owners of Land* of the 1870s. Bateman provided information as to how much land was held by each peer, where it was located, and its value in rents in the 1870s. This material allows a rough comparison to be made between the diehards and the rest of the House of Lords on the basis of income from agricultural rents. Because of the sales of land and the general erosion of rents during the years studied, the comparison must be an approximation. For all that, it can answer the question whether, on the basis of landholding statistics, one should assume that the diehards as a group experienced the agricultural depression in significantly different ways than the other landowners of the Upper Chamber.

An unusually high proportion of the diehards were landowners as compared to the rest of the membership of the Lords in 1911. Bateman's list included approximately 88 percent of the future diehards and 76 percent of the remainder of the 1911 peerage. The distribution of estates in terms of size was not dramatically different, although diehard estates tended to be slightly larger. According to a nineteenth-century authority, "a man who only wanted all the conveniences and comforts that London and the country could give, could have them for £10,000 a year."[4] Comparing the diehards with the rest of the landowning portion of the 1911 House of Lords reveals that the difference was not profound in terms of income derived from agricultural land.

Of the one hundred diehards included by Bateman, 63 percent held land worth at least £10,000 per year in agricultural rents. Approximately 72 percent of other landowning peers had such incomes from their land in the 1870s. Thus before the onslaught of the agricultural depression, landowners from both sections of the peerage were fairly equal with respect to their relative numbers, size of landed estates and agricultural income from those estates (see Table 3.1).

The depression may have had a greater effect on the diehards' incomes from agricultural rents. It began in the 1870s with increased importation of foreign foodstuffs due to improvements in transport, and was aggravated by a series of bad seasons for domestic farmers and by rising costs. Cheap foreign grain drove down the price of grain on the protected domestic market. The effects of the depression, however, were not uniformly severe throughout the United Kingdom. The price of meat, livestock, and dairy produce did not fall as drastically as did that of grain. In fact, the fall in the price of cereals actually aided livestock producers because it reduced the price of feed and also meant that the consumer, able to spend less on bread, could turn to more meat and dairy products.[5]

Table 3.1.   Size of estates of peers eligible to sit in the 1911 House of Lords

	Diehards		Other peers	
	Number	Percent	Number	Percent
To 2,000 acres	3	2.7	22	4.5
To 5,000 acres	16	14.3	43	8.7
To 10,000 acres	18	16.1	65	13.2
To 15,000 acres	13	11.6	58	11.8
To 25,000 acres	18	16.1	64	13.0
To 50,000 acres	21	18.8	67	13.6
To 100,000 acres	6	5.4	30	6.1
Over 100,000 acres	5	4.5	24	4.9
Not listed by Bateman	12	10.7	119	24.2
Total	112	100.0	492	100.0

Source: John Bateman, *Great Landowners of Great Britain and Ireland,* 4th ed. (London, 1883).

Note: In 1882, when Bateman's calculations were made, only twenty-three of the diehard peers of 1911 had succeeded to their estates. This applies likewise to Table 3.2 and 3.3.

Any comparison of agricultural incomes based on landholding must take into account the fact that arable farming and dairy and meat production tended to concentrate in separate geographical areas. While the pattern was far from rigid, arable farming generally predominated in the south and east of England, and pasture in the north and west.[6] This division was reflected in rents. The eastern and southeastern counties of Scotland, areas of high arable farming, were almost as hard hit as the worst regions of England. In Wales there were few permanent reductions of rent, except in the arable farming areas of the north.[7] The estates of the diehard peers were concentrated to an unusual degree in England, which contained nearly 50 percent of their holdings, as compared with 34 percent for the rest of the House. While nearly 30 percent of diehard land was in Ireland, compared to 20 percent for the other peers, only about 22 percent was in Scotland and Wales, compared to approximately 49 percent of the land for the rest of the peerage.

The diehards owned approximately 25 percent of all the land held in England by members of the 1911 House of Lords. If England is divided into eleven regions, following Henry Pelling's method in *Social Geography of British Elections,* in only five of these regions did the diehards hold proportionately more land than did the other peers. While two of these regions (the South-East and Central areas of England) were badly hurt by the agricultural depression, three (Devon and Cornwall, Yorkshire, and North England) were among the most prosperous. Only about 10 percent of all diehard land in the United Kingdom (20 percent of their English land) was in the hard-hit South-East and Central regions, while over 20 percent (42 percent of their English land) was in Devon and Cornwall, Yorkshire, and North England (see Tables 3.2 and 3.3).

An investigation of the "Celtic fringe" also reveals no significant evidence of unusual problems for the diehards in terms of agricultural rents. In the most severely depressed regions of Scotland, the South-East and the North-East, the diehards owned just 5 and 4 percent, respectively, of land held by the peerage. In Wales, where they owned 21.5 percent of the land held by members of the Lords, a study of the three principal areas shows that in Mid-Wales very little land was in diehard hands, while in South and North Wales diehards owned about 26 percent of the land. Finally, in Ireland where they owned about 23

Table 3.2. Geographical distribution in 1882 of lands owned by members of the 1911 House of Lords (by percentage)

	All members of the House of Lords	Diehards	Other peers
England	33.5	48.6	30.5
Wales	3.4	4.3	3.2
Scotland	41.2	17.6	46.0
Ireland	21.8	29.5	20.3
	99.9%	100.0	100.0

Sources: Pelling, *Social Geography;* Bateman, *Great Landowners.*

percent of the land held by the peerage, the diehards owned 14 and 40 percent of the land in Munster and Connaught respectively, the two areas of Ireland most seriously affected by the agricultural depression and the struggle over rents. As a group the diehards were not isolated from the experience of other aristocrats. If they did endure a diminished income from their agricultural properties, they did so in good company and to the same degree as did the other landed members of the 1911 House of Lords.

Detailed information on agricultural rents and incomes which has survived for some of the diehards generally confirms the impression that they were quite typical in their experience of the agricultural depression, with respect to reduced rents and increased costs. It also suggests that there was much diversity among the individual estates and that generalizations about the disastrous effects of the depression were not uniformly applicable. While rents on the Earl of Coventry's Worcester estate were reduced from the mid-1870s by an average of approximately 30 percent on arable land and 10 percent on pasture, on Lord Stanhope's Derbyshire lands the rental actually increased between 1880 and 1911 from £3,731 per annum to £4,298.40. Yet on the Marquess of Bristol's Suffolk property, gross rental was reduced between 1879 and 1894 by 50 percent; his smaller Lincolnshire estate also suffered losses, the net income from rents having declined 47 percent. In contrast, Lord Mowbray's Allerton Park, Yorkshire, estate rental books tell a story of relative stability. In 1871 his rent for the full year was £4,826. By 1911, after several years of difficulty, it had declined only 10 percent, to £4,324. The rental for Lord Leconfield's

Table 3.3. Location and proportional acreage of lands owned in 1882 by members of the 1911 House of Lords

	Diehards	Other 1911 peers
England		
South-East (Kent, Essex, Sussex, Surrey, Middlesex, Hertford)	151,628 (28.6%)	377,836 (71.4%)
East Anglia (Cambridge, Norfolk, Suffolk)	72,640 (22.0%)	258,481 (78.0%)
Central (Bedfordshire, Berkshire, Buckinghamshire, Huntingdonshire, Oxfordshire)	95,167 (32.0%)	202,307 (68.0%)
Wessex (Dorset, Hampshire, Wiltshire)	70,240 (15.0%)	388,659 (85.0%)
Bristol (Gloucestershire, Somerset)	29,020 (11.7%)	218,745 (88.3%)
Devon and Cornwall (Cornwall, Devon)	104,250 (39.7%)	158,168 (60.3%)
West Midland (Hereford, Shropshire, Warwickshire, Worcestershire, Staffordshire)	114,081 (20.7%)	436,290 (79.3%)
East Midland (Northamptonshire, Leicestershire, Nottinghamshire, Lincolnshire, Rutland, Derbyshire)	109,606 (13.6%)	698,961 (86.4%)
Lancastria (Lancashire, Cheshire)	72,943 (23.2%)	241,719 (76.8%)
Yorkshire (North, East and West Ridings of Yorkshire)	187,375 (31.6%)	405,814 (68.4%)
North England (Cumberland, Durham, Northumberland, Westmoreland)	219,131 (36.9%)	375,410 (63.1%)
Wales		
South Wales (Monmouth, Glamorgan, Carmarthen, Pembroke)	57,899 (25.6%)	168,332 (74.4%)
North Wales (Anglesey, Carnarvon, Denbigh, Flint)	39,909 (26.6%)	109,892 (73.4%)
Mid-Wales (Brecon, Cardigan, Merioneth, Montgomery, Radnor)	11,492 (8.6%)	121,743 (91.4%)
Scotland		
Northern Highlands and Islands (Orkney, Shetland, Caithness, Sutherland, Inverness, Ross)	221,205 (10.5%)	1,894,496 (89.5%)
South East Scotland (Peebles, Selkirk, Roxburgh, Berwick, East Lothian, Midlothian, West Lothian, Stirling, Clackmannan, Kinross, Fife)	36,730 (5.0%)	668,734 (95.0%)

Table 3.3   (cont.).

	Diehards	Other 1911 peers
North East Scotland (Nairn, Elgin, Banff, Aberdeen, Kincardine, Angus, Perth)	74,484 (4.0%)	1,768,181 (96.0%)
South West Scotland (Argyll, Bute, Dumbarton, Ayrshire, Wigtown, Kirkcudbright, Dumfries, Lanark, Renfrew)	111,896 (8.0%)	1,353,818 (92.0%)
Ireland		
Connaught (Galway, Leitrim, Mayo, Roscommon, Sligo)	218,285 (40.5%)	319,975 (59.5%)
Leinster (Carlow, Dublin, Kildare, Kilkenny, King's Co., Longford, Louth, Meath, Queen's Co., Westmeath, Wexford, Wicklow)	225,955 (25.3%)	666,495 (74.7%)
Munster (Clare, Cork, Kerry, Limerick, Tipperary, Waterford)	123,444 (14.0%)	760,656 (86.0%)
Ulster (Antrim, Armagh, Cavan, Donegal, Down, Fermanagh, Londonderry, Tyrone, Monaghan)	176,630 (19.0%)	755,135 (81.0%)

Sources: Pelling, *Social Geography;* county names as listed in Bateman, *Great Landowners.*

Petworth, Sussex, estate actually improved in the early years of the twentieth century.[8]

Essex has been identified as the most depressed English county of all.[9] Lord Rayleigh, with 8,632 acres, was by far the most important diehard landowner in this county. By 1878 his tenants had fallen in arrears, and land began to revert to the landlord's hands as the tenants gradually fell away. Between 1882 and 1893, income from the Terling estate plunged from £9,212 to £3,091. However, this did not mean financial ruin for Lord Rayleigh. Under the direction of his brother and agent, Edward Strutt, the estate turned to dairy farming and entered the London milk market, using the name "Lord Rayleigh's Dairies," in the late 1890s. Acreage in hand continued to increase to about 6,000 in 1914 and profits rose from an average of £2,352 for the

ten-year period 1887-1896, to an average of £6,364 for the next eighteen years, and in the last two years before the Great War, Rayleigh's
profits were over £9,000 per annum. As his successor wrote, after
1899, "Rayleigh was not further troubled by financial difficulties."[10]

It is difficult to gauge the effect of declining rents on the landowner
in this period. The catastrophic results pictured in contemporary
books and in royal commission reports were not always mirrored in the
correspondence of agents. It is also important to note that most of the
diehards did not control their estates throughout the agricultural depression and that many of them were accustomed to somewhat reduced incomes by 1911.

It had become apparent to most observers by the late nineteenth
century that unless the landowner had a source of income apart from
his agricultural estate, his financial situation, if not as disastrous as
often suggested, would be more precarious than earlier in the century.
Anthony Trollope observed as early as 1874:

> If a moderate estate in land be left to a man now, there arises the question whether
> he is not damaged unless an income also be left to him wherewith to keep up the estate.
> Land is a luxury, and of all luxuries is the most costly. Now the Carburys never had
> anything but land. Suffolk had not been made rich and great either by coal or iron.
> No great town had sprung up on the confines of the Carbury property. No eldest son
> had gone into trade or risen high in a profession so as to add to the Carbury wealth. No
> great heiress had been married. [11]

He identified most of the major sources of wealth other than agricultural income (except for market rights): minerals, urban and town
land, business and investment, and marriage. The possession of any or
all of these would frequently enable a landowner to surmount his estate
difficulties without meeting disaster.

Minerals, chiefly coal and iron, were the source of enormous profits
to landowners in this period, especially in South Wales, the north of
England, and certain parts of the Midlands and of Scotland. Income
was derived from royalties and from wayleaves (charges on the trans-
portation of coal).[12] Several of the diehards were among the greatest
mineral proprietors in the United Kingdom, and other diehards possessed smaller but profitable holdings. Three of the great coal proprietors of South Wales, the Marquess of Bute, Lord Dynevor, and
Lord Plymouth, were diehards. Bute had the largest mineral workings

in South Wales on his Glamorganshire estate, from which he received about £25,000 each year after taxes. He also had collieries in Durham and on his Ayrshire estate.[13]

The diehard Duke of Northumberland received large mineral revenues from his property in Northumberland. Testifying in 1919 before the Coal Industry Commission, the eighth duke, whose social and political views were those of his diehard father, stated that his annual average income from coal royalties from 1913 to 1919 was £55,391, and had been even greater before the higher wartime taxation. The Liberal Sir Leo Chiozza Money put a series of hostile questions to him, including whether he did not believe that it was wrong for one man to own the giant quantities of coal which his mines produced. Northumberland replied firmly, "No, I think it is an excellent thing in every way."[14]

The Duke of Norfolk and Earl Fitzwilliam owned the two largest mineral properties in the West Riding of Yorkshire. Lord Fitzwilliam's Wentworth Woodhouse estate, the largest in the West Riding, in 1899-1900 yielded over £145,000 gross, two-thirds of which (nearly £98,000) was produced by coal and iron-ore mines. His total income during the same period, from estates and investments in Ireland, Yorkshire, and the East Midlands, was over £280,000 gross, or £148,319 net.[15] Lord Mowbray, Lord Scarbrough, and the Duke of Leeds also received mineral incomes from Yorkshire properties. In 1880 royalties due Mowbray from the Rothwell Haigh collieries equalled over £8,000, but by 1910 they had declined to £4,500 because, as mining engineers explained, "a lessened demand for Coal, and the declining output of Way-leave Coal, consequent on the gradual exhaustion of Coal, is responsible for the reduced production."[16] Lord Scarbrough's mineral revenues increased during the early years of the twentieth century and helped extricate him from financial difficulties. During the 1870s coal near the Sandbeck Park estate had produced over £10,300. When the diehard tenth earl succeeded in 1884, however, outlays for several large dowries and bad times for agriculture had reduced the prosperity of the estate. Lord Scarbrough let Sandbeck Park for twelve years. His fortune was restored by marriage to a wealthy widow in 1899 and, more importantly, by the discovery of new coal on his estate in 1908.[17]

The Earls of Abingdon and Crawford profited from coal properties in Lancashire. The diehard Lord Crawford, called by the *Times* "one of the most accomplished members of the peerage," was an astronomer (sometime president of the Royal Astronomical Society), an explorer, a book and stamp collector, and a noted yachtsman.[18] The wealth which made these varied activities possible came primarily from the coal revenues on his Haigh Hall estate in Lancashire. Other diehards who received significant income from mineral properties included the Duke of Newcastle and Lords Shrewsbury, Stanhope, Bathurst, Leconfield, Loudoun, and Rosslyn.[19]

Urban land constituted another important source of non-agricultural income to the landed aristocracy. The diehards included some of the most substantial urban landowners, a group of men at whom much of the fiercest Liberal invective and some of the 1909 budget's provisions were directed. The Dukes of Bedford, Norfolk, and Westminster, the Marquess of Salisbury, and Lords Ebury, Kensington, and Southampton were important London landlords. Westminster owned about three hundred acres in Mayfair and Belgravia. Income from this property alone totalled more than £250,000 per annum by 1899, when the first duke died.[20] Perhaps the next most valuable of all London estates was that of the Dukes of Bedford, which extended over more than a hundred acres of Bloomsbury, Covent Garden, and St. Pancras. The income of this land increased tremendously during the last years of the nineteenth century. By 1898 it earned over £167,000, or approximately three-fifths of Bedford's gross income from all his landed estates. The sixteen-acre Covent Garden property was the most lucrative portion of the estate. Extensive improvements which were carried out between 1890 and 1914 increased the market's rents and receipts from almost £54,000 in 1890, to £103,807 by 1912. The Dukes of Bedford sold some of their London land from time to time, and in 1914, after a long series of negotiations, Sir Joseph Beecham purchased the Covent Garden estate for £2,000,000.[21]

Norfolk was the other ducal London landlord among the diehards. He held a small but valuable property in the Strand. In 1902 and 1903, Lord Kensington sold two portions of his Earl's Court estate at auction for £565,000 and £300,000. The first sale set a record "in the annals of the property market, for on no previous occasion has so large a bid been received for a property in one lot."[22] Lord Southampton held property in the Euston Road and Kentish Town, part of which he sold during 1919-1920 for almost £200,000.[23] Lord Ebury, a relative of the Duke of Westminster, owned a valuable estate in Pimlico.[24]

Diehards also owned urban and town land and market rights outside London. The Marquess of Salisbury possessed extensive properties in Liverpool, and the Duke of Westminster controlled much of Chester. Lord Fitzwilliam, the Duke of Newcastle, and Lord St. Levan held land in Peterborough, Nottingham, and Devonport respectively. The Duke of Norfolk owned 20,000 acres of Sheffield, including the industrial district of Brightside.[25] His market rights there were the most valuable in the United Kingdom apart from those of the Duke of Bedford in Covent Garden, and from them he received about £10,000 per annum. Negotiations for their purchase by the Sheffield Corporation began in early 1898. At first the duke maintained that he preferred to keep the markets, both because he believed they had strong potential for further development and because of emotional ties of long standing between his family and the tenants. Despite this, and after prolonged haggling, the corporation eventually persuaded the duke to part with the market rights and buildings, and about 39,000 square yards of land, for £530,000.[26]

Diehard landholding ranged from large cities to seaside resorts. The Marquess of Bute and Lord Plymouth were heavily involved in urban areas of South Wales. Bute owned much of Cardiff, and the Duke of Northumberland owned large tracts of town property around the Tyne. Bute sold his Aberdare town land in 1919 for £124,000.[27] Fraserburgh, a newly industrialized fishing village belonging to Lord Saltoun and near his Aberdeen country seat, brought him rents of £48,625.[28] Seaside resort towns were owned by the Duke of Northumberland (Alnmouth), the Earl of Scarbrough (Skegness), and the Earl of Radnor (Folkestone). The rental at Folkestone had increased from £838 in 1851 to £8,222 in 1886.[29] Other diehards also owned market rights and town property throughout England, Scotland, and Wales.[30]

Ireland, although not often considered a source of wealth in this period, was also the site of some lucrative urban property for the diehards. Lord Fitzwilliam, whose huge Irish estates were otherwise not very profitable in the late nineteenth century, owned a large estate in Dublin, as did the Earl of Meath. Meath also owned property in the town of Rathmines.[31] The Earl of Limerick owned almost the whole freehold of the city of Limerick, ground rents totalling almost £6,000 per annum, sold in 1907 for over £113,000.[32]

An economically advantageous marriage was another source of income for the landed aristocracy. An heiress might be sought within the nobility and gentry or among families of comparatively new wealth, although there has perhaps been an over-emphasis, beginning with contemporary comments, on the marriage of peers with new wealth (especially Americans). Most of the peerage married their own kind even up to 1914. A comparison of the first marriages of diehards and the rest of the 1911 House of Lords reveals that only a small minority married either commoners without links to the aristocracy or gentry, or foreigners (see Table 3.4). In this respect, the diehards were somewhat more conservative than the other peers. Fully 90 percent of the diehards married daughters of the nobility, gentry, or military officers (or of relations of these groups), while about 80 percent of the rest of the Lords did so. Only 4 percent of both sections of the peerage married Americans.[33]

Most famous of the four diehard matches with Americans was the Duke of Marlborough's marriage to Consuelo Vanderbilt, whose dowry was reputed to be £2,000,000, probably the largest single sum of the kind.[34] The other diehards who married wealthy Americans were Viscount Falkland, Lord Leith of Fyvie, and Lord Bagot. Lord Northcote married the adopted daughter of Lord Mount Stephen, the Canadian railway and banking tycoon. Other diehards stayed in Britain to pursue their quest for financial assistance through marriage. Both Lord Abingdon and Lord Clifford of Chudleigh married heiresses of the extremely wealthy coal-mining Towneley family of Lancashire. The Earl of Portsmouth married a Quaker heiress, Lord Bathurst married the daughter of the proprietor of the *Morning Post,* and Lord Leitrim married a daughter of a director of the Bank of England.[35]

Many of the diehards married daughters of wealthy members of the landed aristocracy and gentry. For example, the Marquess of Bristol, when still Frederick W. F. Hervey, married the daughter of George Wythes, who was listed in *Burke's Landed Gentry* but was also a former contractor for public works. This marriage enabled Bristol to do a great deal for an estate which was in serious economic condition.

Table 3.4. Marriage patterns (first marriages only)

	Diehards		Other peers	
	Number	%	Number	%
Nobility or relation of nobility	50	50	193	45.4
Gentry and officers of armed forces (relatives)	40	40	151	35.5
Commoners	5	5	58	13.6
Americans	4	4	17	4.0
Other foreigners	1	1	6	1.4
Total	100	100	425	99.9

Sources: Burke's, Debrett's, Complete Peerage.

As Lord Wharncliffe, a trustee for the fourth marquess' predecessor wrote in 1896, "it is most fortunate that the large fortune which your fiancée has, and will inherit, renders . . . further encumbrances unnecessary."[36] Lord Meath's wife was the daughter of the eleventh Earl of Lauderdale, a predecessor of the diehard thirteenth earl. Her dowry was essential for the Meaths' social work, as she noted in her diary in 1886: " 'Just eight years since the death of my father . . . It is his economy that has enabled us to do much which otherwise would have been quite an impossibility. I don't think R.'s philanthropic schemes could have prospered so well without it.' "[37]

Not all of the diehards married for money or were so financially successful in their choices. Daisy, Countess of Fingall, was the daughter of a relatively poor Irish landowner, and the earl married her for love when she was seventeen, to the dismay of his tenantry: "Of course it was a disappointment to them all that Fingall had not married some great and rich lady to bring money to the Castle and estate which so badly needed it." To marry wealth was the expectation, however, and Fingall was an exception in marrying someone who could not help him materially to weather the financial storms. To marry for money was accepted as proper; indeed, many believed that the owner of an encumbered estate would be derelict in his duty to his family and tenants if he failed to do so. Lady Fingall's parents told her that she "was not fitted for the position, and that Fingall should marry someone with money . . . that Fingall with his old name and impoverished castle should look for a richer bride."[38]

Aristocratic participation in business and investment in the stock market were the subject of much discussion at the turn of the century and have continued to provoke debate. These methods of securing a non-landed income touched on the social issue of the supposed influx of new wealth into "Society" and readier acceptance on a more-or-less equal plane by the older aristocracy of new men, so long as they were moneyed. However, the question of business and investment concerned the very basis of the landed aristocracy, not merely its social relations. Many contemporaries believed and regretted that the aristocracy was moving toward plutocracy and abandoning its essential character. T. H. S. Escott suggested that the trend was already of long standing by 1880, and that "our territorial nobles, our squires, our rural landlords great and small, have become commercial potentates." The conservative W. H. Mallock described what he saw as the rotting away of the best of the aristocratic values in *The Old Order Changes.* The socialist, Foreman, informs a representative aristocrat: " 'You, the gentlemen of the country, the old landed families . . . you no longer stand on your own proper foundations. You are reduced financially to mere hangers-on of the "bourgeoisie." Your material splendour, which once had a real meaning, is still, no doubt, maintained. But how? . . . You could no longer live like seigneurs if you were not half tradesmen.' " Lord Benthorpe, a character in Hilaire Belloc's novel, *Emmanuel Burden,* is a peer who has lost all his wealth in the agricultural depression and becomes a front man for international financial organizations, while remaining an active politician. The financiers use his name and he continues to live at his ancestral home, on sufferance of his mortgagers, who tightly manage every aspect of his finances.[39] Benthorpe was Belloc's harshly satiric characterization of what he viewed as a totally emasculated aristocracy.

Contemporary observations suggest both the prevalence of aristocratic business activity and a certain nostalgic disapproval of it. In considering the social and economic position of the diehards vis-à-vis their peers, the first question is whether the diehards participated in business as fully as their fellow aristocrats, and whether they began to invest heavily in stocks and bonds in the late nineteenth and early twentieth centuries. The second question, perhaps more fundamental, is, what effect these activities had on the character of the diehards as landed aristocrats. What was the purpose and result of these financial activities? In the mid-1950s Evelyn Waugh wrote, in response to a comment by Nancy Mitford, "You should have said, not that aristocrats can't make money in commerce, but that when they do, they become middle-class."[40]

Business activity on the part of the aristocracy was not new to the late nineteenth century. What was new was the quantity and quality of this activity. Company directorships, especially, were an increasingly popular means of supplementing landed income in the period following the onset of the agricultural depression. The revenue from a directorship required no outlay and, frequently, if the company merely wanted the prestige of a title to grace its board, little effort. Peers had long been directors of railway or canal companies which ran on or near their estates, but during the 1880s and after more aristocrats took posts with companies with which they had no prior connection.[41] By 1896, 167 peers had obtained company directorships, and by 1920 there were 232 titled directors. A large proportion of the diehards participated in this activity. Many diehards had not yet succeeded or were too young to be directors in 1896, but by 1911 forty-one diehards were directors of one or more companies. By 1920, fifty-four had been directors of companies at some time, a proportion which compares favorably in terms of business activity with that of the whole House of Lords.[42]

Diehard company directorships were spread over several types of companies. Most popular were railways (the traditional field for aristocratic directors), assurance or insurance companies, and ventures overseas.[43] Some of this activity was purely nominal, but many diehards were much involved in the companies on whose boards they served. Viscount Churchill was chairman of three railways, including the giant Great Western Railway. His son noted that "business was his real interest . . . My father's associates seemed to have found out that he had ability, and that as well as his name he himself was an asset."[44] Lord Shrewsbury, the chairman of three companies, wrote to his sister in 1903, "Everyone makes their own Role in Life I have taken up the commercial side & I venture to say there is no Landlord or Colliery Proprietor who knows more about his own business in their respective districts than I do — Commercially . . . [I have] my own houses in Paris, Brussels, Turin, Milan & Nice — 2 Factories in London, 4 Retail Houses also & a Company in Manchester — and as in London alone I had sales of Forty Thousand Pounds in July . . . I am not quite idle — ."[45]

Several of the diehards were involved in business on levels other than that of chairman or director. The fifth Lord Sandys was a younger son who had worked for years as a member of the London Stock Exchange, not expecting to inherit the family estates. Lord Leitrim owned hotels, and Viscount Templetown was for several years in business as an electrical engineer.[46] One of the more eccentric characters among the diehards, the eighth Earl of Hardwicke, defended the peers in January 1910 against the charge of being out of touch with problems of business and trade, asserting that many peers had a detailed knowledge of such matters: "he himself was for ten years engaged in mining engineering, and for two of those years he worked as an ordinary miner. That day thirteen years ago he was working night shift on a ten hundred feet level at union wages in a gold mine in Montana, in the United States of America. He was known as 'Charlie,' and as No. 126 to the management."[47]

Although many diehards participated actively in business, only two of them, Merthyr and Leith of Fyvie, were among the rapidly growing number of ennobled industrial magnates. W. T. Lewis, who became Lord Merthyr in 1911, had been the Marquess of Bute's principal estate agent in South Wales for many years. On Merthyr's death in 1914, the *Times,* in an obituary subtitled "A Great Captain of Industry," commented that he had been "more prominently identified than any other man with the development of the South Wales mineral field in collieries, railways, and docks for the last 50 years."[48] Lord Leith's career corresponded more exactly than that of Merthyr's, who had made his fortune in the service of another aristocrat, to the image of the industrial tycoon. Leith came from an old Scottish family and went to good schools. While serving with the Royal Navy in the early 1860s he met and married, in San Francisco, the daughter of a St. Louis businessman. He began his commercial career in his wife's home city and by 1885, through a series of shrewd financial deals, Leith had become president and principal owner of the Joliet Steel Company and an immensely wealthy man. In May 1890 he formed and became president of the Illinois Steel Company, a giant steel trust with authorized capital of over ten million pounds. Leith was one of the principal factors in the formation of the United States Steel Corporation in 1901, and his plan was adopted in the organization of the Federal Steel Company in the late 1890s. He bought Fyvie Castle in 1889 and was raised to the peerage in 1905.[49]

Most of the diehards had no doubts about the value of business for the landed aristocracy. Lord Rayleigh, who operated an extensive milk supply operation on his Essex estate and in London stores, was once asked by a guest at Terling Place, " 'Do you really keep shops, Lord Rayleigh?' 'Yes,' replied . . . Rayleigh . . . and added: 'You would not be here if I didn't.' "[50] Of course, some aristocrats indulged more fully than others in business affairs. For instance, Lord Fingall acquired an option in a gold mine in western Australia which proved worthless. Upon discovering this, he immediately sent a telegram to London to this effect and gave back as much money as he could to investors. This action was regarded as extraordinarily ethical, and he was offered many directorships. He refused them all, however, maintaining, "City honour is not my honour . . . I don't know anything about business."[51] Fingall was an exception, however, in his unwillingness to be identified with business. Most diehards were willing to serve as company directors or in other forms of business as the opportunities offered themselves. They were not much troubled with the fear of becoming bourgeois. Many, like Lord Rayleigh, realized that business activities could help them preserve their ancestral estates.

Investment in stocks and bonds by the diehard peers and their families was probably, as in other areas of economic activity, quite representative of the peerage as a whole. Detailed information on investments is difficult to obtain, and often fragmentary, but it appears that most investment was intended to be a supplementary source of income, a means of bolstering the landed estate, rather than a total replacement of that estate.[52] At least until 1914, the major exceptions to this statement appear to have been landowners with extensive holdings in Ireland, where various land purchase acts were in effect. Though conclusive evidence is not available, investments seem to have been regarded by most of the diehards simply as a viable and rational source of income, not as a blanket rejection of their role in landed society. This is not to deny that these relatively new efforts to diversify the source of aristocratic income could lead to some conflict within the management of an estate. Alfred Michelmore, the Duke of Somerset's Devon estate agent, wrote to the duke after receiving an offer of £400 from the Totnes Town Council as compensation for laying a sewer on Somerset's property: "I was hoping this money might have been available for expenditure on the Estate, but I enclose a letter from Mr. Williams who says it must be invested."[53]

Diehard investment in the money market varied widely in terms of both quantity and variety. Railroad stock, foreign or colonial stocks and bonds, and government bonds were particularly favored. By 1892, the Earl Fitzwilliam had invested almost £213,000. His largest holdings were in railway shares, both foreign and domestic, but he had also invested in breweries, utility companies, in India Stock and Province of Quebec bonds, and in other corporations. A decade later, the diehard Fitzwilliam had inherited stocks and shares valued at over £470,000, including a large quantity of Guaranteed Irish Land Stock and Local Loans Stock, and a greatly reduced amount of railroad investments.[54] Another active investor among the diehards was the Duke of Bedford. At the end of 1898, for example, the balance of stock in the hands of the trustees of the Bedford estate was worth over £116,000. Similar amounts were recorded for the preceding and following few years, but these did not include stocks held by Bedford personally or investments, often very large, made and then sold during the same year. By 1911, the trust stock alone included a large quantity of consols, approximately £110,000 of Midland Railway and Great Northern Railway debenture stock, and between £22,000 and £36,000 of Local Loans Stock. Another relatively active investor in the diehard ranks, Lord Leconfield, received over £3,700 from interest on investments in 1909. From the 1860s on, the third Marquess of Salisbury invested heavily in stocks and bonds.[55]

There is evidence that several other diehards invested in the stock market. In 1913, for example, Lord Plymouth's estate agent forwarded to his London solicitors a check

for £10,000, being the proceeds of sale of £11,000 Barry Railway Deferred Stock which realised £9,359:3:2 . . .

You will recollect that you forwarded me Certificates for £15,000 Barry Railway Deferred Stock, so that there still remains £4,000 of this stock to be disposed of . . .

I presume that the enclosed cheque will enable you to redeem some of the other securities which are at present deposited at the London Union & Smith's Bank.[56]

Lord Dynevor invested approximately £20,300 in Metropolitan Water Stock, New South Wales and Dominion of Canada Stock, and London County Council Stock after sales in late 1911 of part of the Dynevor Castle Estate for over £32,500. He used the remainder to pay off a mortgage and death duties. Lord Sondes and Lord Bathurst were active in the stock market, and Lord Rosslyn had invested £100,000 by 1896, chiefly in South African shares.[57] Investment overseas was especially popular after the Liberal party came to power in 1905. According to Lord Portsmouth, "no astute business man is now [1909] investing his money in enterprises at home."[58] The Duke of Bedford's agent for his Bedfordshire estate reinforced this opinion: "It is the security of their capital which landlords are so frightened about. They prefer the security they get in Canada to the security they get in the British Isles."[59]

The Irish diehards were perhaps more active investors than many of their English and Scottish counterparts, due to the operation of the land purchase acts, which many utilized to a large extent. A common pattern, as in the case of Lord Kilmaine, was to sell land in return for Government Land Bonds and then cash these in to buy stock, especially railway stock. In 1887, Lord Kilmaine purchased shares in four railways and diversified by also buying consols and India Stock. By 1907, after most of his Irish estate had been sold, Kilmaine's holdings in funds and securities had increased to a total of over £50,000, with railway stock alone valued at £22,000. The Earls of Devon also bought large quantities of railway stock, and the diehard Lord Clonbrock left over £50,000 in various stocks and bonds at his death in 1917. The Marquess of Clanricarde was financially independent of his Irish rents and clung to every acre as long as possible. One of the wealthiest diehard investors, he owned over £560,000 worth of shares, yielding nearly £60,000 for the two and one-half years ending in October 1918.[60] An enormous amount of Clanricarde's investment was in railway stock, but he also owned a large variety of other shares, including foreign and city corporation stocks and bonds.

Before World War I, investment offered a means to support landed society in the midst of financial difficulties. There are some indications, however, that the amount of investment increased after 1918. For example, a comparison of two diehard wills with those of their predecessors reveals an expansion of investment in shares and securities of all types. The ninth Earl of Northesk died in 1892 owning £50,000 of shares in the British Linen Company. The diehard tenth earl, at his death in 1921, had raised his total investment in shares to nearly £130,000, including almost £95,000 of War Stock. Similarly, during his lifetime the diehard Lord Saltoun increased his holdings in the stock market over his predecessor's £4,500 or £76,698. Shares in his own incorporated Philorth Estates accounted for a large part of this new total, but the increase in other stocks was still considerable. It included over £14,000 of war and other government bonds, some purchased only the year before Saltoun's death in 1933.[61]

The diehards thus appear to have participated in business and in the stock market in much the same way as did their fellow aristocrats. Some of the diehards mixed socially with leading business figures. Lady Fingall later recorded that "Sir Ernest [Cassel] was always wanting to invest money for me. If I had accepted his offers I should be very rich to-day. But finance, like other gambling, never attracted me at all."[62] Other diehards did not share her hesitation, and even her traditionally minded husband owned over £5,000 of stocks and bonds before his death in 1929.[63]

A crucial question about the diehards during the period before the Parliament Bill crisis is to what extent they remained members of the landed aristocracy. In addition to the complaints regarding aristocratic participation in business and finance was the contemporary accusation that the great landowners were abandoning both their land and their traditional roles in rural society. The motivation for the sales of estates and the extent of such sales were much discussed prior to 1914. An examination of the degree of the diehards' liquidation of their landed property is therefore essential for an understanding of their economic status and activities, and of their social and political functions and attitudes. Grumbling about the unfair treatment of land and the burdens of landownership was heard frequently during the 1880-1914 period. Landed aristocrats and their allies argued that reduced agricultural incomes, higher taxation, the democratization of politics, legislative interference in the landlord-tenant relationship, and the fear of further injurious legislation made the position of the landowner uncongenial and untenable.[64]

The Duke of Bedford wrote the most sustained complaint by any diehard about the burdens of land. He published *A Great Agricultural Estate* in 1897 after delivering it as a speech before the Thorney Unionist Association, an organization composed primarily of people resident on his Cambridge estate. Bedford argued that "while the circumstances of the labourers had improved, taxation . . . had increased; that rent had disappeared, not only from Thorney, but also from the

Bedfordshire and Buckinghamshire estates; and that the possession of these properties . . . now involved upon their owner a heavy annual loss." Blaming politicians for enacting threatening legislation, Bedford stated that "confidence in the sanctity of property in land" had to be restored in order to encourage investment. He remarked that death duties would be enormous at his death and that his expenditures on his estate had not diminished. Agriculture faced disaster, and the democracy "tries to hasten the catastrophe by convincing every landlord, in a concrete and practical manner, that he is foolish to hold land."[65] However, Bedford's Liberal relative, George W. E. Russell, sarcastically reviewed the book in the *Nineteenth Century,* referring to the "Workhouse" as "that bourne to which the Duke of Bedford's possessions seem to be hurrying him"; at Thorney there could be "little doubt that the dewdrop of sensibility twinkled in the eyes of the struggling farmers and laborious ploughmen who listened to this tale of woe."[66]

The Harcourt death duties were perhaps the single most frequently cited burden on the landowner. These inheritance taxes were introduced in 1894 by the Liberal chancellor of the Exchequer, acting on the advice, ironically, of a future diehard, Sir Alfred Milner, chairman of the Board of Inland Revenue. Despite the relatively low rates of the duties, which many landowners were able to meet out of income or insurance policies, they were the subject of great and, to some observers, exaggerated attack.[67] Death duties did not mean disaster for diehard estates before World War I. There is no evidence that major sales of estates directly resulted from the pressure of the duties. Of the 112 diehard peers, 57 succeeded to their estates before the imposition of the Harcourt duties. For them the problem was one of planning for future contingencies. Discussion of methods to avoid or reduce payment began almost at once. The Earl Percy, later the diehard Duke of Northumberland, wrote Salisbury in August 1894: "My father is very anxious to know whether you can give him any points as to the best way of circumventing the Finance Act. Report says that you have been taking some steps yourself in that direction, & any advice you can give us we should be most grateful for."[68] Lord Fitzwilliam's solicitor advised that settlements be made during his lifetime, because no duties could be charged on property handed over before death. Following similar advice by his solicitors, the diehard Lord Dynevor's father surrendered part of his estate to his son in 1905. Other methods of avoiding death duties existed: investment abroad, gifts made as marriage settlements, or gifts of any type within a specified time before death. After the passage of the Companies (Consolidation) Act in 1908, a landed estate could be registered as a private company, thereby reducing the value of dutiable property while allowing the landowner to preserve his control. Lord Saltoun, for example, utilized this tactic.[69]

Even those diehards with the best advice were often unable to avoid payment of the death duties completely, and that payment occasionally required liquidation of property.[70] Lord Sondes sold stock as part of a complicated financial arrangement in order to meet the duties assessed after his father's death. Lord Stanhope told his mother about his arrangements concerning death duties in May 1907: "I have to pay within 21 days the sum of £9485-12-9, & the remaining £13,000 & interest in the way that I desired — in biennial instalments of £1000 each. I am now corresponding with Archer re sale of stock." Two days after this letter, Stanhope wrote that "all outstanding questions with Somerset House are now settled I think & it only remains to Pay, pay, pay."[71] There is no reason, however, to believe that the diehards were affected more severely by death duties than the rest of the peerage. They were as a group at least as prosperous as other aristocrats and were usually able to meet their payments without any great hardship, if not without inconvenience.

The market for agricultural land was poor from the late 1870s until 1910. Although the Settled Land Act of 1882 gave life tenants the power to sell property, demand for land remained weak, due mainly to the belief that agriculture was a bad investment risk, but also because of the supposed decline in the amenities enjoyed by the landowner.[72] The market improved with the revival of agriculture about 1910 and continued to be active until World War I. Observers agreed that even during the best years large estates were difficult to sell and that most sales generally involved sections of larger properties.[73] In most cases, diehard sales outside Ireland were designed to consolidate an estate or to obtain cash for a specific purpose, rather than to liquidate the entire landed property of a family.

Despite the many complaints voiced by diehards about landholding during the years preceding the Parliament Bill, there appears to have been no general effort, except by some Irish landlords, to sell their lands. Certainly they sold no more frequently or in larger quantities than other peers. Between 1895 and 1914 the *Estates Gazette,* which recorded most major sales of estates in England and Wales, mentioned only eighteen diehard sellers. It should be recalled in this context that the diehards owned over 50 percent of their land in England and Wales. During 1911 and 1912 — very active years for the land market, when the *Quarterly Review* noted over 440,000 acres sold at auction in England and Wales — the diehards sold 61,000 acres in those countries.[74] This amount was small compared to the more than 1,300,000 acres which the diehards had held in England and Wales since the mid-1870s.[75] Much of the acreage sold in 1911-1912, as well as in other years, had been owned by diehards who retained a great deal of their land. During the years preceding the Great War, the diehards predominantly remained landed aristocrats, as their families had been before them.

Sales of diehard land were occasionally important to a family's social or economic position. As early as 1888, the Whittlebury, Northamptonshire, estate of the young Lord Southampton was sold for £335,000. This early sale reduced Southampton's property by over two-thirds and left him with less than two thousand acres of agricultural land. However, he continued to live the life of a landed aristocrat in the pre-war years and retained his large London estate until after the war.[76] Lord Churchill also sold the principal portion of his estate. His successor was later unable to offer an explanation for the sale but did state that it was not because of poverty or death duties.[77]

Land sales increased in number after the turn of the century, but never reached massive proportions except on some individual estates. During several different years, in quantities ranging from 1,000 to 7,000 acres, Lord Londesborough sold a total of more than 26,000 acres, almost half his estate. Approximately 12,000 of Lord Portsmouth's 34,500 English acres were sold at different times, nearly half of the sales taking place after the Parliament Bill battle. Willoughby de Broke, whose main property lay in Warwickshire, sold 3,000 acres in Staffordshire and Lincolnshire for £90,000 in 1906. The Duke of Westminster allowed the tenants of his Halkyn Castle, Flintshire, estate to purchase their land in 1911. In the same year, Lords Harlech, Shrewsbury, Sondes, and Abingdon sold various amounts of land, yet each retained extensive acreage. The Dukes of Somerset and Marlborough, the Earl of Malmesbury, and Lord St. Levan all sold small quantities of land before World War I.[78]

The Duke of Bedford has been credited with beginning the increased activity of the land market by selling much of his agricultural property, starting with his Thorney estate in Cambridge, purchased by the tenants in 1909, and continuing with land in Bedfordshire, Devonshire, and Dorset.[79] The duke, in common with other diehards such as the Duke of Westminster and Lord Harlech, lent money to tenants to enable them to buy land, and it was suggested that the interest on these loans might actually have been more profitable than the rents formerly received.[80] In Bedford's case this was true, for income from Thorney estate rents had been marginal for years; after 1909, interest on the tenants' mortgages totalled thousands of pounds annually, with no outlay.[81] Financial opportunities such as this made the sale of land attractive, especially when sales involved outlying property or secondary estates which allowed continued full participation in landed society. The Duke of Bedford's example did in fact inspire some other landowners, including the Earl of Devon.[82]

The Earl Stanhope was another diehard landlord who sold large amounts of land in the years 1910-1912. He expressed fear of Liberal legislation and believed that the sale of land in Devonshire and Derbyshire would be a simple way to meet payment for death duties. Stanhope cited privately to his agent the advantages of investment in shares which would require no annual expenditure, but in his public farewell letter to his Devonshire tenants, he lamented the destruction of the "warm relationship which in the past had existed between landlord and tenant . . . and that the tendency of politics will be to make the holding of large estates in the future a matter of impossibility."[83]

By the early twentieth century Irish land had become a very unattractive investment to most landowners due to political and agrarian unrest. The Land Purchase Acts of 1885 (the Ashbourne Act), 1891, and 1903 enabled landlords to rid themselves of unwanted land with reasonable ease, though not without furious complaints. Sales were especially common after the passage of the Wyndham Act of 1903, which provided for a bonus to landlord vendors. Many diehards, especially those with both British and Irish estates, took advantage of these land purchase acts before they considered the sale of anything like a comparable amount of their other land.[84] Lord Fitzwilliam inherited a huge estate in Wicklow valued at more than a half million pounds in 1902. The estate had already been somewhat diminished in acreage, and the diehard Fitzwilliam recommenced large sales in 1904 at the

same time he was purchasing an English estate from the Duke of Bedford.[85] Lords Devon, Deramore, Stanhope, Leconfield, Portsmouth,
Digby, and Harlech were other diehards with extensive landed property elsewhere in the United Kingdom who sold a great deal of their
Irish land in this period.[86]

Those diehards who considered themselves Irish were sometimes
more reluctant to sell their estates. Several of them sold land prior to
1903, some did so after the Wyndham Act, but others clung to their
estates with extraordinary tenacity. Even those peers who did participate in the land purchase scheme did not always sell their entire estates. The diehards did not play a particularly outstanding role in the
flood of land sales after 1903 and remained landed proprietors as long
as possible. At least outside of Ulster, this commitment often was more
a matter of embittered opposition to Home Rule than of sound economic sense.

Some of the Irish diehards did sell all or most of their Irish land.
The fourth Lord Kilmaine was among the first to take advantage of
the Ashbourne Act and sold the major portion of his entire estate following the passage of the Wyndham Act. Kilmaine told his son in
August 1907 that the sales meant that, in contrast to earlier times,
"Money is very plentiful now, bonuses coming in daily, & you can have
any amount to insure comfortable travelling etc. —"[87] Other diehards
who sold on a large scale in the years 1903-1911 included Lords Wicklow, Ranfurly, Massy, and, to a lesser extent, Fingall and Meath.
Lords Erne, Templetown, and Limerick began to sell portions of their
estates from 1912 to 1914, and Lord DeFreyne, a symbol of landlord
resistance to Home Rule, yielded his Roscommon estate to the Congested Districts Board and sold lands to tenants from 1911.[88] Other
Irish diehards continued to resist sales longer even than the determined DeFreyne. Lord Clanricarde held his huge Galway estate until
forced by the land court to sell in 1915.[89] Lord Clonbrock began to
make small sales in 1915 but retained most of his land until his death
in 1917. Lords Ashtown, Muskerry, Gormanston, and Erne also resisted change in the pre-war era.[90]

The evidence of sales of property suggests that for the most part the
diehards remained proprietors of large landed estates up to the Great
War. Portions of estates were sold quite frequently for investment purposes or to meet financial obligations, but the diehards had not be-

come "plutocrats" by 1914, if that term implies, as it did to their contemporaries, a wholesale abandonment of the land and the traditional
pattern of aristocratic life. In fact some diehards actually purchased
land during this period.[91] Far more common, however, than the purchase of new land was the effort to remain a landed proprietor, to preserve the family estate by any means, even if these involved the sale of a
portion of it.

Several of the estates of the diehard peers, like those of a large part
of the aristocracy, were heavily encumbered by the beginning of the
twentieth century. These encumbrances included mortgages, jointures
for widows, portions for younger sons and daughters, and pensions.
Mortgages were usually the largest debts charged to the estates of the
diehards. Some contemporaries, notably Hilaire Belloc in *Emmanuel
Burden,* regarded this fact as evidence that the landed aristocracy was
in thrall to the moneyed interests, that it had become the creature of
the plutocracy in cases where it was unable to join it through the possession of wealth. In reality mortgages were not always obtained from
financial institutions or from men of new wealth and power. The for-
tunes of other landed aristocrats were frequently the source of the
mortgages for their financially troubled fellows. Mortgages were seen
as a suitable area for investment by the landed aristocrat who possessed
sufficient liquid assets, an alternative to stocks and bonds as a supplementary source of income. The sixth Earl Bathurst sold a house in
1879 and told his estate agent that he was "quite ready to put £6000 in
a good mortgage." Lord Fitzwilliam by 1902 held mortgages on three
different landed estates. The Marquess of Clanricarde invested heavily
in mortgages.[92] Clearly, the dramatic picture of an old-fashioned rural
society hopelessly in debt to a modern plutocracy is too simple. Men
with large landed estates could also be men of business and finance.

With rare exceptions, the diehards who held heavily charged estates
in the early twentieth century had inherited those encumbrances from
their predecessors — not necessarily, of course, from their immediate
predecessors. To a great extent these debts were amassed either before
the onset of the agricultural depression or in its first years, in an age of
prosperity when both landowners and their creditors regarded the
financial future with optimism.[93] When the first Earl of Londesborough succeeded in 1860 to £100,000 in rentals per year and
£2,000,000 in stocks and shares, he "set himself to its dispersal, itself

the work of a life-time, with zest and abandon . . . Yachts, races, coaches, carriages, sport of every kind, especially shooting, speculation and the stage were the chief channels he had found for ridding himself of his earthly burden."[94] His successor sold nearly half of the estate in an effort to restore his finances. The diehard Lord Lovat inherited a heavily mortgaged estate in 1880 and the first Lord Halifax spent too freely for years, necessitating retrenchment by his diehard son.[95] The sixth Duke of Newcastle declared bankruptcy in 1870. Despite this, the diehard seventh duke, through judicious management and income from minerals, retained about 35,000 acres at his death, almost the same amount as Bateman had attributed to the family in the 1870s.[96]

The diehards' role was one of retrenchment, of consolidation of the often manifold and confusing debts, and of an attempt to pay off some or all of the charges on the estate. The goal in almost every case was the preservation of the estate in a profitable financial condition. Sentiment and a ruthless approach to the problems of business were frequently combined in an effort to save a traditional way of life in a form which would not sacrifice the pecuniary interests of the diehard family. Retrenchment was not universal among the diehards and it would be misleading to imply that all of them were in any sense struggling. The degree of difficulty encountered even by those who were financially troubled can also be greatly exaggerated. For example, the predecessor of the diehard Earl of Radnor, due to the extravagance of his father, had to mortgage his property at Folkestone in the late 1890s. In the same year he was able to hire a special train to Windsor from Woking when he and his wife were invited to the castle by the queen.[97] The diehards avoided adding new encumbrances to their estates whenever possible and worked with great determination in a businesslike manner, for the most part without self-pity (except in statements meant for public consumption), to preserve their position or to restore their estates to financial health.

On some heavily encumbered estates efforts at reform had already begun with the predecessors of the diehards. The sixth Earl Stanhope, father of the diehard, succeeded to the title in 1876 and almost immediately began a program of reform and rationalization. He sold the Hoggesten estate in Buckinghamshire to Hannah Rothschild (later Lady Rosebery) for £100,000. The sale provided him with the funds to pay off the mortgage on the estate and to pay £40,000 of the four younger children's portions. He later sold the Irish estate under the Ashbourne Act. The estate accounts were clarified, and Stanhope centralized the disbursement of funds. He also had his land surveyed and, in the late 1880s and early 1890s, commenced an extensive building and drainage program. He consolidated his property in Devon by sales and one purchase, and made several purchases of land in Kent.[98]

In the midst of a steady succession of bad years for agriculture, the third Earl of Morley, father of the diehard, invested a great deal in estate improvements, attempted to reduce and consolidate his debts, and diversified his sources of income. One of Morley's most profitable holdings was the clay company located on his land. In 1880, for example, receipts from clay alone equalled nearly £4,000. In the early 1860s a large portion of the clay company's shares had been accepted by the Naval Bank and the Earl of Leitrim as collateral for a mortgage obtained by the second Earl of Morley. The third earl worked with great determination from the early 1870s to regain sole control of the company and thus to increase his income. After becoming a member of the Liberal government in 1880, he talked at great length with the bank and Lord Leitrim, persuaded them to reduce their asking price, and in 1884 bought their shares with £6,000 obtained from the sale of three paintings. Morley purchased the few remaining outstanding shares in late 1888 and noted in his journal: "It is certainly when I look back at 1864 wonderful to think I can have accomplished this. the purchase of shares at various times has cost me £7019. this is certainly money well spent—."[99] Left at his succession with a financially straitened estate, Morley had restored one sector of it to health and independence. He continued to work on other areas in a successful effort to pass on the estate, virtually intact in its English acreage, to his diehard son.

The diehard Lord Shrewsbury inherited a financially troubled estate in 1877: "When I came of age I inherited a watch & chain, 2 guns & an overdraft at every bank . . . & then I had to pay a large sum to Mother." He worked successfully at various enterprises "to make commercially enough to pay off all charges mortgages etc before I die."[100] In his case, as in others, business was a means to supplement rather than replace landholding.

Other diehards strove to improve the condition of their estates by retrenchment and economy. The Lords Fingall, Cathcart, Scarbrough, and Willoughby de Broke, among others, leased one or more of their

country seats at various times to reduce expenses.[101] Lord Saltoun fell
heir to "a broken landed estate" in 1886. For years he labored to restore it to financial health, using income from his land for improvements and to repay mortgages: "the discipline of that early period was
never forgotten and became habitual to him."[102] The Earls of Devon
battled with a heavily encumbered estate from the 1870s. The Devon
Estate Act of 1884 allowed for powers to sell as much land as was considered necessary and clearly enumerated all liabilities. In memoranda
prepared for Lord Devon in 1887 his solicitor and Viscount Halifax, a
trustee, argued that large sales of land were necessary and that investments and company directorships were essential. They took a businesslike approach. Halifax warned that the death of the eleventh earl
would be the signal for creditors to descend:

I submit that there is every reason for considering, now, *during Lord Devon's life,* . . .
the whole question of what it will be most advantageous to do in the interests of Lord
Devon, Lord Courtenay and in those of Mr. Henry Courtenay and his family. Whatever is best for the Estate must be best for them and no false delicacy, or fear of what
such an investigation may disclose, ought to be allowed to stand in the way of making
such an investigation thorough & complete.

By the end of 1891 the encumbrances on the estate had been reduced
from their 1884 level of more than three-quarters of a million pounds
to under £500,000 by a combination of sales and good management.[103] The next two earls of Devon were both careful in their expenditure, and the fourteenth earl was an example of a diehard landowner saddled with debts accumulated before his succession, who
continued to act in the traditional manner on his landed estate,
despite the complicated legal and financial dealings which were necessary to maintain it.

Lord Sondes faced an array of mortgages charged upon his estate
before he succeeded in 1907. During the next few years he and his solicitor, A. R. Farrer, worked steadily to reduce and consolidate these
charges, some of which dated back to the eighteenth century. The
strategy adopted for reduction of the debts included the sale of some
land, especially Elmham, Norfolk (not completely sold until 1919),
leasing of the Lees Court residence, reduced expenditure, investment
in the stock market, and a search for minerals on the estate. The sale
of a Gainsborough for £20,000 helped in these efforts. Sondes and his
solicitor were successful in their endeavor to restore the estates to a

better financial condition. Just five years after Sondes' succession, Farrer told him that since the death of the first earl in 1890 there had been an attempt to reform the finances of the estate, "though you have done more in your time in this direction than those who went before you." Not only had many of the mortgages and charges been consolidated into a less confusing number, but others had been altogether eliminated.[104] As in the case of other diehards and their families, good management beginning at different times in the period from the late 1870s to 1914 reversed the trend toward deeper indebtedness, which had been established for well over a century among the landed aristocracy.

The financial arrangements and disputes in the late 1890s between the third Marquess of Bristol and his nephew and diehard successor, the then Frederick W. F. Hervey, over control of the estate illustrate not only the businesslike determination and skill which many of the diehards manifested in the handling of their estates, but also a ruthlessness and fierce practicality in negotiations which were designed to keep the family estate intact. Personal communications between Hervey and Lord Bristol ceased for months in 1899 when they accused each other of bad faith. Hervey described Bristol's conduct as "dishonorable." The conflict centered on Bristol's freedom of action as life trustee of his heavily encumbered estate. His belief that he was near bankruptcy was the root cause of a long and impassioned argument about minute details of various clauses of a business agreement. In late 1897, Hervey, newly married to a wealthy woman, took over the management of the family estate's mortgages and charges, in exchange for full title to the real and personal property. He then began to apply himself expertly and energetically to the reorganization of the estate's finances. By 1902 Hervey had advanced over £220,000 to consolidate various mortgages, as well as additional funds to clear other charges off the property.[105]

The future fourth Marquess of Bristol was determined to preserve the traditional landed estate of his family and to live eventually as his predecessors had done. His method had nothing old-fashioned or sentimental about it. Hervey's strong sense of practicality, his desire to retain the estate intact for future generations, and his disinclination to add new debts to the old ones found expression in a letter rejecting the notion of a pension for a dismissed agent:

I am afraid your plea of 'custom' for a retiring pension does not appeal to me — . . . I can imagine no more pernicious habit than for a tenant for life saddling an estate with pensions which ought to come out of the yearly income of the estate . . . This principle applies most aptly in this case for should anything happen in the near future to Lord Bristol & myself, if I die without a male heir, I do not see how without a large sale of property my successor would ever have a penny piece of his own for income & the possibility of his ever being able to live at Ickworth on the revenues of the estate is absolutely nil without external aid. [106]

Bristol's modern technique and businesslike spirit (not in reality ever foreign to the landed aristocracy) were typical of many of the diehards who had inherited financially troubled landed estates after the onset of the agricultural depression.

Some historians might question the general applicability of conclusions drawn from a study of diehard landholding and finance, believing that a large proportion of the diehards were relatively poor members of the House of Lords and that their motivation for resistance to the Parliament Bill of 1911 was anger at both the Liberal government and the Conservative leadership for ignoring their plight. This version of the "backwoodsmen" thesis argues that these peers did not simply choose to stay away from London society and national politics, but were forced to do so because of their poverty. When they came to Parliament in 1910, they were "returning with the frustrated bitterness of long exile imposed by agricultural depression."[107]

A large proportion of the peers who opposed the Parliament Bill were in fact relatively prosperous, some even being among the wealthiest men in the United Kingdom. While it is undoubtedly true that the diehards' perception of the social and economic changes wrought by the depression sparked a psychological crisis of sorts and helped to shape their view of society, it is the nature of their response to the crisis which is significant. Their willingness to adopt new methods to preserve their traditional way of life was characteristic of the landed aristocracy as a whole. It was a rational and reasoned approach, rather than an emotional reaction based on an unexamined sense of frustration. The diehards were, perhaps, somewhat more traditional than landed society in general, in that they tended not to sell so much land so soon as did many other landowners in the years just before World War I. In investing in the stock market and participating in business, they were not untypical of their fellow aristocrats. Frequently, diehard landlords and their agents devoted their efforts to clearing away old debts and setting their estates on a more efficient and orderly footing.

The diehards recognized clearly the threat which the agricultural depression presented to their economic position. They responded to this imminent danger in a tough-minded, realistic fashion. Although their goal in diversifying their sources of income was to preserve landed society as far as possible, they did not hesitate to use new methods to accomplish this end. It was this quick readiness to adopt controversial, sometimes drastic means to insure the maintenance of their traditional way of life which also characterized the diehards' behavior in the political arena of the early twentieth century.

During the last two decades of the nineteenth century the British landed aristocracy experienced another attack on its status and influence in the countryside in the shape of the increasing democratization of the franchise and local government. In 1884 the Third Reform Act granted household suffrage, accompanied by the ballot, enfranchising the agricultural laborer for the first time. Elective county councils were established in 1888, parish and district councils in 1894. These three new local governing bodies consolidated the previously confusing array of local authorities and removed administrative power from the hands of the magistrates, the traditional, appointed rulers of the countryside.

Democratization of local government and extension of the franchise seemed to many observers to have profoundly disturbing implications for the landed aristocracy. As a class, both its continued power in local politics and its influence in national affairs appeared threatened. In addition, frequent assaults on aristocratic authority were thought to have effected a psychological change in the governing class. Mrs. Humphry Ward suggested this in *Marcella,* a story of rural life published in 1894, the year of the parish councils bill. In the novel, Lady Winterbourne remembers how her grandmother, "as good and kind a woman as ever lived," put a laborer in the stocks because he had not, when drunk, removed his hat to her, and how she went home conscious of having done her duty. Lady Winterbourne tells her friend Lord Maxwell, a leader of county society, that things have changed since her grandmother's time: " 'But if the power of the stocks still remained to us, my dear friend . . . we could no longer do it, you or I. We have lost the sense of right in our place and position—at least I find I have.' "[1]

Suggestive as the perceptions of the novelist may be, the evidence must be examined to determine how successfully the landed aristocracy in general and the diehard peers in particular resisted or adapted themselves to the inroads of democracy and maintained their influence

on local government and politics.* The degree of continued influence
and activity at the local level may, as some authorities have suggested,
have had an important effect on political and social behavior at the
national level. The diehards might have been influenced in their actions on the Parliament Bill both by the conditions they experienced in
their home counties and by their perceptions of these changes. They
may have felt inordinately threatened by increasing democratization
on the local front and resolved to make a final stand for their prerogatives in the arena of the House of Lords.[2] On the other hand, changes
in local government and politics might have spurred the diehards to
greater positive efforts in both national and local affairs in order to
maintain their position.[3]

The price of a deferential society was, to some extent, philanthropic
expenditure. Contributions to local charities, donations to schools,
churches and hospitals, subscriptions to clubs and other organizations,
and pensions for retired employees had come to be expected from
landed aristocrats and were essential to the maintenance of influence
in local affairs. Nor did they decline with the onset of the agricultural
depression. The landowner was "expected to head every subscription
list, to take the lead in every philanthropic movement within the district, to assist his church, and to be the general almoner of the distressed of the neighborhood."[4] Despite such laments about the demands made upon landowners, both Conservatives and Liberals recognized the political advantages to be gained from such activity.

During the last two decades of the nineteenth century, however, the
agricultural depression had begun to hit landed incomes with great
force. Some authorities have suggested that the pressure of events and
other demands on landed incomes reduced philanthropic expenditure.
Such a decline, coming at the same time as the democratization of
local government, might have weakened the landed aristocrat's position in local politics and society. Diehard estate papers indicate, however, that the trend toward smaller philanthropic contributions was by
no means universal. In this respect, it is possible that the diehards form
a somewhat unusual case. They were frequently among the more pros-

---

*Contemporary observers differed over the degree of success of the landed aristocracy in main-
taining its local political power in the late nineteenth and early twentieth centuries. They divided
on the basis of their political allegiance — Conservatives lamenting the weakened condition of the
aristocracy, Liberals noting continued "tyranny" in local affairs.

perous landowners, often possessing non-landed resources, and were also slow to sell land. The diehard peers may have had both more ability and more determination to keep up the flow of monetary benevolence than many landed aristocrats. Their interest and activity in politics may also have led to their desire to maintain their charitable contributions.

Charitable activities ranged from Christmas gifts of venison and beef, coupled with visits by the lady of the house, to the support of churches, schools, and hospitals.[5] Many subscriptions and donations came in the form of annual payments, and these seem to have been kept up very well by diehard peers. Requests for money came in a constant barrage. For example, in April and May, 1913, Lord Plymouth gave small amounts to the Cardiff Institute for the Blind, to the Missions to Seamen at the Barry Docks, to a golf club at Bridgend, to the Cogan Reading Room, to the Penarth May Day Horse Show, and to the Annual Sports of the Cardiff Schools.[6] Though Plymouth was wealthier than many of the diehard peers, the number and scale of his donations was not unusual, and these examples do not include large amounts spent on annual subscriptions and donations to churches, schools, and political clubs. Another major expenditure for the landlord was pensions for retired laborers or their widows and families. These continued unabated throughout the period. A case which the Duke of Somerset's agent reported in 1901 was typical:

I wish to bring to your Grace's notice the case of Samuel Hodge who has worked on the Estate for over 50 years, he is now 77 years of age and is incapacitated . . . is now dependent on what is allowed him he has always been an excellent workman as a labourer on the Estate and has always borne an exemplary character. He has three sons all of which have families except one and I would suggest an allowance of 10/0 per week which would be in accord with precedent.[7]

Diehard charitable expenditures fluctuated from year to year, but in general remained at a high level. Lord Scarbrough gave £560 in bounties, charities, pensions, and similar contributions in 1885. In 1893, when the total came to £415, the decline appeared almost entirely on the Yorkshire portion of the estate. On Lord Bathurst's Cirencester Park estate, during the lifetime of the sixth earl, subscriptions fluctuated mainly between £200 and £320 from 1878 to 1892. After a marked decline at the death of the sixth earl and again during the

Boer War, a dramatic increase occurred, with contributions exceeding
£1,000 per year from 1908 through 1914. This period coincided with
Lady Bathurst's inheritance of the *Morning Post* and increased political activity on the Bathursts' part.[8]

More detailed records of a wide variety of subscriptions exist for the
Derbyshire estate of the Earls Stanhope from 1890 to 1905, ranging
from about £150 to over £300. Donations and charities for the Duke
of Bedford's estates remained at a very high level for the entire period,
with the annual total coming to several thousand pounds.[9] Like many
other diehards, the duke was not dependent on his agricultural rents
for income and was therefore able to maintain his philanthropic expenditures. It seems that whenever possible the level of diehard benevolence remained high, and that a diminution for some years might be
followed by a resumption of a previously greater total. The diehards
recognized the importance of these contributions for their local status
and were not inclined to let them lapse.[10]

The diehards were slightly more active in local affairs than their
predecessors had been. Almost 71 percent of them held some type of
local office, while only 60 percent of their predecessors had done so.
The diehards were also somewhat more successful than the other peers
in adapting themselves to new local circumstances, just over 70 percent
of them having held some local office, as opposed to approximately 67
percent of the other members of the 1911 House of Lords. The differences in these figures suggest little in the way of dramatically differing
experiences which might help account for the diehards' intransigence
at the national level (see Table 4.1).

The relative success of the old magistrate group in county council
elections could also have been a factor in aristocratic attitudes toward
local government. A rapid change after 1888 in the social composition
of the political rulers of the counties might have exacerbated the inse-
curity of landowners already troubled by franchise reform and agricultural depression. If the areas in which the diehards owned land coincided with those in which the old magistrate group suffered electoral
setbacks, this would tend to support the idea that uneasiness about
local government resulted in increasingly inflexible positions on national issues.

The peers who voted against the Parliament Bill held land throughout the British Isles. There was no clear correlation between the inci-
dence of diehard landholding and the success or failure of the upper

Table 4.1.   Local office-holding

	Diehards		Other peers	
	Number	% of 112	Number	% of 479
Justices of the Peace	54	48.2	279	58.2
Deputy Lieutenants	58	51.8	223	46.6
County Councillors or County Aldermen	28	25.0	70	14.6
Lord Lieutenants	21	18.8	67	14.0
Chairmen of Quarter Sessions	2	1.8	7	1.5
Chairmen of County Councils	6	5.4	10	2.1
Number in local office	79	70.5	322	67.2

Sources: Statistics compiled from *Burke's, Debrett's,* and *Complete Peerage.*

Note: Less than one-third of the predecessors of the diehards had been J.P.'s, only about 40 percent deputy lieutenants, and less than 10 percent county councillors or aldermen (a figure vitiated by the differing dates of succession to the title as compared to the Act of 1888 establishing the county councils). Eighteen of the predecessor group had served as lord lieutenants. These statistics, which do not include parish or district council offices or membership on local boards, may be incomplete for the reason that some local office-holding went unreported.

classes in local government. The diehards did own a disproportionately large amount of land in England, where magistrates were elected more commonly than in the Celtic fringe.[11] They did not congregate in those English counties in which the magistrate class did relatively poorly in county elections, and at least one diehard peer held some land and public office in almost every county. At the level of county, parish, and district councils, and of magistrates, the experience on the part of diehard peers seems not to have been distinctive except perhaps for a slightly greater ability to function within the new elective system of local government.*

*J. P. D. Dunbabin has noted, of "the differences in social composition as between councils — [that] those in the east and north of England were the less aristocratic (in this reflecting their courts of Quarter Sessions)" ("Expectations of the New County Councils and Their Realization," *Historical Journal,* 8 [1965], 361). In the three counties in which the largest number of diehard country seats were located, the magistrates had very little success in county council elections in the West Riding, while in both Hampshire and Devon they did exceptionally well.

There was no clear correlation between the diehard peers and the upper classes with respect to their success or failure in local government. A comparison of the geographic distribution of diehards with the percentage of county councillors and aldermen on each council in 1911 who were included in *Walford's County Families* reveals no pattern which would help to account for the self-selection of peers into the diehard group. See also *County Councils and Municipal Corporations Companion,* 1911.

The diehards took an active part in the most traditional governing bodies of their counties, the bench of magistrates. The functions and social composition of the bench had changed in the course of the nineteenth century. Various local authorities, such as poor law boards, had been created, depriving quarter sessions of certain administrative functions. However, magistrates frequently maintained their influence as ex officio members of the new bodies. During the same period, the social composition of the bench had become more middle-class through a process of assimilation rather than drastic change. The upper-middle classes generally adopted the attitudes of the gentry and aristocracy, who continued to play an active role.[12] Until 1906 a property qualification of £100 landed income per year remained in effect. This provision, and the fact that after the Home Rule Bill crisis of 1886 the great majority of magistrates, lord lieutenants, and the landed and upper-middle classes from which these officials were drawn were conservatives, insured that there would be no rapid alteration in this institution of local government.[13]

Despite the gradual changes which had taken place in quarter sessions, appointment to the bench and selection of the chairmen of quarter sessions remained firmly in the hands of the traditional ruling classes throughout the period 1880-1914. The office of justice of the peace was much sought after, especially as a mark of social distinction. The local judicial power and immense influence which accrued to those who controlled the appointments, at least up to 1914, continued to lie with the landed aristocracy in most counties; and in this regard the diehards were among the most active landowners. The general procedure for appointment to the bench, prior to the Liberal reforms of 1911, was recommendation of candidates by the lord lieutenant to the lord chancellor. The lord lieutenant, generally a great landed magnate, gathered his information from leading magistrates, from friends of his own social class, and, after 1888, from county councils.[14] Landed aristocrats frequently received requests for aid in appointment to the bench. This was particularly true since most lord lieutenants after 1886 were Unionists and belonged to the same social class as the landowners. In July 1898 Lord Cranborne, the future Marquess of Salisbury, received a letter from a political acquaintance asking for help for a potential justice: "Col. Henry Fallowfield Cooper is very anxious to be appointed a magistrate for Kent. Can you manage it with the Lord Lieutenant? He is as you know a person to whom no objection can be made."[15]

Appointment to the bench of magistrates was one of the social rewards landed aristocrats could grant in return for political assistance. In March 1892 Lord Cranborne's election agent in his Darwen constituency urged him to submit the names of his political supporters to the chancellor of the Duchy of Lancaster: "As this is the last time we, possibly, may be able to do the job, would you have any objections to my sending up the names of Pilkington Shinock . . . If appointed it would do good and bend the whole Shinock interest to us."[16]   Some diehard peers exerted influence in the larger cities. In 1901 Samuel Roberts, Conservative M.P. for Sheffield, suggested to the Duke of Norfolk, lord lieutenant of the West Riding and a great landowner in the city, that he exercise his power to recommend appointment to the bench. Roberts noted that there were a number of prominent Sheffield conservatives who had done good work for the party and that the political situation made it possible to reward them. He went on to discuss the qualifications of specific candidates for the duke's consideration.[17]

Prominent landowners and their local lord lieutenants constantly exchanged letters about appointments of magistrates. The favor of a powerful peer was not always sufficient, however, to secure a position on the bench. Especially toward the end of the nineteenth century the political balance of quarter sessions and inactive justices began to be sensitive issues. The diehard Lord Clarendon, lord lieutenant of Hertfordshire, wrote Lord Cranborne in April 1897, in response to the latter's suggestion of a new J.P., that the political ramifications of such an appointment had to be weighed:

Any recommendation from you would have great weight with me in the matter of magisterial appointments, but you will . . . agree with me that there are other considerations besides complying with the requests of a personal friend . . .

One point I like to be quite certain about is whether or no a particular local bench requires additional strength . . . If not, when and if a Radical Government returns to power, it might be said that I had been guilty of favouritism . . . Are you of opinion that the Hatfield Bench requires an additional magistrate.[18]

On the one hand, Clarendon's letter indicates the growing importance of public opinion and the national political situation concerning this aspect of local government, and as such it demonstrates a diminution of aristocratic influence. However, it is clear that the assumption remains that Cranborne is the proper person to be advising Clarendon about local government, that it is even up to him to decide if his own suggestion was a good one. There is no indication that others will be consulted on the issue. This is a private communication between one peer and another, between two members of the same class who are also friends and political allies. This is still decision-making among the "right" people, even if circumstances impinge on them more than in the past. A decline in influence was a purely relative matter. Despite the loss of absolute, unquestioned control, the diehard peers' scope and freedom of activity were still large.

Until after the Parliament Bill crisis, this relative social exclusivity in the process of selecting magistrates seems to have been maintained, although the bench itself became more middle-class. But those consulted as to the suitability of prospective appointees came from a much narrower circle. The twelfth Duke of Somerset, a predecessor of the diehard duke, was lord lieutenant of Devonshire from 1867 until his death in 1885. Throughout this period it was customary for large landowners or a bench of magistrates to recommend possible justices to him. The duke would make inquiries of his friends, prominent magistrates, and then of the Exeter law firm which also handled his Devon estate business, Michelmore and Sons. After receiving information from these few sources, Somerset would decide whether or not to recommend an appointment to the lord chancellor, who invariably followed Somerset's advice. In 1885, for example, the Earl of Morley, the Earl of Devon, and Lord Clifford of Chudleigh all made recommendations to Somerset. A letter from Clifford is typical of the correspondence between these men of local influence, in its emphasis on the social status, economic means, and county involvement of his candidate: "Mr. Robert Dymond is suitably married . . . resides partly at Exeter & partly on his own estate . . . He was for many years in the Land Agency firm of Robert Dymond & Sons of Exeter . . . His younger brother is a magistrate . . . & he has himself been an acting Justice of the Peace . . . He is possessed of adequate means some of which consists of real estate." These landowners displayed no resistance to middle-class magistrates, so long as they had what was vaguely described as an "interest" in county affairs.[19] The aristocrats of the county remained the channels through which men from other classes asked to be appointed to the bench. This important element of social and political influence remained, even as the character of the bench slowly changed. In March 1903, for example, Lords Morley and Clifford were still communicating about magistrates in the same tone as nearly twenty years previously. There had been requests for more J.P.'s at Tynemouth, but Morley perceived "ructions in this bench" and recommended that they pause before complying, until they might find out "the real meaning of all this."[20]

After 1906 Liberal lord chancellors tended to bypass this aristocratic network of influence in many cases. Then, in 1911, the lord lieutenant's power to appoint magistrates was abolished, in an effort to end the aristocratic and conservative hold on magistrates' benches. Advisory committees were to be established in the counties and boroughs. In the counties, at least, they were small, usually included the lord lieutenant, and were "political" in the party sense.[21] The transition could be both slow and moderate, as, for example, in Glamorgan where Lord Plymouth served as lord lieutenant in the years just before World War I. He was still the hub of magisterial affairs and retained a good deal of influence. Even as late as 1913 not all the members of every advisory committee in the county had been appointed, so that much discretionary power remained to him. In addition, though an advisory committee suggested potential magistrates to the lord chancellor, its list was then returned to the lord lieutenant of the county for further inquiry. At this point Plymouth or his agent asked prominent local magistrates for their comments on the proposed list. As of May 1913 the committee was instructed to submit recommendations directly to Plymouth, and only — so he informed the lord chancellor — for individuals who conformed to certain socially restrictive rules established by him: "The Lord Lieutenant would continue to adopt the policy . . . as he had done in the past viz: — that he would not include in his list any retail tradesman or shopkeeper, but only those persons who occupy independent positions, or those who might be expected to perform the duties of Magistrates in an unbiased manner."[22]

Many landed aristocrats continued to exercise great influence in the selection of the chairmen of quarter sessions in the years prior to the Great War. Despite social and political changes it remained usual for the leading magistrate to be chosen from a socially prominent family, and peers retained their predominant role in the selection of candidates. For example, the 1904 correspondence among Lords Clifford, Coleridge, and Ebrington in regard to the vacant chairmanship of quarter sessions in their division of Devonshire reveals aristocratic political jockeying, the persuasion of candidates to run for the post, and an effort to decide the outcome before negotiations became public, as "a contest would be very undesirable."[23] There is an air of traditional political maneuvering about this correspondence, harking back to pre-1832 county politics in parliamentary elections. In a period of apparently drastic change, landed aristocrats remained active and influential participants in the oldest institution of local government.

The Local Government Acts of 1888 and 1894 presented a wholly new problem to the landed aristocracy. For the first time, democratically elected organs of local government had been established in the countryside, which this class had long regarded as its stronghold. There were to be no ex officio members of the county, district, and parish councils. Magistrates would no longer automatically serve on local boards. County councillors would be elected for three years, and from their number they would choose aldermen to serve for six, but all members of the council had to face the newly expanded electorate. At the district and parish level, all members of the councils were officially equal in point of length of service and election. Yet few of the diehards or their predecessors in 1888 expressed apprehension about the effect of the proposed county councils on their influence in local politics — only a small number of them participating in the debates in the House of Lords. The most prominent representative of a diehard family present at the debate, the third Marquess of Salisbury, the prime minister and predecessor of the diehard fourth marquess, supported the Local Government Bill. He emphasized that the bill dealt with prosaic matters, changes that were necessary "in order to make our institutions more acceptable to the people." He expressed uncertainty about the success of magistrates in county council elections, but did not anticipate any disaster in that regard. To Salisbury, as to other Conservative speakers, the county councils were in part designed to ward off future unrest — a sort of safety-valve for the countryside — and it was believed that magistrates and others of their social class would continue to obtain seats on the new county councils.[24]

Arthur Gordon, later Lord Stanmore, wrote his friend the first Earl of Selborne in November 1888 from Colombo, expressing "very great apprehension" about the Local Government Act and the ability of the aristocracy and gentry to continue in positions of importance in local government.[25] Selborne replied in the moderate tone characteristic of most of the diehards' responses to changes in local government. He expressed confidence in the ability of the aristocracy and gentry to get elected to the councils. Selborne also recognized that there was a growing community of interest between the landed classes and the middle classes of the counties, and attempted to reassure Gordon that he saw "no signs of men unfit for the work of county government being likely to be chosen."[26]

Most of the diehard peers faced changes in local government with cautious optimism. They reacted to the Liberal Local Government Bill of 1894, establishing popularly elected district and parish councils, in the same spirit. The third Marquess of Salisbury stated that he saw no great need for the changes proposed in the bill, though the new councils would not do any harm: "I think it was Mr. Morley who said that they would give greater interest to rural life, and when he said that he about stated the amount of the value which they will be to the inhabitants of the rural districts."[27] Conservative peers concentrated their efforts on limiting the proposed councils' powers of taxation and, in the case of the parish councils, their power to create allotments.[28] The peers were divided as to whether the bill would reduce the influence of the magisterial classes in local government. Lord Salisbury expressed gloom over the long-term prospects, primarily because he believed that complications of elective local government would lead the "leisured class" to withdraw slowly from public life.[29] The diehards more generally accepted the idea that the landed aristocracy would retain a significant degree of power despite, and independent of, legislation.

Aristocrats in general regarded changes in local government brought about by the acts of 1888 and 1894 with equanimity partly because of the gradual nature of the changes. Organizations with limited electorates had long before 1888 deprived the magistrates of exclusive control of rural administration. In the nineteenth century, the magistrates themselves had increasingly been drawn from the middle classes, especially in counties with large urban populations. The middle classes did not generally offer a direct challenge to the landed aristocracy, but rather blended as best they could with the old county society. After 1886, with the question of Home Rule and the leftward swing of the

Liberal party, links between landed society and the middle classes tended to become stronger.

The diehards did not necessarily see changes in local government as threats to their interests simply because these changes involved the elective principle. They had been prepared for such changes by alterations in society and government over a long period. They approached the change in a spirit of practical adaptability, realistically determined to grapple with the new circumstances. Like other landowners, the diehards did not feel obliged to retire from the leadership of rural society. They reasoned that adapting themselves to the new institutions would help them to preserve the old ways of life.

The establishment of the county councils and the first elections in early 1889 did not effect a revolution in the social composition of local government. In England, at least, where the diehards held their greatest concentration of land and where they would have felt change had it occurred, the magistrates were returned in large numbers as county councillors and aldermen.[30] The *County Councils Magazine* observed that "the constitution of the authority which will administer county business is . . . to a large extent . . . composed of the same men"; men of local standing were preferred over strangers, preserving the traditional personal character of local government.[31]

Besides the return of a large proportion of incumbent magistrates in most counties, the most striking fact about the first county council elections was the small number of contests.[32] Large numbers of electors stayed away from the polls even during contested elections, and the proportion of contests remained small in the years prior to the Great War.* The common belief that the necessity of competing in elections would drive the landed classes from local government was based in part on the illusion that elections would generally have to be fought. When a man of sufficient local prominence offered himself to serve on the county council, however, he frequently was elected without effort or opposition. Certainly there was no cause for extreme concern among the diehards or other members of their class.

*Of the 3,240 electoral divisions in England and Wales, only 1,749 (54%) were contested in 1889; and, of 2,213,452 county electors on the register of divisions in which elections of county councillors were contested, 1,633,092 (74%) cast their votes. At the second election in 1892, when the number of contests for county councils declined by more than half (to 788), only 725,969 (62%) of 1,173,980 potential electors in contested divisions voted. (1889 *P.P.* 65 [*Returns,* vol.247], "Return of County Council Elections," p. 2; 1892 *P.P.* 68 [*Returns,* vol.268], "Return of County Council Elections," p. 12.)

Even during the years of constitutional crisis, from 1909 to 1911, the diehards evinced no great worries about trends in local government. In March 1910 Lord Willoughby de Broke pointed triumphantly to local government and politics as an area in which the aristocracy and gentry had prospered despite the predictions of Liberals about their downfall:

> Mr. Lecky has said that there is no truer sign of the vitality of a class than the way in which it adapts itself to changed conditions, and that is what . . . the class of country gentlemen has done. There is also a feature about the country-gentleman class which has been a very great disappointment indeed to a certain type of Radical who thought that the County Councils Act, and the Parish Council Acts . . . were going to do away with the domination of . . . the squire and parson once and for all. But they revived again at the last election. [33]

Nearly a quarter of a century after the passage of the Local Government Act of 1888, the country gentlemen retained a large proportion of county council seats. In 1911, on the forty-seven English county councils, over one-fifth on average of the county councillors and aldermen in each county were listed in the socially exclusive pages of *Walford's County Families* for the year. Thirty-six diehard peers sat as members of county councils during the period before 1914. [34] The Duke of Leeds and the Earls of Denbigh, Meath, and Stanhope were on the London County Council, and all the major areas of Great Britain, including Southern Ireland, were represented by diehard county councillors and aldermen.

Many of the diehards exercised their local influence by running for county council seats themselves or in support of a candidate of their choice, as the landed aristocracy had done for centuries. As local notables they were frequently asked by prominent Conservatives in their area to offer themselves to the electorate. In October 1894 Lord Cranborne received a letter stating that both candidates for the Hertfordshire County Council election in March 1895 had decided to retire in favor of Cranborne in the Hatfield area. They believed that Cranborne's candidacy would add interest to the county council election and would ensure a Conservative victory. [35]

The lack of contested elections meant that for many landed aristocrats there was little need for extraordinary exertion and seemingly little change from an earlier system of local government. Offering himself for election to the first Gloucestershire County Council, the sixth Earl Bathurst, father of the diehard earl, placed an announcement — his only campaign gesture — in the pages of his local news-paper:

> I have received a Memorial . . . which leads me to presume that the submission of my name as candidate for the representation of the Urban District of Cirencester on the County Council may meet with your concurrence.
>
> My personal knowledge of those whose signatures are attached assures me that it is not merely an expression of political opinion, and I should decline to entertain it on such a footing; but I venture to hope that the neighbourly feeling which has so long existed in this town towards my family, and the inseparable community of our interests, are guarantees that, if named as your representative, I should discharge the duties to the best of my ability. [36]

Lord Bathurst's faith in the electors of Cirencester, in the shadow of his country house, proved justified. His son, Lord Apsley, the seventh Earl Bathurst, was also returned for an adjacent division of the county. In 1892 the sixth earl retired, but his son was re-elected without opposition, as were the candidates in fifty-two of the sixty divisions in Gloucestershire. Similar figures were obtained in the following years. [37]

The Duke of Bedford interested himself a great deal in the county council of his home county. By 1911, the duke, his relative Lord Ampthill and his head agent Rowland Prothero, had become aldermen of the county council of which the duke was chairman. Bedford had long exercised his influence in an effort to get his candidates elected as councillors in areas in which he held property. This work was handled mostly by Charles Hall, the duke's agent for the Woburn Abbey estate. For example, in 1895 Hall chaired meetings for James Crouch, the county councillor for Woburn since 1889. In addition to active electioneering, Hall also canvassed locally and compiled a list showing the way electors intended to vote, and loaned carriages to transport friendly electors on election day. The duke's influence in Woburn was regarded as decisive, and his wishes were respected. Before the next county council election in 1898, Crouch asked Hall to ascertain the duke's opinion of his candidacy, and offered "to retire in favour of anyone His Grace might prefer." Bedford made it clear that he "would like to have early information if opposition is attempted." [38]

The Duke of Bedford did not confine his efforts in local government to Woburn. Even if his influence was not always decisive in local elections, it was always sought by Conservative candidates and was generously proffered. On the Bedfordshire County Council, his personal influence, with that of his allies, remained a significant factor. He was continually named chairman of the council, generally without opposition. In 1910, however, Councillor Oakley objected vehemently to Bedford's election in terms which suggest that Bedford's influence, though far from absolute, was still important enough to arouse intense animosity:

> Speaking as a democrat . . . he thought they would do well to spread this honour to other parts of the country . . . They often heard what the Duke . . . had done for the county, and also what the county had done for him . . . He knew what a hard battle it was for the poor man to get up and speak against the Duke of Bedford. He represented great power through his wealth and land, in fact more than it was safe to put into the hands of any one man. [39]

Oakley received no support whatever from the other members of the council, and Bedford was again confirmed as chairman.

The diehards, like other Conservative landowners, frequently pictured themselves as the beneficent friends of the lower classes. In 1889 the eighteenth Lord Willoughby de Broke offered himself as a candidate for the Conservative interest in the Kineton division of Warwickshire, which included much of his estate. He responded to Liberal charges that he lacked sympathy for laborers with statements deploring the injection of politics into local affairs (a typical Tory stance) and calling for an increase in the number of allotments and for economy in local government. In the course of the campaign Willoughby de Broke went so far as to condone compulsory purchase of land for allotments if landlords and tenants could not work these matters out among themselves.[40] The *Stratford-upon-Avon Herald,* while predicting a close contest, remarked that Willoughby de Broke had "become quite liberal in his sentiments on county government," and that, "indeed, these County Councils are bringing out views which would have been considered much advanced a few years ago." Even such a staunch representative of the traditional social system in the countryside as Willoughby de Broke was prepared to contest a local election and appeal to the newly expanded electorate in the effort to preserve his local position. Like so many other landed aristocrats, gentry, and magistrates in this first county council election, he was rewarded with success.[41]

Lord Willoughby de Broke was equally successful in subsequent county council elections until he retired because of ill health in 1901.

In 1892 he won a narrow victory over a Liberal challenger, who was thereupon elected a county alderman in order to remove the threat to Willoughby de Broke's seat.[42] Later county council elections saw fewer contests. In 1909 the diehard Lord Willoughby de Broke, who had succeeded his father in 1902, was elected county alderman. He had inherited a love of fox-hunting from his father as well as a taste for politics, and his attendance at council meetings sometimes suffered. "The first Monday in November was the traditional day for the opening meet of the Warwickshire Foxhounds it seemed a pity that the meeting . . . had been arranged for the same day."[43]

Continuity of aristocratic influence marked the election results for the parish and district councils established by the Local Government Act of 1894. Liberals expressed far more disappointment and bitterness than did Conservatives, despite the election of a substantial number of men from the working classes to the parish councils, especially in northern counties.[44] The Liberals lamented that the parish councils were too weak and that both the district and parish councils were dominated by farmers and men of the rural middle classes.[45] There were also complaints that the unpaid status of councillors and the amount of time involved in government work discriminated against laboring men and even some farmers. By contrast, many Conservatives, including the diehards, professed pleasure with the elections and believed they could work very well with the new councillors. Charles Hall compiled and analyzed a list of the councillors elected in areas of Bedfordshire where the Duke of Bedford had interests, and expressed satisfaction with his findings.[46] The *Wilts and Gloucestershire Standard,* published in Cirencester and faithfully reflecting the views of the Bathursts, whose seat was located at the edge of the town, regarded the results of the 1894 local elections as a triumph for the traditional rulers of the countryside over those who had been trying to teach the agricultural laborers "to look upon the parson and the squire and the farmer as their natural and mortal enemies . . . The elections show, either that 'Tory tyranny' existed only in the heated imagination of party grievance-manufacturers, or else that the down-trodden electors hug their chains with provoking complacency."[47]

The Earl of Clarendon, like other aristocrats, recognized that the parish councils brought additional problems and responsibilities but believed that he would continue to play an important role in his area. He declined Salisbury's invitation to chair an anti-disestablishment meeting in December 1894, with the explanation that he had to attend the first meeting of his parish council: "it would be indiscreet to cancel this previous engagement, especially as I have amongst my Colleagues . . . some political firebrands who hold diametrically opposite views from myself . . . and it is possible also that I may be selected as Chairman."[48] Similarly, in 1909, Lord Ampthill told L. J. Maxse that he could not join him on a Tariff Reform platform because he had to attend a parish council meeting: "to the simple folk of my village it is an important occasion and they would be pained if the Chairman . . . (the important post which I now occupy) were absent."[49]

The social composition of the parish councils remained approximately the same up to the Great War, and there were rarely contests. The eighteenth and nineteenth Lords Willoughby de Broke participated as effectively in parish council elections and business as they did on the county council level. In December 1894, after a preliminary meeting at which arrangements were made to avoid contests, the eighteenth Lord Willoughby de Broke was elected chairman of the Kineton Parish Council. Joining him on the council were his sister, the Hon. Mabel Verney, a doctor, a farmer, a tradesman, a postman, and a laborer.[50] In 1901 Lord Willoughby de Broke retired from the chairmanship and was replaced in that position by his son, the Hon. Richard Greville Verney, later the diehard Lord Willoughby de Broke, who remained chairman during the remaining pre-war years.[51] One of the two local newspapers in the Kineton area, the *Stratford-upon-Avon Herald,* lamented that, "those who thought that the labourer would take an interest in and find a position on the Boards have not had their expectations realised. The labourer is nowhere."[52]

It was not necessary for the landed aristocrat himself to sit on a local governing body in order to exercise influence in local government. There were frequently candidates for these councils whom the local diehard landowner would be willing to support. If an independent man's views closely paralleled those of the landowner, then the latter would have no objections to his being elected, especially since this arrangement would reduce the amount of time and perhaps expense involved in a diehard's personal candidature. Such was the case with the Duke of Bedford's support of James Crouch in the Woburn constituency. Another route to indirect political influence was for the great landowner's agent or representative to win election to local governing bodies. This common practice further augmented the amount of influence the landed aristocracy continued to exert. The diehard peers were among those who realized the advantages of representatives, bound by employment or relation, sitting on local councils. The fourth Marquess of Bute testified to this effect in 1919, when a member of the Coal Industry Commission asked him whether "generally speaking your Factor whenever an opportunity presents itself gets elected to every County Council?" The marquess replied, "Yes, it is generally done. If one is a big ratepayer one is represented in that way. I am on the County Council myself."[53]

Rowland Prothero, later Lord Ernle, became chief agent to the diehard Duke of Bedford in 1898 and was quickly elected to the Bedfordshire County Council. In 1903, at the duke's request, he accepted the chairmanship of the Higher Education Committee of the council and two years later become a county alderman, serving on several committees. Prothero accepted an invitation in 1907 to stand as the Unionist candidate for the Northern Division of Bedfordshire. Although he failed to win election in 1910, in 1914 he became a Member of Parliament for Oxford University. "My whole-time service," Prothero later recalled, "was at the disposal of the Duke of Bedford. On my own initiative . . . I should have undertaken none of this public work."[54] The Duke of Bedford's Woburn agent closely observed the first county council elections in 1889 and sent the duke a list of the councillors elected from the fourteen districts in which the duke had interests; five of the fourteen were his tenants.[55] Charles Hall was himself involved in representing Bedford's interests in local government — as a member of the Woburn Parish Council throughout this period and as a military member of the local Territorial Force Association.[56]

Other diehard peers had agents or close relatives representing their interests in local governing bodies. Lord Plymouth's Worcestershire land agent, Lionel F. Lambert, sat as a county councillor and, along with the diehard peer Lord Sandys, as a member of the Worcestershire Standing Joint Committee of councillors and magistrates.[57] Robert Forrest, Plymouth's chief Glamorganshire agent from 1874, was a J.P. since 1879, had been high sheriff of Glamorganshire in the early 1890s, had served as chairman of the Cardiff Rural Sanitary Authority and the Llandaff Highway Board for many years, was the district representative for the Board of Agriculture, chairman of the Llandaff and Dinas Powis Rural District Council, and a member of his county council since 1889.[58] Walter Mynors, land steward for the Earl of

Shrewsbury and Talbot's Staffordshire property, was a magistrate, chairman of the Stafford Rural District Council, and a member of the county council.[59] Representation of great landowners by their agents or relatives was extremely common throughout England and provided an effective means to exert influence in local affairs.[60]

Robert Anderson, Lord Bathurst's estate agent, won a seat on the Cirencester Urban District Council at the first election and held it at subsequent contests.[61] By 1906 he had become a member of the Gloucestershire Education Committee, along with Lord Bathurst and other county notables.[62] Throughout this period Anderson regularly delivered political speeches and engaged in controversies in the local newspapers on behalf of his employer.[63] He was, like many other land agents, both land steward and local political agent for his employer.

The Barons Willoughby de Broke were well represented in the areas near their Warwickshire estate by their agent William Hutton and by their relatives. The eighteenth Lord Willoughby de Broke's brother and sister were members of local rural district and parish councils.[64] While the Rev. L. Goodenough of Kineton, who held a living in the gift of Willoughby de Broke, sat on the Stratford Rural District Council and on the Kineton Parish Council,[65] Hutton was vice-chairman of the Stratford Rural District Council for several years.[66] In this capacity he was responsible, in the decade before 1914, for investigating and improving housing and sanitary conditions in Kineton, a village principally owned by his employer, Lord Willoughby de Broke. As the nineteenth baron's agent, Hutton worked successfully at the same time to safeguard the interests of the estate in matters such as leases of land by the district council for sewers and other improvements.[67]

In Scotland, Wales, and Ireland representation of diehards and other landed aristocrats in local government by their agents or relatives was much less usual but not unknown. Andrew Ralston, agent for Lord Strathmore's Glamis estate, was a magistrate, chairman of the Glamis School Board, and a county councillor for Forfarshire.[68] J. T. Garrioch, Lord Lovat's agent, was county councillor for Inverness, chairman of the Kilmorack School Board, and of the Kilmorack Parish Council, and an active magistrate.[69] Nationalist strength made it extremely difficult for agents or for the diehards themselves to win election to local office after the Irish Local Government Act of 1898. Victor Le Fanu, for example, estate agent for the Earl of Meath in county Wicklow, served for some years on the Bray Urban District Council but was defeated in a bid for re-election in 1909 by a Nationalist.[70] However, it is clear that, on the local level, especially in England, the diehards maintained a high degree of influence, either directly or through their agents, despite changed political circumstances.

The extension of the franchise in 1884 to agricultural laborers, the secret ballot, and the agricultural depression threatened the influence of the landed aristocracy in parliamentary elections. The diehards, however, experienced no drastic change in this activity. Over 20 percent of them had been M.P.'s, as compared to just under 25 percent of their titled predecessors. The number of members of diehard families in the House of Commons from the time of the 1832 Reform Act only diminished gradually.[71]

There was no correlation between national political trends and the geographical distribution of diehard estates. Diehard conservatism on the national level cannot be explained by frustration with Liberal preeminence on the local level. The diehards did not include a disproportionate number of peers with estates in areas of Great Britain which tended to vote against the Conservatives in the post-1884 period. Only about 22 percent of their land was located in predominantly Liberal Scotland and Wales. In England, where the diehards held most of their land, voting patterns were mixed. The diehards held about 23 percent of all Irish land owned by the peerage, but a substantial portion of it was located in Unionist Ulster.[72]

The character of local party politics and local elections changed somewhat after the reforms of 1884-1885. The number of public political gatherings increased enormously during the late nineteenth and early twentieth centuries because of the need to reach the expanded electorate. Rather than withdrawing from the changing political arena, the diehards exploited new political opportunities to the full. Many were active in the Primrose League, the aristocratic Conservative organization which cultivated the electorate and attempted to foster a feeling of unity between different classes through common membership in political clubs.[73] The Stanhopes, for example, held Primrose gatherings every year from 1887 at their Chevening estate in Kent. Like other landed aristocrats, they organized innumerable "school treats," bazaars, cricket matches and other non-political gatherings at which they almost always appeared and frequently made speeches. The diehard seventh Earl Stanhope, who enjoyed the excitement of public politics, admitted on occasion that the enthusiasm generated by his own speeches "was worth living for."[74]

Formal political meetings were by no means the only occasions at which diehard and other peers exercised their powers of political and social persuasion. The everyday round of life in the countryside provided them with countless opportunities to speak at sporting events such as puppy shows and hunt dinners, at rent audits and tenants' dinners, and while distributing the customary largesse of the great landowner. On one Christmas Eve, for example, when Lord Denbigh had distributed the usual gift of beef to all the cottagers on his Newnham Paddox estate he took advantage of the moment to defend the Conservative position on old age pensions.[75]

The diehards remained prominently involved in their local Conservative party politics throughout the period before the Great War. Contemporaries, including those critical of the diehards, recognized that despite changes in the political system many members of the landed aristocracy retained a good deal of local power. Gladstone and the first duke of Westminster conducted an acrimonious correspondence on the subject of the duke's influence in Chester after the former political allies split over Home Rule in 1886. Gladstone attributed to Westminster the power to change the political complexion of Chester from Liberal to Conservative despite the introduction of a wider franchise. In 1890 the Conservative whip in the Lords, the third Earl of Limerick, urged the prime minister to fill a vacant post with "some peer of great local influence and property who can be of use to the party. When the general election comes it will be necessary to urgently appeal for pecuniary and general support to the principal peers."[76]

Politicians realized that influence was important even if it implied less than absolute control of a constituency. The assistance of a peer could add many votes even if it did not assure victory. For instance, the Fitzwilliam interest, powerful in Yorkshire for decades before 1884, had generally controlled the Southern Division of the West Riding and the boroughs of Malton and Peterborough.[77] Although the Hon. W. H. Fitzwilliam, the second son of the sixth earl, was defeated in 1885 for the Southern Division of the West Riding, the Fitzwilliam interest was still powerful enough to have him continue as the Conservative candidate for the Doncaster Division. In addition, the diehard seventh Earl Fitzwilliam served as M.P. for Wakefield from 1895 to

1902 when he succeeded to the title, and a relative, B. C. V. Wentworth, was the unsuccessful Conservative party candidate for the
Barnsley Division in both 1886 and 1889.[78] Joseph Chamberlain appreciated Fitzwilliam's power in local affairs and, in 1904, urged
Arthur Balfour to appoint the young earl to a vacant under-secretary-
ship for India: "Fitzwilliam is ambitious, and as you know, influential
in the old sense of the word throughout his part of Yorkshire."[79]

The career of F. W. F. Hervey, later the diehard fourth Marquess of
Bristol, was an example of traditional influence and modern politick-
ing used to aristocratic advantage. He served as M.P. for Bury St.
Edmunds, the long-time stronghold of his family. In July 1904, at the
urging of his uncle, the third Marquess of Bristol, and of Captain
Lionel Wells, the principal agent of the Conservative party, Hervey
agreed to stand for Bury St. Edmunds at the next election. The local
Conservative Association unanimously confirmed his nomination.
Shortly thereafter Hervey received a letter of campaign advice from
Lord Francis Hervey, who had represented Bury St. Edmunds from
1874 to 1880 and again from 1885 to 1892. Lord Francis advised him
about the most important aspects of an election campaign:

> *Dinner and meetings.* now and again you will do well to put in an appearance . . . But
> don't make yourself *common; especially at the outset.*
> *Subscriptions.* The major things were in the nature of capital expenditure I think . . .
> church repaired; organ provided; important alterations to hospital, minor things,
> and contrib. to football & cricket club; sports at the Grammar School, E. Anglian
> School & so on; prizes to schools £1 a year or in small cases 10/ — Friendly Societies
> and their *outings* — the subscrips to the *Societies* were chiefly small; the outings £1
> or so — Then there will be a certain number of . . . artisans provident societies . . .
> Don't overdo it.

In 1906 Hervey was opposed at Bury St. Edmunds by a Liberal. Despite the relatively safe nature of the constituency, Hervey began to
make himself known very soon after he was selected by the Conservative Association. He went on to win election to the House of Commons
by a combination of his willingness to campaign and the influence of
his family. Shortly after his victory Hervey wrote letters of thanks to his
supporters. One canvasser replied, giving credit to Hervey's uncle,
Lord Bristol, for making a small gesture which won votes for Hervey:[80]

Last August I had a nephew from London a lad of 14 stay with me for his School Holiday. We did not know what to do to pass away the time, so I wrote to the Noble Marquis asking permission to fish in the lake at Ickworth Park. His Lordship wrote me a
letter himself granting us two days fishing for two weeks, when I went round to Can-
vass for you, I carried that letter to show waverers so that they could see what sort of an
English Gentleman the Noble Marquis is that done it, almost every one that seen that
letter said I'll vote for Hervey and to show the truth of it . . . in Counting up the votes
on the Night of the Poll the For's was 131 majority in your favour and this is a Liberal
ward.

The old customs survived despite the new political conditions.

The fourth Marquess of Salisbury was another diehard peer who
remained influential in local parliamentary politics. As Viscount
Cranborne he had been M.P. for the Darwen Division of Lancashire
North East from 1885 to 1892 and for Rochester City from 1893 to
1903, when he succeeded to his father's title. During the 1890s he
served as chairman of the Mid-Hertfordshire Conservative and Unionist Association and had been engaged in local disputes and practical
matters of party finance and election strategy.[81] He was also president
of the Conservative Association of East Dorset, where a family estate
was located. In December 1902 Charles van Raalte, the newly selected
Conservative candidate for East Dorset, appealed to Cranborne for
assistance: "A word from you will help very much I am told."[82] Upon
van Raalte's death in 1908, the local Conservatives appealed to the
then fourth Marquess of Salisbury for his advice in choosing a successor.[83]

During the years of Joseph Chamberlain's protectionist campaign,
Hertfordshire was a battleground of tariff-reformers and free-traders. Lord Salisbury, president of the East Hertfordshire Unionist Association at the time, was allied to the free-traders, yet both sides recognized this power in local affairs. Henry Page Croft, a tariff-reformer,
asked his permission, which was denied, to contradict "a rumour
amongst the members of the Hatfield Tariff Reform League that your
influence is being used to persuade certain members to resign."[84] Salisbury himself realized that his public statements in the 1906 Mid-Hertfordshire election were "likely to have great weight." At a crucial
moment in the contest he assured the "tottering" agricultural laborers
in an open letter that he would never countenance a food tax unless it

was "acceptable to the labouring classes."[85] This statement satisfied
the electorate and the Unionist candidate triumphed. Abel Henry
Smith, the Unionist free-trade M.P. for East Hertfordshire from 1900
to 1910, provided Salisbury with full reports of his battles with the
tariff-reformers and asked and received Salisbury's advice as to tactics.[86] When, in October 1909, both Smith and the protectionist candidate retired from the field on the advice of the Conservative Central
Office, the compromise candidate requested Salisbury's assistance
almost at once.[87] Although local politics were by no means peaceful,
Lord Salisbury remained both actively involved and secure in the
knowledge of his importance in local affairs. He did not always emerge
victorious either in intra-party disputes or in elections, but as the head
of the Cecil family he always played a leading role.

In 1895 Richard Greville Verney, later nineteenth Lord Willoughby
de Broke, was elected to Parliament for the Rugby Division of Warwickshire in an election which combined elements of the old aristocratic England with the new conditions of the post-Third Reform Act
era. The Conservative candidate was the young son of a peer who
owned a great estate within the constituency. His father, the eighteenth Lord Willoughby de Broke, president of the local Conservative
Association, and the diehard Earl of Denbigh, an important political
figure in the Rugby Division for many years, were his chief supporters.
Verney was selected as the candidate of the Rugby Conservative Association in the time-honored manner of a decision by a meeting of the
chief Conservative figures in the constituency, the management committee, prior to the general party meeting.[88] Verney triumphed not
simply because the old political methods still worked so well, but also
because he was able, indeed very willing, to engage in the numerous
public appearances and speeches demanded by a larger electorate. It
was an easy thing to be selected by the Conservative Association but
much more difficult to be elected from a division which, as Verney
later wrote of his country house, was "too close to Birmingham to be
pleasant for a peer."[89] Difficulties did not cause him to flinch from the
battle. He spoke often and bluntly for over a year on topics of national
importance, especially Home Rule and death duties.[90] Verney, like
other diehard peers, recognized that new conditions required new and
sometimes radically different methods and programs. He dealt in the
more active politics of the platform because he realized that it was the

only way that the position of the aristocracy might possibly be maintained.

In his introduction to *The Sport of Our Ancestors* Willoughby de
Broke summarized the attitudes of some of the landed aristocracy in
the 1890s:

> They perceived that if they were to keep their influence, their service to the State
> could no longer be confined to having a good luncheon four times a year at Quarter
> Sessions, and sitting on the local Bench once a month on a non-hunting day. The
> whole paraphernalia of local government compelled their attention, if even from no
> other instinct than that of self-preservation. Parliamentary elections ceased to be a
> choice between a Whig and a Tory landlord; the squire was opposed by the Radical,
> who was not ashamed to confess that he was out to demolish the existing order . . .
> The electors ceased to take things for granted . . . Leaflets, pamphlets, and all the
> other horrors of that terrible thing called propaganda were brought into full play. The
> comfortable evening at home had to give way, with distressing frequency, to the village
> meeting. A wise and witty Tory "grande dame" is said to have remarked that unless
> this privation were cheerfully borne, "the eight o'clock dinner would ruin the Con-
> servative Party." [91]

Willoughby de Broke was not alone among the peers in recognizing the
need to remain actively involved in local politics and government in
the face of threatening changes. The diehards were at least as successful as the rest of the peerage in adjusting to the new structure of local
politics. The picture of the "backwoods" peer, muttering impotently
against impoverishment and the loss of his influence, does not apply to
the peers who opposed the Parliament Bill of 1911. The motives for
the diehards' opposition to the Parliament Bill and revolt against their
own political leadership must be sought in their attitudes and activities
touching on national and imperial affairs.

5 / The Armed Forces and the Empire

The diehard peers' deep concern about the maintenance of British power in the increasingly competitive atmosphere of early twentieth-century international relations was a major factor in their attitude toward the Liberal government and their own Unionist leadership. The vast majority of conservatives feared for the continued safety of the British Empire during this period and demanded stronger measures of national defense. The diehards were not alone in their concentration on the need for action. Several of them, such as Lords Milner and Roberts, were exceptionally prominent in the movement for a more powerful military establishment, a more unified empire, and "efficiency" in domestic administration and imperial affairs, and were willing to promote great changes in order to achieve their objectives. Dissatisfaction with the policies of their government and their leaders in regard to these vital matters contributed to the diehard peers' general alienation from traditional parliamentary practices and to their opposition to the Parliament Bill of 1911.

An unusually high proportion of the diehard peers had military experience and interests, a fact which may explain their much remarked use of military metaphor to describe political activity.* Many of the diehards spoke frequently in Parliament and at political meetings on military and imperial issues. They were active in organizations designed to promote a big army and navy, national service, and tariff reform. Several of them provided funds to finance these organizations. Others supported and associated with propagandists for military and imperial causes. A few called for physical and racial "regeneration" and adopted the programs of the eugenicists. The diehards approached the issue of Britain's role in international affairs in a serious and technical manner. Their tone was urgent and highly moralistic. Along with other Conservatives, they believed that Great Britain faced national disaster unless drastic steps were taken to alert her people to the dangers she faced from rival powers. The diehards' attitude toward

*Even before the 1911 Parliament Bill vote one Conservative M.P. observed that "ex-soldiers were a large proportion of the gathering" of seventy of the diehards in Ashburton Street, August 9, 1911 (Willoughby de Broke Papers, H.L.R.O., Hist. Coll. 142, WB/2/112, p. 7).

society and politics in general was strongly colored by these militaristic and imperialistic preoccupations.

The influence of military attitudes and experiences on members of the upper classes in Victorian and Edwardian England has not been much discussed. There has been perhaps a tendency to regard the military experience of the aristocracy as a form of finishing school with little effect on the behavior of its members. For many aristocrats, including a large proportion of the men who voted in the Lords against the Parliament Bill of 1911, this was not the case. It would be a mistake to confuse the lack of uniforms with a disregard for the problems of the military and the empire. The diehard Earl of Denbigh was one of those who spoke in praise of military virtues and "the spirit of militarism . . . which impelled a man to defend his country, if called upon to do so."[1]

Conservative aristocrats were conscious of the threat to Britain's position during the years before the First World War, and their concern was reflected in their handling of issues which seem somewhat removed from national defense. In 1911 Lord Selborne stated his support for women's suffrage in the *National Review:* "I believe that the whole of our national life depends on the existence and solidarity of the home, therefore I want to admit to the ranks of the voters and the supporters of the country and the home, women whose influence, I believe, will be to that end." Lord Ebury's reply attacked female suffrage but also used the national defense issue. He complained that already too many people had the franchise: "in a country like ours, where men do not admit the obligation of service to qualify them for national defence in case of need, they are less fit than the men of other countries who do so to exercise political power."[2] Concern for military and imperial questions thus affected behavior on a large variety of issues, even if, as in the case of women's suffrage, it did not necessarily determine an individual's position.

Exposure to a military ethic began early for most aristocrats. The public school, a great formative influence in many ways for the aristocracy, instilled a sense of duty, of the importance of working as a team, and, especially in the last decades of the nineteenth century and the early twentieth century, a fervent patriotism and respect for the military virtues.[3] In this regard, it is notable that the diehards included a greater proportion of relatively young peers than the rest of the membership of the House of Lords in 1911 (see Table 5.1). Thus a

Table 5.1.   Birth dates (by decades)

	Diehards		Other peers	
	Number	% of 112	Number	% of 479
1880-1890	6	5.4	18	3.8
1870-1879	21	18.8	49	10.2
1860-1869	26	23.2	87	18.2
1850-1859	27	24.1	118	24.6
1840-1849	17	15.2	128	26.7
1830-1839	12	10.7	55	11.5
1820-1829	3	2.7	23	4.8
1810-1819	0	0.0	1	0.2
Summary				
1860-1890	53	47.4	154	32.2
1850-1859	27	24.1	118	24.6
1810-1849	32	28.6	207	43.2

large number of the diehards were approaching maturity, attending public school, and becoming aware of contemporary affairs, at a time when Britain faced increasing competition from the rest of Europe and from the United States. Edmond Warre, headmaster of Eton from 1884 to 1905, was the great figure associated with the growth of patriotism and militancy in the public schools. He emphasized the importance of games to an unprecedented degree and spoke frequently about the danger of war and the need for preparation for defense. Lord Willoughby de Broke, an old Etonian, described the Eton of those students born between 1865 and 1875 as part of his portrait of the altered circumstances of the landed aristocracy:

There was a very slight draught, almost imperceptible, when Dr. Warre of revered memory succeeded Dr. Hornby, the effect of which can only be appreciated by those who were at Eton when the change took place. The nature of the change was the substitution of a certain flavour of the orderly room for the dignified, flexible, country-house compromise that prevailed when Hornby was headmaster.[4]

Eton was the most popular school of the aristocracy, and its increasingly rigid and military spirit spread to other schools. In early 1900 a committee of the Headmasters' Conference, an organization of the heads of public schools, unanimously adopted a resolution that all students at universities and public schools "should be enrolled for the purposes of drill and manoeuvre and the use of arms" (see Table 5.2).[5]

Table 5.2. Secondary education of members of the 1911 House of Lords

	Diehards		Other peers	
	Number	% of 112	Number	% of 479
Eton	48	42.9	192	40.0
Harrow	9	8.0	45	9.3
Other public schools	8	7.1	48	10.0
Other institutions	3	2.7	22	4.6
Military colleges (Sandhurst or Woolwich)	12	10.7	23	4.8

Sources: Burke's, Debrett's, and Dod's.

Many aristocrats, including an unusually large number of the diehard peers, had been introduced to military matters at their public schools and followed up by drilling with the Oxford or Cambridge Volunteers. After university, or directly after public school, many of them obtained commissions in the army, preferably in a fashionable Guards regiment, or sometimes served brief apprenticeships with the militia to facilitate entrance into the army (see Table 5.3). George Cornwallis West followed a typical path. His family decided in 1892 he should make a career in the military. Since he had applied too late to go to Sandhurst, "it was decided that I should get in at what was then known as 'the Back Door,' i.e. the Militia. As Lord Lieutenant of his county, my father was able to give me a commission."[6] Already a militia officer, Rosslyn went up to Magdalen College, Oxford, in 1888 but became "rather bored" there and left to join the Royal Horse Guards. He left the Horse Guards because of his marriage and later joined a reserve troop. "The excitement of joining a crack regiment and being a soldier of the Queen was intense, and I very much regret I did not make my career a military one."[7] Viscount Mahon, later the seventh Earl Stanhope, attended Eton in the 1890s and proudly participated in the Eton College Volunteer Corps. He continued his interest in things military at Oxford, but was disappointed in the Oxford Volunteers. Stanhope left Oxford after three terms and was commissioned into the Grenadier Guards in 1901.[8] Some aristocrats varied this rather leisurely pattern by attending the military colleges of Sandhurst or Woolwich. Of the 35 members of the 1911 House of Lords who had attended a military college, 12 were in the diehard camp.[9]

The large percentage of young aristocrats who entered the Brigade

Table 5.3.   University education of members of the 1911 House of Lords

	Diehards		Other peers	
	Number	% of those at any university	Number	% of those at any university
Trinity College, Cambridge	15	31.9	82	36.6
Other colleges, Cambridge	1	2.1	14	6.3
Christ Church, Oxford	11	23.4	53	23.7
Magdalen College, Oxford	7	14.9	3	1.3
Other colleges, Oxford	10	21.3	58	25.9
Scottish, Irish, or other English university	3	6.4	14	6.3
Total who attended university	47 (42% of 112)		224 (46.8% of 479)	

Sources: Burke's, Debrett's, and *Dod's.*
Note: Statistics should be treated with caution on account of the incomplete nature of the data in the sources cited.

of Guards for their military service did not have a particularly hard time of it. In London their duties were light, and they spent much time at the Guards and Marlborough Clubs and at balls during the Season. It cost a great deal for an officer to keep up appearances, and for this purpose most men received an allowance from their families to supplement their meager pay. This tended to keep the officers' mess satisfactorily exclusive. Sir Osbert Sitwell noted that the Brigade of Guards — the first adult, independent world for many young aristocrats — was a "curious and enclosed world . . . full of luxury, hardship, and privilege, and hedged with shibboleths, traditions, and formulae."[10] This shared experience in the military, however relaxed it may have been, was, along with the public school, a powerful formative influence on the late Victorian aristocracy.

Several of the diehards served for a number of years in the regular army or the navy, some achieving high rank (see Table 5.4). Earl Roberts was field marshal and commander-in-chief of the army from 1900 until the office was abolished in 1904; the Earl of Erroll and Lord

Table 5.4. Military service of members of the 1911 House of Lords in the regular army or navy

	Diehards (112)	Other peers (479)
Army	77	192
Navy	4	16
Service in the brigade of guards	25	38
Total serving in regular army or navy	81 (72.3%)	208 (43.4%)

Sources: Burke's, Debrett's, Complete Peerage.

St. Levan (both of whom at different times commanded the Grenadier Guards), rose to the rank of brigadier general; and many diehards served as A.D.C.s to colonial governors or to the royal family. Lord Raglan was one of those who considered that "soldiering was really his 'job,' and to the end of his life his chief pride was to regard himself as a soldier."[11] He had been a captain in the Grenadier Guards, served in the Afghan War of 1879-1880, worked as A.D.C. to the governor of Bombay from 1880 to 1883, and had been under-secretary of state for war, 1900-1902. Among the most unusual military experiences of the diehards were those of the Earl of Kinnoul, who served as chief of staff for Baker Pasha in Egypt, and Lord Clifford, who, while visiting family friends in the United States, participated in an expedition with General Custer against the Sioux.[12]

The landed aristocracy dominated the officers' ranks of Great Britain's reserve forces (see Table 5.5): the militia, yeomanry, volunteers, and the reserve established by Haldane's army reforms of 1907.[13] The diehards were especially active in the Territorial Force Associations, and participated also in local rifle associations, Boys' Brigades, and other organizations designed to promote military arts.[14] The actual work involved with these lesser organizations varied a great deal. Sometimes officer status was purely honorific, but it almost always included a good deal of speaking, with opportunities for political and social commentary and exhortations. When Lord Denbigh spoke at a 1909 meeting of the Monks Kirby Air Rifle Club, which used a range at Newnham Paddox, his Warwickshire seat, he used the occasion to warn his audience of the danger from Germany and urged the neces-

Table 5.5. Military service of members of the 1911 House of Lords in reserve organizations

	Diehards (112)	Other peers (479)
Reserve or Militia	37	100
Yeomanry	9	92
Volunteers	8	39
Territorial Force Association		
(including chairmen)	21	59
Chairmen, T.F.A.	18	50
Total who served	56 (50%)	220 (45.9%)

Sources: Burke's, Debrett's, Complete Peerage.
Note: Statistics should be treated with caution on account of the incomplete nature of the data in the sources cited. In all probability, the proportion of those serving in reserve organizations was considerably greater for both groups.

sity of Sunday rifle practice.[15] Another of the diehards, Lord Meath, as part of his constant quest for strengthening England, established the "Lads' Drill Association" in 1898, becoming its first chairman, with Lord Roberts as vice-president.[16]

The reserve forces were important county social institutions. Their officers were chosen from the leading men of the county, and frequently knew their troops from the villages on or near their country estates. The reserves were socializing institutions which, along with the public schools and the regular regiments, helped establish a sense of close kinship within the upper classes. "An officer in one regiment usually found that a proportion of the officers in every other regiment had been at school or the University with him."[17] For certain periods each year the landed aristocrats turned their attention to military problems and activities, frequently allowing their parklands to be used for drills, and Lord Salisbury noted that at Hatfield, in September 1909, his family had forgotten "all about Tariff Reform . . . and our conversation is entirely about flank movements and extended lines."[18]

The Boer War was a crucial experience for many aristocrats, including the diehards. Among those who served in important capacities in the years 1899-1902 were many diehards whose later political, military, and imperial attitudes were influenced by these years of service.[19] Of the 112 diehard families, 92 contributed men to the battle or, in a few cases, to home service in World War I. Lords Abinger and Brabourne were killed, as were the successors of DeFreyne and Kesteven;

thirty diehards lost a successor, a son (Denbigh, two; DeFreyne, four) or a brother (St. Levan, two) to the war.[20] The diehards, universally advocates of a strong military, did not spare themselves or their families from combat.

Throughout the years prior to the outbreak of the Great War, the diehards were prominent among those Conservatives who hammered at the theme of Britain's unpreparedness for battle, especially against Germany. Demands for an increased military establishment became particularly strident after the Liberals came to power in late 1905, but they had been made much earlier. Viscount Milton, later the diehard Earl Fitzwilliam, had stated in 1898 that "if we wish to avoid war, the safest and surest way to do so is to allow the world to observe that our military resources, as well as our naval resources, are adequate to the task of defending our colonies, our commerce, and all our rights."[21] The Boer War was the occasion for the most ominous warnings about the state of Britain's defenses. From the end of the war in South Africa to the outbreak of the general European war in 1914 the experiences of the colonial conflict were continually referred to as justification for more military and imperial efforts. Conservatives drew a picture of an isolated British Empire, surrounded by hostile powers, gravely endangered from within by subversive forces and by dull-witted people who failed to perceive the danger. The diehards adopted an apocalyptic tone, a "now-or-never" attitude which emphasized the extremity of the peril and the necessity for supreme effort. Lord Denbigh, presiding at a meeting of a local Conservative Club, stressed that Britain faced a crucial period of testing, that to fail to assist the British settlers in South Africa "would practically sound the death knell of the British Empire, and were the people of this country prepared to stand calmly by and see the empire reduced to the two islands on which we lived and a few small isolated colonies scattered about the world?"[22] The Duke of Somerset's maiden speech in the Lords, in 1900, emphasized the threat from other countries: "My lords, we have won half our splendid Empire with the sword. We have only to look at the nations around us, armed to the teeth and jealous of our prosperity and freedom, to see that we must be prepared to defend the whole of it by the same means."[23]

The diehards and other Conservative peers reserved their harshest criticism about military and imperial affairs for the Liberal government of Campbell-Bannerman and Asquith. They believed that the

Liberals were weakening Britain's defenses at a time of great danger of war and possibly of invasion. They repeatedly stressed that negotiations were no substitute for powerful armed forces as a means to keep the peace. Lord Roberts' speech to the London Chamber of Commerce in the summer of 1905 emphasized England's "unpreparedness for war" and warned that "the only true safe-guard is that the armed forces of the Crown should be in such a state of readiness and efficiency that it would not be to the interests of any power to risk War with us."[24] Roberts' message was echoed throughout the country by those who professed both their faith in military power and their fear of the Liberals' intentions. Some months later Lord Bathurst averred that the Liberals seemed to wish to cut down on military spending and thus reduce Britain's power in the world. This would be disastrous, he continued, because "it was the strong man who walked safest through the crowd, and he thought they would all agree with him that they wished this country to be a strong man armed . . . that we might not suffer from our neighbours."[25] The diehards were never shy of using the strongest language to express their distaste for the Liberals, and national defense was a topic which aroused some of their bitterest comments. In *The New Order,* a collection of conservative essays which the Earl of Malmesbury edited in 1908, he denounced socialism as a "malignant" growth, "a poisonous weed of huge proportions" which was "destroying our national defences and warping the strength of the nation . . . Socialism — narcotic-like — has drugged the spirit of patriotism into a forced slumber."[26] In 1912 the Duke of Somerset went so far as to allege that the Liberal ministers were "using the revenues as a huge fund for bribing their supporters by giving them posts . . . It annoys me to see how helpless we are to stop all this & to put our Navy and Army into a condition wh. will enable them to do their duty when the storm bursts — which with our present rulers I fear will not be long."[27]

It was not unusual, of course, for Conservatives to use the issue of national defense as a stick with which to beat a Liberal government. The diehards were different from most of their fellow aristocrats not so much in their opinions — though these tended to be more extreme than most — but in their persistence, the strength of their commitment, and in the leading role which many of them took in military and imperial controversies. The problems of national defense were not simply political weapons for the diehards. They believed that they faced a new and crucial international situation, one which demanded powerful arms and a watchful attitude. They did not waver in their call for larger armed forces even in the midst of the constitutional crisis, and their concern was not solely for public consumption. Milner told Lord Roberts in 1909 that "National Defence is more important than any of the things we are fighting about, & my principal reason for wishing to get the Liberals out is that they are even more apathetic about it than the Unionists."[28] Diehards did not confine their activities to general comments or public attacks on Liberals during political campaigns. Their concern led them to participate fully in current controversies about Britain's power and role in the international arena.

The navy was the focal point of important disputes about size and tactics. The Duke of Somerset was for some years president of the Navy League, while Willoughby de Broke led the Imperial Maritime League. The latter organization was founded in 1907. One of its main objectives was the removal of the first sea-lord, Admiral Fisher, whose reforms of the navy, especially his reliance on dreadnoughts, had met with much opposition. Other members of the Navy League included the Duke of Westminster and Lords Ampthill (who was especially active), Roberts, Fitzwilliam, Denbigh, Malmesbury, Meath, and Ranfurly.[29]

Lord Selborne, first lord of the Admiralty from 1900 to 1905, was the diehard most closely associated with national developments in the navy in the years before World War I. Selborne was responsible for the appointment of Fisher to second and then first sea-lord, in 1902 and 1904 respectively, and he remained a staunch supporter of the controversial admiral despite the attacks by much of the Conservative press and several of his fellow diehards. Like other diehards, Selborne was willing to change, even in the realm of class privilege, if he was convinced it would ultimately strengthen the empire, and the "Selborne Scheme" for navy modernization provided for a system of common entry and training for all executive officers to replace the old, socially discriminatory system of separate entry for different fields of the service. Archibald Hurd, one of the leading naval journalists and propagandists of the pre-1914 period, paid tribute to Selborne as "heart and soul 'a big Navy man'" who "never received the acknowledgement due to him for the courageous step he took in deciding that the old order had to give place to the new."[30]

In his preface for Hurd's short history, *Our Navy* (which appeared in 1914), Selborne adopted a gloomy, "now-or-never" attitude about the close link between the security of the empire and the strength of the navy. He argued that the very survival of the empire depended upon the power of the navy to maintain control of the seas. "It does not matter where the great battle is fought . . . if the British Fleets win that battle, then every part of the Empire . . . are all alike saved."[31] Selborne also expressed doubt about the preparedness of the navy for war. Other diehards showed similar concern. Both Bristol and Dynevor, while members of the House of Commons, had spoken often and at length on the necessity of the maintenance of the two-power standard, and had raised questions about the efforts of the Liberals in this area. Captain Frederick W. F. Hervey, later fourth Marquess of Bristol, urged in his speech on the 1906-1907 navy estimates that "our sole guarantee was our strength in battleships," not ententes, and that "what we needed were the biggest battleships with the biggest armaments in order that this country might wipe the floor with any nation which had the temerity unnecessarily to come into collision with it."[32] Subtlety of expression was not the strong point of most of the diehards' speeches. In 1910, W. F. Rice, later seventh Lord Dynevor, accused the government of failing to maintain the two-power standard and warned, "If you have a big Navy, you will have peace, and you will not have peace without it."[33] The specter of potential disaster and national humiliation loomed over many speeches and activities in all areas of national defense, but nowhere more prominently than in discussions of the navy.

The Duke of Bedford, although active chiefly in army affairs, was also interested in the navy. He was closely associated with Arnold White, a leading specialist in naval matters, who wrote for the *Daily Express* and advocated a strong navy through columns of *The Referee* under the pseudonym of "Vanoc" (Merlin's son in Arthurian legend). White conducted a long correspondence with Bedford on naval and military affairs, supplied him with information, and acted as his political agent. Bedford in return became White's generous patron.[34] White had warned for several years of the dangers of the strengthened fleets of the Continental powers, and in 1898 collaborated on *When War Breaks Out,* a novel in the form of a series of letters which dramatized England's unpreparedness for war.[35] Both White and Bedford, like their contemporaries, came to fear Germany most during the early years of the twentieth century. German industry, imperial adventures, and naval building programs all seemed to threaten Great Britain and its empire. Superior British power was the only safeguard against disaster.[36]

The Earl of Selborne and the Duke of Bedford were among the most prominent speakers in the Lords on naval problems, but other diehards were also active. Lord Muskerry, an Irish yachting enthusiast who lived on his boat anchored in the Thames while Parliament was in session, was the chief spokesman in the Upper Chamber on merchant marine affairs for three decades prior to the Great War. Muskerry and Lords Meath and Abinger introduced various restrictive bills by which British coastal and imperial trade would be reserved for British ships and property. They argued that it would be folly to allow aliens to gain an intimate knowledge of the British coast.[37]

It was the army rather than the navy, however, with which most aristocrats were actively concerned. The two military controversies which predominantly occupied their attention in the pre-war period were those over the Haldane army reforms of 1907 and the campaign for national service led by Lord Roberts. The diehards were not unanimous on these issues. In fact, both the Duke of Bedford, the leading opponent of Haldane's reforms insofar as they touched on the militia, and the Earl of Portsmouth, the Liberal under-secretary of state for War responsible for piloting those measures through the Lords, were to join together in voting against the Parliament Bill in 1911. During the committee stage of the debate on Haldane's Territorial and Reserve Forces Bill, for example, the future diehards were almost the only peers taking a major part in the debate on both sides.[38]

The reforms of R. B. Haldane, secretary of state for War in the Liberal government which took office in 1905, were designed to make the army into an efficient fighting force for service overseas. Instead of relying on a field force put together as occasion demanded, Haldane created a permanent expeditionary force. This change encountered little opposition.[39] However, Haldane believed that all parts of the army should be thoroughly integrated and he went on to reform the various reserve forces to achieve this goal. It was this measure which aroused the furious opposition of many peers. They were prominent officers of the three different auxiliary force organizations — the militia, volunteers, and yeomanry — which Haldane proposed to alter drastically. His plan, embodied in the Territorial and Reserve Forces Bill of 1907, was to dissolve the militia and to replace it with a special reserve which would be officered by members of the regular army and whose recruits, obtained from the same sources as the old militia, would pledge to serve abroad if the need arose. The purpose of the special reserve would be to maintain the expeditionary force for service in the field, rather than as a separate force.[40] The special reserve would thus be a part of the regular army, under the control of the War Office. The yeomanry and the volunteers, together with some of the old militia, were to be combined to form a new territorial force, organized into county units.

The traditional leaders of county society were firmly in control of the new territorial force. It was to be made up of representatives of county councils and secretaries of trade unions, presided over by the lord lieutenant of the county. The county councillors in the associations were nominated by the army council, not elected by the county council. The officers of the force were volunteers recruited from public school and university men who had participated in officers' training corps and from officers of the old auxiliary forces. The new reserve force organization actually reversed the whole trend toward democratization in the countryside:

For more than half a century the landed gentry had been progressively dispossessed of local government and the Radical victory at the polls in 1906 had seemed likely to accelerate the process. Now however at one point Haldane's initiative had not merely slackened but reversed it. The landed gentry were invested with new functions of military local government. [41]

However, many aristocrats objected strenuously to the formation of the territorial force and the special reserve, accomplishing as it did the destruction or amalgamation of the old auxiliary forces. Their opposition to Haldane's reforms did not stem from the simple issue of democratization versus continued control by the landed aristocracy. The latter was in any event to be maintained or even augmented, and both supporters and opponents of the reforms realized this. The controversy actually centered around questions of tradition and military effectiveness. The diehard Duke of Bedford was the leading figure in the Lords' resistance to the Haldane reforms. Bedford, an intensely traditional, immensely wealthy peer, commanded the militia in his own county. Along with Lords Roberts, Ampthill, Raglan, Lovat, and Bathurst among the diehards, he participated in the meetings called by Haldane in 1906 to discuss his proposed changes in the reserves. Lord

Roberts believed Haldane was moving in the right direction, but Bedford and the other diehards, representing the militia colonels, resented the disbandment of the militia and its use as a supply of men for the expeditionary force.[42] However, Bedford was a controversial figure, even within his own Unionist party, and resistance to Haldane's schemes was not Unionist policy. He had a deep respect for and interest in military matters. When his son and heir, the pacifist Hastings, refused to enter the army in 1914, Bedford wrote that he never wished to see him again and took steps (eventually unsuccessful) to disinherit him. Hastings did not visit Woburn Abbey again for almost twenty years.[43]

The need to reform the militia had been recognized since the days of the Boer War with its problems of mobilization and supply of reserves. In 1904 a royal commission chaired by the diehard Duke of Norfolk considered the issue but failed to come up with any promising suggestions.[44] In 1904-1905 the Unionist secretary of state for War, H. O. Arnold-Forster, proposed to divide the regular army into a general service army and a home service army, with the militia to be absorbed into the latter.[45] This plan ended with the fall of the Unionist cabinet, but not before the Earl of Selborne and the Duke of Bedford had expressed their disapproval. Selborne, then the first lord of the Admiralty, deplored the proposals on the grounds of both tradition and politics, arguing that the Unionist party, as the conservative party in the state, should preserve at least the name, if not the exact form of the militia, "one of the oldest institutions in the country."[46] The Duke of Bedford agreed that certain changes were needed in the militia, that methods of recruiting had to be improved, and that the duration of the annual drill should be increased.[47] He did not idealize the existing situation but he did claim that the militia system was the only viable alternative to conscription for raising a national army. Along with Lord Roberts, he urged that greater control be returned to the lord lieutenants and deputy lieutenants. Opposition by the diehards to changes in the militia thus varied in intensity and focus, but none wished simply to maintain the status quo.[48] Selborne wanted to preserve the form and name while allowing for major changes, while Bedford demanded the restoration of the militia to a supposedly more effective past state, with all militia institutions intact. Lord Lovat was correct in his belief that the two great issues, apart from tradition, were whether the militia would become a feeding organization for the regular army and would consent to serve abroad (which had not been required of the militia previously) and whether recruitment could be made more adequate.[49]

Haldane's decision that these problems could not be met under the existing reserve forces system provoked much of the opposition. Bedford and other diehards argued that the new system would be less efficient than the old in providing an effective military force. The duke complained that in disbanding the militia the government was doing away with a "sure and solid foundation . . . in order to catch at the phantom forces of a speculative Army."[50] The idea that the training of the proposed new force would be inadequate and too slow in case of a national emergency was constantly reiterated from 1906 until the outbreak of the Great War. Colonel the Earl of Erroll wrote disparagingly of "Mr. Haldane's Dream of a 'National Army,' " and Willoughby de Broke warned that "the six months' training after war breaks out that Mr. Haldane postulates for the Territorials nullifies our value as a land force to any ally in the event of a European conflict."[51] The diehards stressed practical military problems, often in technical terms.

The idea that the militia and the other reserve forces would become merely sources of supply for the regular army also troubled the diehards. The issue of foreign service was crucial to this question. "If I can get the Militia to back me up," the Duke of Bedford wrote Arnold White in June 1906, "now is the time to strike a bargain with the war office on foreign service enlistment. But the Militia must make a definite offer and if refused (which I hold to be impossible) must be prepared to resign and be replaced by the paid volunteer."[52] Bedford maintained that no officers would be attracted to the special reserve or the territorial force if they were not allowed to command their forces in the field, and that the quality of the enlisted men would decline because many mature men would refuse to serve at all if they were forced to pledge themselves to go overseas as part of the regular army. Bedford warned that the commanding officer of a special reserve unit would be in an intolerable position: "He is to ask his men to serve under his command in peace, and to hand them over to someone else in time of war, presumably because he himself is considered incompetent to go with them." Lord Ampthill added that to take men piecemeal from the militia battalion, or even to take companies rather than the whole battalion for service abroad, would destroy the strength of the battalion and would also deprive it of the chance to develop the tradition of service and valor which was considered essential to the morale of the troops.[53]

Behind these arguments in favor of the preservation of the militia battalion while on active service was the landed aristocracy's belief in the importance of the county and the necessity of long-standing personal and social relations to establish discipline and the proper military spirit. As a contemporary commentator noted, "The Militia is the most feudal force there is. At the head of the battalion the most prominent man in the county is very often found; the officers are drawn from the families who in former years might have ridden to war in his suite; and the men in civil life often work on the estates of their officers."[54] The diehards and other aristocrats who testified before the Norfolk Commission placed great emphasis on the desirability of having men of local prominence command the auxiliary forces. The "habit of command" was essential: "Officers from the county are in close touch with your men; they know the whole of the command personally . . . the men enlist readily with gentlemen they know and respect."[55] The Duke of Northumberland observed that long service with the same officers promoted the "habit of discipline" within a regiment.[56]

The belief in the virtue of having militia officers drawn from the ranks of local country gentlemen was coupled with the idea of the superiority of the agricultural laborer over the townsman as a recruit. Many aristocrats, including the diehards, held to a rather rigid city versus country attitude, that the city could contaminate the country if too close contact were allowed. The countryman was less rambunctious, more deferential, though perhaps less intelligent, and could be depended upon to be available year round. In addition, of course, the military discipline garnered from militia camp could prove useful to the aristocratic landowners in ordinary affairs. Viscount Wolmer, later the diehard Earl of Selborne, praised the simple residents of the countryside, who "give no trouble whatever. They are never cheeky; they are never insubordinate; they do not get drunk; they seem to like their work and enjoy their soldiering . . . With the townsmen it is otherwise . . . the localisation of the companies of the county volunteer regiments should be applied also to the militia. In this way the greater part of the contact between the agricultural labourers and the town roughs would be avoided."[57] By 1905 Selborne, who had commanded the Hampshire regiment since 1899, recognized that it was becoming increasingly difficult, due to rural depopulation and the growth of the cities, to separate recruits from the city and the country, ideal as that would be. "The town element is not a good one in a country battalion. If you keep the town element together they do very well, but don't mix them with the countrymen."[58] Lord Bathurst, whose own militia battalion was disbanded in 1908, feared that as a result of the reforms, "the country would . . . lose the services of many of the best type of young fellows from the country district . . . and the Special Reserve battalion would be filled with street corner boys . . . of not half the physique."[59] Many of the diehards believed that Haldane's reforms meant not only that the military power of Great Britain would be weakened, but also that the efficacy of military service as a force for social discipline and the maintenance of the status quo in the countryside would be destroyed.

Despite the fact that the county associations were dominated by the upper classes, the diehards were unsatisfied with this provision of Haldane's plan. They worried about the efficiency and added expense of a large number of new local organizations, and Bedford dismissed the entire idea with the comment that "nobody wants the County Associations."[60]

Although many peers protested Haldane's scheme, most of them took part in its implementation once the bill had passed. Colonel Charles à Court Repington, an important military correspondent, noted that even the most bitter critics "belied their criticisms by their patriotic acts. I cannot help laughing now at the remembrance of the Radicals trooping into one lobby to place the Second Line under the County families, and of the Tories trooping into the other lobby to prevent it."[61] Haldane toured the country to explain the new plan to county authorities and to persuade them to assist in its work. The irony of the spectacle of Haldane asking for the assistance of the county families, despite their early opposition to his plan and the general atmosphere of political mistrust which existed between the Liberals and the aristocracy, was not lost on the diehards. They seem to have relished the sight. Nevertheless, as the Earl of Erroll predicted, "they [the landed aristocracy] will play up, and will do their best to make the scheme workable, and will thereby heap coals of fire upon his head."[62] The peers used this circumstance as political capital for years after the plan went into effect, often repeating that, when things had to be done, both political parties looked to the landlords for help.[63]

Although the diehards and other Conservatives supported and often headed the territorial associations, many of them did not forgive Haldane for abolishing the old auxiliary force organizations. This was a contributing factor, along with his fondness for German culture, in Haldane's downfall in 1915. The Unionist campaign against his reforms intensified after the resignation of the conciliatory Balfour as leader of the party in 1911 and his replacement by Bonar Law. The latter made the army issue a straight party matter, and his attacks on Haldane were supplemented by Leo Maxse in the *National Review*.[64] When Arnold White, Bedford's political agent, wrote to congratulate Maxse on the commencement of the "Balfour Must Go (BMG)" campaign, he suggested an attack on Haldane as well. White reported that Bedford planned in the next month to assault "Haldane's veracity . . . But the Duke will probably make little impression on the public unless his attack is preceded by a general effort to get rid of the man who is the Jesuit of the Cabinet." White himself wrote condemnations of Haldane's policies in the columns of the *Daily Express* and the *Referee*. Lord Lovat and the Duke of Bedford continued to be among Haldane's most persistent critics in the Lords throughout this period. After the beginning of hostilities in 1914, the duke expressed the hope that White would "be successful in [his] pursuit of Haldane."[65]

An alternative proposed for Haldane's scheme was universal military service, a sharp break with British traditions of voluntarism and a notion which found little favor among the Unionist leaders. The impetus for discussion and action along these lines came from the experiences of the Boer War. In articles, parliamentary debates, and before the Norfolk Commission, diehards argued that some form of universal service was necessary in order to train men adequately for defense and to recruit sufficient numbers. Several diehards suggested that enforcement of the old militia ballot system would answer the need, but most believed that a new system and an intensive propaganda campaign were essential.[66]

The leading role of the diehard peers in military controversies was nowhere more apparent than in the National Service League, which they founded and led. It was the most militant and by far the most important organization which campaigned for universal military training in the pre-war years. It demanded four years of light (compulsory) training for home defense for all men between the ages of eighteen and thirty.[67] Lord Raglan was the league's first president, but its leading figure and second president was Lord Roberts, who had resigned from the army in 1904 to speak out on military issues.[68] Raglan's letter offering Roberts the presidency in 1905 reflected the members' fear of delay and their faith in the response of the people:

we shall never have the army we require till it is brought home to every man that it is his duty to make himself proficient in soldiering.
   Universal Service in some shape or form is bound to come sooner or later. I can't but think that there is grave danger in postponing it. That it would be unpopular with the working classes I do not believe. It is the middle classes who have done nothing from time immemorial for the defence of the country who shriek at the idea.[69]

The diehards advocated universal military service not only for its value for national defense but also for its social purposes. Many of them stressed the ability of universal service to bring different classes together and to revive the spirit of discipline and patriotism which they believed had faded badly. Through universal training for boys, "the spirit of patriotism and the sense of duty would be quickened in the nation, and in time of difficulty young men would rush to the ranks and compulsion would be unnecessary."[70] Universal service would "revive the disappearing manliness of our race" and, in the opinion of many diehards, could save the nation from weakening and divisive forces.[71] It was Roberts' belief that

the Army is not a perfect medium of education, but it does accomplish two things thoroughly: it demolishes class prejudices and teaches self-discipline. Of late years . . . the education of the nation has been singularly unsuccessful in these two respects. Apathy toward one's duties, "envy, hatred, and malice" towards other classes, do not make for a strong, happy, and united people, nor for a desirable Empire.[72]

The diehards' attitudes toward universal training were thoroughly integrated with their attitudes about society and politics as a whole. The diehards, like other aristocrats, viewed the army as an instrument to revive and preserve the traditional values and social order of the nation. Willoughby de Broke even introduced a bill in 1914 which would have required "young men who have either inherited or acquired a comfortable place in society . . . to justify this place by the performance of military duty."[73]

Fear of Germany and of a possible invasion of Great Britain underlay many of the demands of the National Service League.[74] Coupled with this fear was a strong belief that the navy alone was not sufficient for national and imperial defense. Roberts argued that the feeling of security prompted by "our island isolation" was "a false security."[75] Many of the diehards believed that if Britain relied only on the navy and the regular army it would be denuded of defenses in the event of a major war. The solution of this dilemma, they thought, lay in the formation of a large and thoroughly trained body of men for home defense. Lord Milner deplored the single-mindedness of the Liberal government and its military advisers:

> They never seem to think that we might be attacked . . . *when we already had* our *hands full,* with our small army all abroad, as it was in the Boer War, & our Navy engaged in keeping *distant* seas open for our communications.
> Fisher gives away the whole case in a simple sentence, "Arrangements are made, that the force at home, *under any circumstances,* will *never* be less than sufficient to cope with Germany."
> That is to say, however great the need of our fleet abroad, we *must always keep* more than half of it "tethered like a goat" in home waters, *because* we should be helpless, as no other nation would be, in case of invasion.[76]

The diehards' primary concern was the possibility of invasion. They did not see this as a remote contingency, but as a disaster which could easily occur in a few years or even months. This belief lent stridency to their statements about defense.

In July 1909 the House of Lords debated Lord Roberts' National Service (Training and Home Defence) Bill. Diehard peers took the major role in this debate, as they did in nearly all those related to military matters, although they were by no means united on the merits of compulsory universal training for home defense. Roberts, Milner, Lovat, Erroll, Ampthill, Norfolk, and Willoughby de Broke spoke in support of the bill. They argued that an adequate number of men could not be obtained without the implementation of Roberts' plan.[77] The Unionist party leadership opposed the bill, as did the diehards Bedford, Northumberland, and Salisbury. The Duke of Northumberland, who prided himself on his non-party stance, argued vigorously that the country would not stand for compulsion, that it was unnecessary, and that it would be harmful to herd the youth of all classes together in "one general hotchpot." Profoundly conservative, Northumberland opposed the introduction of the novel practice of compulsion as "a very momentous and far-reaching change, striking deep into the foundations of society, and affecting the whole character of the nation."[78] It was he who introduced the successful amendment rejecting the bill.

The Earl of Meath defended the voluntary principle during the debate, although he supported the idea of universal training with great vigor. He recommended that the people be given time to develop their imperial spirit: "You must remember they do not possess ancient coronets and musty title deeds; and, after all, education and the franchise are but recent events in the life of a nation." While picturing an England whose people had grown soft and irresponsible, Meath advocated

discipline in the upper classes, discipline in the middle classes, and discipline in the lower classes. If we had more discipline we should not have such a large number of men and women who think nothing of the State and of the community, whose sole idea is pleasure, pleasure, pleasure; and we should not have those "slackers" in the lower classes whose whole idea is how much money they can get out of their employers and how little work they can do. [79]

For Meath, as for other diehards, universal service would both improve national defense and be an effective force to mold society in a desirable manner.

During the years before and after the debate on Roberts' bill, many meetings were held in the provinces to support national service. The league was a convenient issue on which to attack the Liberals. As Willoughby de Broke recalled in his memoirs, "A provincial audience in the home counties nearly always contained enough high and dry Tories to warrant the success of an appeal to the crusted tradition of the Constitution in Church and State, not forgetting to mention Lord Roberts and the National Service League."[80] The diehards were among the leaders of local efforts to rally support for the league. Lord Stanhope invited Leo Maxse to join Lord Ampthill and himself at a gathering at his estate in February 1910: "Kent has done splendidly. We have taught England how to play cricket, we have taught her how to vote, & now with the exuberance of youth I hope to go one better still & make Kent an example as a hotbed for National Service."[81] Lord Roberts, intensifying his propaganda campaign after the passage of the Parliament Act of 1911, relied to a large extent on the assistance of his fellow diehards. For example, in August 1913, he wrote Lord Bathurst that he intended to hold a great London meeting in December, and he asked Bathurst to organize and speak at as many provincial meetings as possible between October and December.[82]

The National Service League became a major political issue for several of the diehard peers. It contributed to their hostility toward the Liberal government and the Conservative leadership of Balfour and Lansdowne. This was especially true of two of the most influential of the diehards, Lord Milner and Lord Roberts. Milner was convinced that the league's program should be adopted by the Unionist party and that "the National Service question is more important than any other"; "the alternative before this nation is 'Compulsory service or climb down.' "[83] Even Lord Roberts' bill, just defeated in the Lords, was insufficient although a step in the right direction. Compulsion would come eventually, even though "two or three years ago a proposal like that of the Bill would have been scouted by almost everybody. To-day *that* proposal would only need the support of some leading party politician to go down."[84] Milner strongly implied that a change in the attitude of the personnel of the Conservative leadership was necessary to secure the safety and strength of the nation. Lord Roberts was more explicit:

The small amount of success the N.S.L. has achieved is mainly due to the action of the Leaders on both sides of politics. Balfour, when in power pooh-poohed the idea of an invasion . . .

I had hopes at one time that the National Service League might be kept clear of politics, but of this there now seems little chance, and if it is to become a Party question, it is essential that the Leader of the Party should believe in it.[85]

Balfour's temporizing, even before the Parliament Bill crisis, had led Roberts, and other diehards, to the belief that a new Unionist leadership was essential.

Closely tied to problems of defense were those of the empire. The same feelings of foreboding which impelled the diehards to interest themselves in military affairs moved them to play an active part in imperial matters. Many of them were closely associated with the movements for national efficiency and for tariff reform. In Lord Milner their ranks included the leading prophet of the former creed and one of the most influential imperialists of the day. Tariff reform claimed many converts in the diehard group of peers and their support was important for the Chamberlain program. The Boer War had a tremendous impact on the British image of their power and position in the world. By the late nineteenth century, in the face of the so-called Great Depression and competition from Germany and the United States, much doubt and alarm were felt about Great Britain's status. The Boer War intensified these fears because it revealed Britain's isolation and the inefficiency to its organization for war. Politicians and journalists clamored for improvements in administration, asking that more power be given to experts and attacking the bungling of the political leadership. The critics hoped to establish the British government upon a more efficient basis in order to compete more effectively against Germany and to preserve Britain's power and influence.[86] This drive was symptomatic of the impatience with the old leaders of the Unionist party, such as Balfour and Lansdowne.

The diehards were prominent in the search for national efficiency. In 1901 Arnold White wrote *Efficiency and Empire,* one of the books which served to keynote the movement. He pressed for efficient administration, which he believed demanded a strict merit system, good pay and training, thorough definition of duties, and constant supervision. He attacked what he called "the Deterioration of our Rulers," holding up Lansdowne and Sir Michael Hicks Beach as examples of this phenomenon. White was no revolutionary, however, and his program for reform, like that of many other advocates of efficiency (and certainly of those diehards involved), was essentially a very traditional call for the aristocracy to regenerate itself, to take its rightful place as the leadership of the nation. White's thesis was that change must occur at once or disaster would strike—an attitude which many of the diehards shared. He lashed out at the influence of the "Smart Set" and of "foreign Jews," and vehemently assaulted the defects of all governmental departments. At the conclusion of *Efficiency and Empire,* White called for a "Man" to improve the administration of the armed forces and to provide a strong lead in national and imperial affairs.[87]

Lord Milner was one man to whom many looked for leadership. As a leading advocate of efficiency, Milner distrusted democracy and exalted the "scientific administrators." He believed that the English system of government was especially unfit to rule a far-flung empire.[88] He and his "kindergarten," a circle of young disciples originally formed from among his assistants during his tenure as high commissioner in South Africa, advocated a more tightly knit empire organized on the most efficient possible lines. They disliked democracy, regarding it as inefficient and changeable, exalted the strong administrator and the expert, and advocated imperial preference.[89] These ideas were attractive to most of the diehard peers, though not to all of them. After speaking with Milner in May 1908 about national service, Lord Salisbury remarked that "he does not believe in freedom in this, or I suspect in any thing."[90] However, Milner's authoritarian views and his dedication to strengthening the empire pleased many who thought that Britain faced its most severe test in the first years of the twentieth century.

A close relationship with or fervent admiration for Lord Milner, and an unusual degree of participation in South Africa or Africa in general, were among the links which helped to bind the diehards loosely together and to distinguish them from other members of the aristocracy. Firsthand knowledge frequently led to impatience with the traditional rulers who had nearly bungled the Boer War. Strongly imperialist sentiments also increased animosity toward the Liberal governments of Campbell-Bannerman and Asquith. In addition to military service in the Boer War, many diehards had official or family links with South African affairs. Lords Milner and Selborne served in succession as high commissioners of South Africa from 1897 to 1910. The diehard second Lord Rosmead was the son of Milner's immediate predecessor as high commissioner, Sir Hercules Robinson, first Lord Rosmead. Robinson had been a personal and official friend of Cecil Rhodes and was implicated in the Jameson Raid. Rhodes's patronage made Robinson's fortune, and he and his diehard son were dependent financially on African investments.[91] The second Lord Rosmead, who succeeded in 1897, took an active interest in imperial affairs.

When Lord Selborne replaced Milner as high commissioner of South Africa in 1905, Balfour predicted that he would "be a dreadful loss to the Government and the Party here; but he will be a great gain to South Africa." For Milner, "it was the greatest possible relief" to know that Selborne would succeed him.[92] Milner's faith in Selborne was justified. The new high commissioner enthusiastically supported Milner's and the "kindergarten's" pro-unification politics in South Africa. The Selborne memorandum of 1907, which advocated early unification, was drafted by Lionel Curtis, a member of the "kindergarten."[93] Selborne remained an advocate of many of Milner's ideas and later became an associate of the Round Table group, formed before World War I to promote imperial cooperation by means of discussion and publication of a journal.[94]

Diehards took the major roles in debates in the House of Lords about "Chinese Slavery" and Milner himself. The Duke of Marlborough, under-secretary of state for the Colonies, replied for the government to Liberal attacks in early 1904 on the Chinese slavery issue. The Marquess of Winchester, Lord Lovat, and other diehards were also firmly in the high commissioner's camp.[95] However, on this as on other military and imperial issues, while the diehards were prominent in debate, they were not necessarily agreed on the issues. In the case of Chinese labor in the Transvaal, the Earl of Portsmouth, who was to be under-secretary for War in the first years of the Liberal government, was one of the two most persistent critics of Milner in the Lords.

The vast majority of the diehards and other peers disagreed with Portsmouth's assessment of Milner. In March 1906, after the passage of a vote of censure against Milner in the Commons, the diehard Viscount Halifax moved a resolution in the Lords in praise of Milner. He identified Milner as the symbol of the British Empire and claimed that the censure had angered those who sided with the British in the Boer War. Halifax asked the peers to reaffirm their determination to maintain the power of the empire by their appreciation of Milner. Lords Ampthill (seconding the motion), Roberts, and Halsbury followed Halifax to speak on Milner's behalf. The resolution passed 170 to 35. Those opposed included the future diehards Portsmouth and Stanmore, both of whom counted themselves Liberals at this time.[96] At the same time, a public address in support of Milner was signed by over 370,000 people and presented to him by the Duke of Somerset, chairman of the Address Committee.[97]

Several of the diehards, in addition to Lord Rosmead, had business interests in Africa. Lord Lovat, an early supporter of the "kindergarten" and Round Table group, had campaigned for land settlement in South Africa as early as 1902 and formed a private company for this purpose in 1907.[98] The Marquess of Winchester was heavily involved with Rhodes's British South Africa Company and was chairman of two other African companies. Ten other diehards held positions in 1911 with companies operating in Africa.[99]

Joseph Chamberlain's tariff reform campaign, which began in 1903, was the center of the most important pre-war controversy about imperial affairs. Serious worries about the state of national defense were among the most important factors leading many of the diehards to take a prominent part in the effort to secure tariff reform. Some expressed the fear that without such reform Britain would soon lose its place among the great powers of the world. The Earl of Selborne wrote a Conservative M.P. in 1903 that, "The more I study the question the more I am convinced that, if this country is to maintain herself in the years to come in the same rank with the U.S., Russia, & Germany, the unit must be enlarged from the U.K. to the Empire."[100] The following year the Duke of Bedford published "one of the most suggestive contributions to the present controversy," in which he argued that military, imperial, and business considerations required tariff reform: "The alarming increase in our national expenditure, an increase which must continue if we are to hold our own — and I cannot accept any other position in the world for Great Britain except that of first — must be met by an increase in taxation."[101]

Speeches on tariff reform frequently included references to the German threat. By 1909, for Lord Bathurst, "the whole question [had] resolved itself into this — was Britain going to exist as the greatest Empire in the world, or was she to fall into the insignificance of a petty state: There was no middle course."[102] Fabian Ware, editor of the *Morning Post,* wrote Lady Bathurst, the newspaper's proprietor, that Spencer Wilkinson, his naval correspondent, was not fervent enough in his demands for a bigger navy and for tariff reform, despite the fact that "he and all men in his position now see that the Imperial solution (towards which Tariff Reform is the first step) is England's only chance." Ware reported to Lady Bathurst that Wilkinson "has been wanting to write saying that there are no causes for misunderstanding between England & Germany at present — but I *won't* let him; to allay fear of Germany is to throw away our *only* chance of getting the people here to bestir themselves." The German threat was thus both a very real concern and a political tool. For Ware and the Bathursts the concern for the strength of the empire was coupled with the fear that Englishmen would be too slow to deal with the problem. They felt a strong sense of crisis. "*The* thing that wants shouting from the housetops at present is that if the whole Empire does not combine we cannot keep up this naval rivalry . . . That is why we must have Tariff Reform — the only practical Imperial link."[103]

The Duke of Westminster, an active tariff-reformer, published an article in 1912 which summarized much of what had been said over the past years about the dangers to the empire and the possible solution. "The rule of the middle class has come to an end," he announced.

"Democracy has arrived. A democratic national policy has taken the place of the ancient utilitarianism, and Imperialism is merely the latest, and I think the highest, incarnation of our democratic nationalism." Westminster warned of the dangers threatening the empire and stated that, "During the last fifty years the comparative strength of Great Britain has declined while the vulnerability of the British Empire has greatly increased." Common tariffs and a valuable market were the best ways to bind the diverse areas of the empire together. Westminster stressed that the time had come when the intense competition from other nations could no longer be ignored. "We have come to the parting of the ways. We must either unify the Empire or allow it to disintegrate."[104]

"Unify" or "disintegrate" were the stark alternatives offered by worried imperialists by the early twentieth century. Forebodings of disaster, the desire to halt what appeared to be a downward slide in Britain's relative position in the world, led some writers and political figures to look beyond purely military questions in order to salvage English power. The British Empire had been founded and maintained partly on the assumption of racial superiority: that the British "race" was more fit and moral than its subject peoples, whether Irish or African. This easy assumption was called into question soon after it became known that a high proportion of recruits for the Boer War were unfit for service.[105] The most usual reaction among both Conservatives and Liberals, including most diehard peers, was to demand measures to improve health and physical fitness. A strong people would insure a strong empire. Lord Meath was particularly prominent for his activities to promote physical fitness and his constant emphasis on the necessity of what he called "Grit."[106] He and his wife sponsored an impressive variety of charities and schemes for social improvement. From 1904 on, he advocated the establishment of an annual Empire Day during which students would engage in patriotic activities. Meath hoped that such a day would help prevent the "growth of enervating luxury and of the spirit of selfishness" which he believed were weakening the British people.[107] Puritanical strains united with patriotism in an effort to promote ruggedness, strength and self-sufficiency. The ill-nourished, weak, and luxury-loving people were to be transformed into warriors ready to stave off national disaster.

Increased exercise and better diet were not, however, the only solutions proposed to halt the decline of the British people's fitness. More drastic than Meath's traditional paternalist stance, or even than that of the Liberal social reformers, was the emphasis on race and breeding. Only the strongest and most intelligent members of English society should be allowed to have children. Armaments and imperial acquisitions were of no avail if the quality of the race degenerated.[108] The eugenicists and their followers, who included a very few diehards, stressed a curiously gloomy, pessimistic racialism which well suited their allied perceptions of threats to national security. They did not dwell on the exalted status of the British race, though they all acknowledged its past greatness and potential for the future. Instead, they concentrated on its degradation and the danger of imminent collapse of the empire, which this fall from racial health portended. Arnold White, the diehard Duke of Bedford's associate, urged that the unfit not be allowed to marry and warned that "race improvement to-day is not a question of philosophy, but existence . . . If the first law of life is self-preservation, England must choose between State suicide and race-improvement."[109]

Lord Willoughby de Broke was by far the most devoted and outspoken eugenicist among the diehard peers, the vast majority of whom had nothing to say on the subject. A friend of C. W. Saleeby, the founder of the Eugenics Society, he published several articles and delivered numerous speeches in which he emphasized in the strongest terms the need for physical improvement. He referred to social reform legislation as "measures for the improvement of the race" and supported various legislative proposals, including women's suffrage (the "effective advice of the mothers of the future race") and national service, on the grounds that they would benefit the "health of the nation." The maintenance of a secure Britain depended on "breeding from the best stocks and bringing to maturity the greatest possible number of mentally and physically sound men and women, reared among healthy surroundings, in the ideals of Religion and Patriotism, equipped with a trade education, protected by a Tariff from unfair foreign competition, [and] trained to bear arms."[110] Though only a few diehards would have spoken enthusiastically about biology and breeding, the vast majority of them shared Willoughby de Broke's concern for fitness, universal training, and social class.

The diehard peers were leaders among Conservative aristocrats in the military and imperial controversies of the early twentieth century. While it could be used as a political weapon, the issue of imperial defense was far more than that for the diehards. It shaped their political views at least as much as it served as a political tool. Along with other Conservatives, they saw their empire as a dangerously enervated giant. They demanded, with increasing shrillness as the new century wore on, that steps be taken to remedy what they believed was a crisis situation. At the same time that they faced an attack on their traditional way of life from within, they were convinced that the nation was in imminent and extreme danger of assault from without. This feeling of danger led many of the diehards to regard their established Unionist leaders with distrust, since it seemed they had done little to improve the situation while in power and because they seemed disinclined to fight for the more extreme military and imperial measures while in opposition. It also intensified the diehards' dislike for a Liberal government which, on top of its other sins, seemed to ignore the most urgent needs of national and imperial security.

6 / The Politics of Unionist Discontent

The Parliament Bill of 1911 abolished the power of the House of Lords to veto financial legislation and allowed the Upper Chamber to delay other measures for no longer than three years. The official policy of the Unionist leadership, faced with the Liberal threat to create enough peers to pass the bill, was to abstain from the division on the measure. The diehards' furious dissent from this policy and their vote against the bill gave the group of 112 peers its name. They have been pictured as old-fashioned aristocrats who longed for former days and whose revolt was an effort to restore a traditional way of life and method of governing.[1] This analysis is partly correct. The diehards did believe they were living through an age of national and international crisis and were profoundly disturbed by trends which had been gathering momentum since the mid-nineteenth century. Undoubtedly they preferred the security of the old ways to the uncertainties of the new. Viscount Halifax, prominently involved in church affairs for many years, had expressed his fear of the future in an article on "The Crisis in the Church" in 1903: "The twentieth century will not be as the nineteenth. We are on the eve of great changes. It is in more senses than one *le fin d'un siècle*. There is a movement of unrest and expectation on all sides. The foundations are being shaken everywhere."[2] There was a strong desire to preserve as much of the old order as possible, to salvage what could be salvaged of the power and social authority of the aristocracy. However, the method by which the diehards hoped to accomplish this has not generally been assessed by historians. The question, to continue Halifax's metaphor, is whether the diehards relied on repairs to the old foundations to shore up the ancient edifice of aristocratic influence and national strength, or wished rather to place the edifice on substantially new foundations. It was their stress on novel means for preserving the old system which characterized the diehards' approach to the problem. It also led them to propose great changes in the realm of personal finance and in military affairs, where many advocated the innovation of national service. The diehard peers exhibited no hesitation in using radical methods to maintain their position. Nor did they allow tradition to restrict their plans of action.

In this respect the diehards resembled what has been termed the "radical right" of the present day. Their objective was not simply the restoration of the old ways of life and politics. In fact, they were the leaders within the Unionist peerage of those who called for new plans to meet modern challenges. The foremost advocate of national efficiency, Lord Milner, wrote in 1911 that he wanted "a body of political doctrine, having some . . . *inner unity,* which will take account of all the great needs of our national life . . . and propound an orderly and coherent plan for dealing with them as a whole."[3] Milner was not the only diehard to demand new solutions from the Unionist party. The Earl of Malmesbury, who edited the radical conservative publication, *The New Order,* asserted that, "however difficult it may be for the more rigidly Conservative cast of mind to accept it, the necessity for new institutions and new movements in harmony with the changing spirit of the time has never been more imperative . . . and just in proportion as the Unionist Party proves itself capable of this adjustment will be its power of continued usefulness to the Country."[4] The cry for clarity and strong principles to serve as guides for action had been a constant refrain among the diehard peers for many years before the Parliament Bill crisis. It extended to all phases of national life. In the early 1880s, Lord Halifax had warned that, for the Church to survive and to influence the common people, "the religion she puts before them must be definite and distinct."[5] In 1911 Willoughby de Broke was insisting that "First principles, First principles, and again First principles are what we must preach. That is the only way to save Tariff Reform & everything else besides. No more utility."[6]

The diehards' sense of unease with the political and social trends of the time had developed over a long period before the crisis of 1909-1911. Successive franchise reform acts, Home Rule bills, and the development of the centralized party system seemed to most of the diehards to portend further sweeping and dangerous changes. They feared democracy and the possibility of socialism. Lord Percy, later the diehard seventh Duke of Northumberland, despaired of the future in 1883, even before the third Reform Act or the first Home Rule bill. Defining revolution as "the rejection of certain principles of political science which have . . . been regarded as the foundation of political power and of social rights," he believed that "a real, though not as yet a complete revolution" had already occurred.[7] Arthur Gordon, Lord

Stanmore, for many years a Liberal, had come increasingly to distrust Gladstone's policies. In early 1890 he expressed alarm "that there is on all sides a practical acquiescence in the inevitable destruction of our present institutions." Like Northumberland, Stanmore believed that the slide toward the Left had already gone very far. His "alarms as to the immediate political future in England" were by no means assuaged by Selborne's prediction that reaction would follow. "Yes, — no doubt there will be such a reaction, but will that reaction be an *ebb* of the tide, or only that reflex and momentary lull which follows the bursting of a succession of large breakers?"[8]

The fear of socialism was widespread long before the "People's Budget" of 1909. Several of the diehards believed that socialist doctrines fell on ready ears wherever there was high unemployment or poverty. The Earl of Meath had warned in 1899 that the increase in the population of Great Britain would lead to the creation of a poor and hungry stratum which would, "driven to desperation and beguiled by the honeyed words of Socialists and Anarchists, endeavour to improve their miserable lot by the general destruction of society."[9] It was the mark of the diehards' distrust of democracy that they believed that large masses of men could not possibly govern as well as a trained aristocracy, and that ordinary men would use their new-found political power to secure economic advantage. The voters of a democracy would "take keen interest in a subject for a moment, but to continue a sustained interest in *any* subject that does not directly touch their persons or pockets is impossible."[10] The Duke of Northumberland was persuaded that democracy led inevitably to socialism:

There never has been a period . . . when masses of men . . . have been persuaded that it is good that they should be compelled to work for a daily wage while others should not. Our ancestors were wise enough to see this, and kept the political power of the State in the hands of those who had property. We have destroyed their systems, & placed political power in the hands of the multitude, & we must take the consequences.[11]

The diehards were convinced that Great Britain faced a critical situation which demanded drastic, perhaps radical, action. In 1907 Selborne warned that "the social system *is* out of joint," and "it is our business to save the Constitution from immediate overthrow."[12] This conviction grew out of the onslaught of Liberal legislation in the post-

1906 period and the feeling that social changes were rapidly over-
taking the aristocratic way of life and mode of politics. There was a
desperate tone to many of the diehards' utterances. They expressed a
willingness to take radical conservative action long before the Parliament Bill upheaval. Several of Lord Halifax's speeches in the mid-
1890s, for example, strongly prefigure—in their angry language and
defiance of the will of the Commons—the speeches of the diehards
against the Parliament Act and the Home Rule bills of 1912-1914.
Halifax spoke often as a representative of the English Church Union,
an organization which had long advocated independence for the
Church in theological affairs. His choice of language was close to that
later used by the diehards against the Liberals. Halifax, as well as
other diehards, believed increasingly that the will of the nation could
not be expressed by a parliament controlled by tightly knit party organizations or "caucuses." In 1895, when he moved his Divorce Amendment Bill—designed to repeal a law forcing the Church to bless marriages of those who had been divorced for adultery—he suggested that
clergy and laity of the Church of England would be justified in refusing to obey statutes passed by such a parliament.[13] Halifax noted during the 1906 debate on the Deceased Wife's Sister Bill that some of its
measures "would provoke a quarrel between the civil law and con-
science, the result of which would be very much to the misfortune of
the law."[14] Advocacy of resistance to the law was not a traditionally
popular attitude among English conservatives, but it became a common stance for the diehards.

The diehards were not an organized or unified political faction
before the Parliament Bill crisis of July and August, 1911. During the
years of Liberal governments from 1906 through most of 1911 they
generally voted with Lord Lansdowne and the Unionist leadership. On
only a few issues—the military, Irish, and religious questions, to which
some of them were particularly sensitive—did significant numbers of
the future diehard peers oppose their Unionist leaders. Even on these
issues, just four bills in all, the diehards were far from unanimous in
their opinions. Thus while division lists for the period 1906-1911 reveal
that some of the diehards occasionally opposed their leaders, they do
not reveal a unified political faction preparing for a contest in which
112 peers were eventually to unite against the official policy of their
party. The lists do suggest frustrations with the Unionist party on cer-

tain specific matters which led disparate groups of dissatisfied peers to become the diehards of August 10, 1911.

Two of the four bills on which differences with the leadership had already become apparent were intimately connected with religious issues. Both the Education (England and Wales) Bill of 1906 and the Marriage with a Deceased Wife's Sister Bill of 1907 aroused strong emotions from such prominent High-Churchmen as Lord Halifax. There were thirty-one divisions of the House of Lords over the Education Bill, and on all but five of these divisions almost all of the diehards voted with Lord Lansdowne. In those divisions in which several diehards voted against Lansdowne, a considerable number of diehard peers voted with him. Thus on an amendment offered by Lord Clifford of Chudleigh and opposed by Lansdowne, seventeen future diehards voted against the amendment and seventeen for it. Those voting with Clifford included many of the diehard Roman Catholics and High-Churchmen. A similar mixed voting pattern obtained on the other divisions of the bill. Divisions over the Deceased Wife's Sister Bill went much the same way, with almost equal numbers of diehards ranged on each side of the issue. Some followed Lansdowne and others, mostly Roman Catholics and High-Churchmen, refused to do so. To the latter, both bills were matters of principle which overrode party considerations — a favorite theme of all the diehards during and after the Parliament Bill debates.

The National Service Bill proposed by Lord Roberts in 1909 was the only other bill, besides those in 1910-1911 which involved reform of the House of Lords, on which a significant number of the diehards deserted the Unionist leadership. The vote on the National Service Bill was Contents, 103; Not-Contents, 123. Thirty-nine diehards voted with those pressing for national service. Only seventeen opposed this plan together with Lansdowne, other Unionists, and the Liberals. This opposition to the official policy of the Unionist party was the largest such display by future diehards before the Parliament Bill itself and was a measure of their commitment to national and imperial defense measures. The vote also underlines the importance of defense issues in contributing to the alienation of a large number of diehards from both the Liberals and their own leaders.

The Irish Land Bill of 1909 also alienated some of the diehards from Lord Lansdowne in one division (out of twelve). At issue was whether the Congested Districts Board should be compelled to hire land for tenants if efforts at voluntary purchase failed. The proposal had been initiated by the Irish diehard, Lord Atkinson, and was supported by the Liberals, Lansdowne, and twenty-five diehards, very few of whom held Irish land. Thirteen diehards, all but one of whom were Irish landlords, voted against the motion and thus against Lord Lansdowne. Irish affairs were of great importance in increasing the tendency of many of the diehards to ignore the will of Parliament and traditional methods. The Home Rule struggles of 1886 and 1893 had alienated large numbers of Liberal peers from their old leaders. Several of these men, or their heirs, became diehards.[15] The various Irish land acts, designed to eliminate the landlord problem from Ireland and passed by both Liberal and Unionist governments, created disillusionment among many future diehards with the leadership of the Liberal and Unionist parties. Prior to the Parliament Bill crisis a large group of peers with Irish interests no longer believed they were represented politically by the traditional leaders of the Unionist party. In their frustration and anger with the normal political process they turned to radical methods to preserve their old status. In this effort they were joined by similarly inclined peers disgruntled for other and allied reasons.

The idea of drastic resistance to Home Rule was not new to the crisis years of 1911-1914. Thoughts of offering armed defiance to the government were current in diehard circles at least as early as the 1890s. In 1892 Lady Monkswell was strongly affected by Edward Ponsonby (later Lord Bessborough) when he told her "with flashing eyes" that Irish Unionists "would fight" rather than agree to Home Rule.[16] She was sympathetic to the idea of radical resistance, as were many English diehards, and this feeling grew with the passage of time and the growing worries about the preservation of property rights and national defense.[17] Bessborough's comments were echoed frequently by Irish diehards. At an Ulster Unionist Convention in 1892, the Earl of Erne warned that, if "Parliament in a moment of madness repudiate our allegiance . . . then we say to them . . . that though Parliament has a right to govern Ulster it has no right to sell her into slavery . . . We tell them . . . that an assembly such as they are seeking to constitute is no place for the Loyalists of Ulster, that we repudiate its authority."[18]

The Unionist leadership's support of Irish land legislation alienated many Irish peers and their English supporters, and several future diehards took a prominent role in attacks on what they considered English Unionist betrayal. In the 1890s Lords Erne, Clonbrock, Muskerry, and Templetown were leading speakers in Parliament on behalf of Irish landlords. In 1896, during debates on a Unionist Irish Land Bill, Clonbrock was particularly outspoken and impassioned in his verbal assault. He and other diehards asserted that Irish landlords were treated unjustly because of their political weakness. Clonbrock noted that "there were but two courses in Ireland by which the attention of English Statesmen could be attracted — by resistance to the law and by votes in the ballot-box." He, like other landlords, had hoped this situation might be changed by a Unionist government, but the outcome had been "not only disappointment, it almost amounted to despair."[19] Given their disillusionment with their traditional leaders, and the impossibility of gaining majorities in southern Irish elections, the alternative of "resistance to the law," noted but not yet advocated by Clonbrock, became increasingly attractive. Conservative and Liberal Unionist peers voted against the proposed land legislation in the Lords. A list of the rebellious peers named seven diehards who voted against their leadership on all six divisions relating to the bill, and twenty-six others who voted against the government on at least one division.[20]

Several Irish diehards expressed varying degrees of anger with George Wyndham's Land Purchase Act of 1903, another Unionist measure. Most extreme and vocal of all of them at this juncture was Lord Muskerry, whose opposition was too unswerving even for the stalwart Lord Clonbrock. On August 11, 1903, Muskerry stated his full case against a Unionist government which he regarded as grievously lax in its support of the Union. He demanded to know whether it was not "time to inquire who are the present custodians of Conservative principles . . . For some time I have been wondering what has become of the Conservative Party? Past Governments who claim to be Conservative have been any thing but Conservative as regards their Irish policy." Muskerry believed that all land legislation had been unjust and dishonest, and had "shown great cowardice on the part of successive Governments, who have prostituted their sense of justice to the outcry of agitators, and for the purpose of gaining a few votes or disarming opposition in the House of Commons."[21] His assertion that the Unionist leadership had chosen opportunism over principle was echoed by other diehards. In 1900 Viscount Templetown asked, "If once it is finally established that in any part of Great Britain you can take property for any purpose, without compensation, where is the security for any man's property? . . . if Socialism is to be the watchword of the Unionist party?"[22]

The more extreme Irish diehard landowners complained throughout this period that they had been betrayed by the Unionist leadership. In 1912 and 1913 Lord Ashtown corresponded frequently with Andrew Bonar Law, the new Unionist leader, and referred to the policies of the old leadership as the root of many Irish problems. In April 1912 he wrote that the "Fighting Unionists" were opposed to "Land Purchase on the Line of Mr. Balfour." Ashtown was one of those Irish diehards who refused to sell their Irish land, and in December 1913 he once again dispatched a letter to Bonar Law with a strong slap at the former Unionist policy regarding Ireland: "The present state of things is 'Sickening'. I and others have fought very hard to keep the flag flying in these parts & we see our weaker neighbours cleared by agitation connived at by the present gov. & by the Unionist gov. when Wyndham was Chief Secretary."[23]

While the Unionist leadership's attitude toward Irish land legislation alienated many of those diehards with Irish property, it was not crucial for other diehards and would not have caused them to break with the leadership. More important for exacerbating the relationship between most of the diehards and the party leaders was the controversy over protectionist tariffs which split the Conservative party in the first years of the twentieth century. During the last two decades of the nineteenth century the traditional dogma of free trade, virtually unchallenged since the repeal of the Corn Laws of 1846, began to be seriously questioned. Increasing competition from other industrial nations, especially Germany, and the onset of agricultural depression, led to demands for protective duties.[24] The entrenched tradition of free trade held firm, however, until 1901, when Sir Michael Hicks Beach, Conservative chancellor of the Exchequer, imposed a small duty on imported wheat in an effort to raise money for the Boer War. This was intended purely as a revenue measure, but it created joy in protectionist ranks and consternation among free-traders.[25] In 1903 the Conservative government repealed the duty on wheat.

Joseph Chamberlain, the colonial secretary, had meanwhile become convinced that the empire must be bound more closely together for reasons of power and economic prosperity. The best means to achieve this imperial goal would be tariff reform and imperial preference. On

May 15, 1903, Chamberlain delivered a speech in Birmingham in favor of tariff reform, including import duties on food. A three-way split quickly developed in the Unionist party between devout free-traders, tariff-reformers, and those who preferred to seek a compromise solution under Balfour's leadership. In July both the Free Food League and the much more powerful Tariff Reform League were founded. In September Balfour, seeking to preserve the unity of his party, succeeded in maneuvering the leading free-traders and protectionists in his cabinet into resigning.[26] The battle between these two groups and their followers raged thereafter, with Balfour generally attempting to hold to a noncommittal middle course. This attitude on the part of the leader of the party distressed both sides, but it particularly infuriated the tariff-reformers, who were much stronger and by 1905 had gained control of both the Conservative National Union and the Liberal Unionist Council.[27]

The diehards included a substantial number of ardent tariff-reformers. The adoption of tariff reform by these peers was a symptom of their fear of changes in Britain's powerful position in the world and of their desire to restore the prosperity of British industry and agriculture. They were not afraid to challenge the traditional creed of free trade and to effect a revolution in tariff policy, if by doing so they could preserve something akin to the status quo in internal affairs and restore Britain to a preeminent position in the international sphere. Frustration with the Unionist party leadership helped to bind the diehards together and to persuade them to take radical action.

Although the landed classes were split on the issue of free trade versus tariff reform, Joseph Chamberlain's imperialist conservatism has sometimes been defined as "the creed of the successful industrialists, of the engineers and technicians."[28] Such an analysis seems to imply that it was the moderate Balfourites who were drawn from the landed interest, while the tariff-reformers and free-fooders came in large measure from manufacturing and commercial groups.[29] The Chamberlain group supposedly experienced an influx of landed aristocrats only after the introduction of the terms of the budget of 1909, when many aristocrats became convinced that tariff reform was the only feasible alternative to socialism.[30]

Although generalizations regarding the disinclination or slowness of landed aristocrats to adopt tariff reform may be partially correct for the peerage as a whole, they do not apply to the actions and attitudes of a large proportion of the diehards.[31] These peers were not slow to see the appeal of protection, nor did they all become converted to tariff reform only after the "People's Budget" was adopted. They did not abandon Chamberlain's cause after the Parliament Bill had passed. A conference of diehards in late 1911 "agreed that the main issues of principle, were Imperial Unity, Defence and Social Welfare, with Tariff Reform as the essential economic instrument."[32]

Protectionist sentiment was strong in diehard ranks even before 1903. Agricultural protection was not synonymous with Chamberlain's full program, but it did provide many of the diehards with a basis for sympathy with the campaign for tariff reform. As early as 1894 and 1895 agents for the Earl of Strathmore and the future fourth Marquess of Bristol told the Royal Commission on Agriculture that some form of protection was needed to restore the prosperity of British agriculture. Other countries had adopted tariffs and it was unfair to continue to uphold the old dogma of free trade alone.[33] The Earl of Coventry was of the opinion that " 'the Chancellor of the Exchequer might have reimposed a shilling duty upon wheat without hurting anyone. Until we in England are placed on even terms with the foreigner, agriculture will never flourish again.' "[34] Lord Halsbury, not a landowner himself and well aware of the internal and external ramifications of protection, later claimed that he had been a "Chamberlainite . . . before Mr. Chamberlain."[35]

Systems of protection and of retaliatory tariffs for use against nations which built up tariff walls were much discussed before Chamberlain's campaign began. Even the fourth Marquess of Salisbury, always opposed to tariffs on food, had suggested in 1901 that retaliation might be necessary to maintain the strength and unity of the empire.[36] Despite his association with the free-fooders (among them his brothers, the Lords Hugh and Robert Cecil), Salisbury was never a rigid free-trader. His resistance to tariff reform was based on political rather than ideological grounds. He claimed to "have no repugnance to Colonial Preference nor do I think that Retaliation is irreconcilable with Free Trade."[37] He was afraid, however, that tariff reform would be a political liability. He advocated a cautious, step-by-step approach, "not with a view of fraudulently committing the country by degree to a policy which they otherwise would not adopt; but because I . . . think it is only a policy of this kind which has the least chance of real approval by the mass of the Conservative Party."[38]

Many of the diehards were early converts to tariff reform, partici-pating actively in the Tariff Reform League long before the sup-posedly crucial experience of the budget of 1909. The executive com-mittee of the league, inaugurated on July 21, 1903, included the Duke of Westminster and Lords Malmesbury and Ranfurly; Selborne was one of the two vice-presidents.[39] Earl Fitzwilliam, whom Joseph Cham-berlain persuaded to become honorary treasurer of the league in 1904, proved himself an excellent fund-raiser.[40] During 1904 the Dukes of Bedford, Newcastle, and Somerset lent their influence to the cause of tariff reform at public meetings near their country seats.[41] Viscount Halifax's biographer identified him as "an early convert [pre-1907] to Tariff Reform,"[42] and the same could apply to Lords Ampthill, Den-bigh, Marlborough, Bathurst, Leconfield, Muskerry, Stanhope, and Milner, among other diehards.

The activities of the diehards in favor of tariff reform varied widely, from speaking in Parliament and public meetings, and fund-raising, to writing controversial articles. Lord Selborne, a pragmatic and non-extremist advocate of protection, announced in Parliament in 1903 that free trade could no longer be considered a part of "revealed reli-gion." Rather, "the question that we now look at is . . . what is the policy which under given circumstances, will best suit this country or that."[43] By 1905, when he succeeded Milner in South Africa, Selborne was Chamberlain's "most trusted friend in the Cabinet" except for Chamberlain's son, Austen. Lord and Lady Bathurst were among the most fervent diehard supporters of Joseph Chamberlain. Their impor-tance in this regard was vastly enhanced by the fact that Lady Bath-urst, the daughter of Lord Glenesk, was the proprietress of the influ-ential right-wing newspaper, the *Morning Post*. The Bathursts, friends of both Joseph and Austen Chamberlain, were typical of the diehards in general in that they did not confine themselves to support of tariff reform from afar. The countess, along with Lady Malmesbury and other wives of the diehard peers, was an early adherent of the women's branch of the Tariff Reform League and founded a local group.[44] Lord Bathurst, like many of his fellow diehards, presided over his local chapter of the league and was also president of the larger Western Counties Tariff Reform Federation.[45]

Lords Selborne and Bathurst were not unique in their active support of protection. The Earl Stanhope became the secretary and treasurer of a fund to finance a speaker who would talk with workers in pubs about the empire and tariff reform, and Stanhope "had to do the work."[46] Lord Leconfield was in close touch with *National Review* editor L. J. Maxse and was an activist in the Tariff Reform League. In March 1907 he recommended that a giant Albert Hall meeting be held while the colonial premiers were in London: "It will not be my fault if a resolution does not go from every Branch in the County as well as from every village meeting that I can hear of. We must make the country ring with Tariff Reform while the Premiers are with us."[47] By 1908, tariff reform, including protection and imperial preference, had become an essential part of a radical conservative program for many of the diehards. In that year the Duke of Marlborough, former undersecretary to Chamberlain at the Colonial Office, urged a policy of preferential trade in the Lords.[48] Also in 1908, a year before the "People's Budget," the Earl of Malmesbury accorded tariff reform a prominent place in the "new order" proposed by Conservatives dissatisfied with hitherto dominant trends in national politics. He noted angrily that the empire was governed by men who called themselves collectivists, yet ignored "the right of the nation collectively to make its own terms in trade-bargaining with other countries and with distant parts of the Empire upon a proper commercial basis."[49]

Many of the diehards were in the vanguard of the Chamberlain campaign for tariff reform. They were joined in 1909 by other diehards who had come to the conclusion that tariff reform was the only alternative to socialism. However, the nucleus of men who were more inclined than most landed aristocrats to accept radical solutions to current problems already existed. The annoyance of many of the diehards with their own Unionist leadership's hesitant stance, their fear of Liberal financial and social legislation and, perhaps most important, their willingness to do something drastic about it, had been recognized for years. By 1909 they had become increasingly frustrated with the methods and results of traditional parliamentary procedure and the forms of British government in general. Events of the succeeding years greatly exacerbated these attitudes.

The protectionist issue was enough motivation for several of the diehards to turn against their leadership. The common complaint, as Lord Ebury, the active president of the Hertfordshire Tariff Reform Federation, later wrote, was that "some of our prominent politicians of the Conservative Party are infected with a philosophic detachment" which seemed inappropriate to the politics of crisis.[50] Although none of the diehard peers were actually members of the "Confederacy" (a secret organization of extreme protectionists dedicated to driving free-traders from the Unionist ranks), as Milner and others were rumored to be, there can be no doubt that many of them sympathized with that group's goal and success. By 1905 the tariff-reformers had captured the National Union. They were increasingly restive with Balfour, especially after the Liberal landslide of January 1906. Ivor Maxse (brother of L. J. Maxse) urged the necessity of drastic action in the face of national peril. He told Lady Bathurst that the question of the Unionist leadership was "merely the outward sign of deep rooted disorder," and that the controversy surrounding tariff reform was part of a larger concern that the "British Empire must be *organised*" for purposes of defense. "The old Tory sees none of these necessities . . . Therefore we must split the party for a time . . . Our idea must be and will be the antidote to socialism."[51]

Most of the diehards in 1906 would not have gone as far as Maxse in his desire to split the Unionist party, but there was a general feeling that new solutions to contemporary problems must be reached. In July 1906, for example, Lord Ebury confessed that he would "be glad a little later on to associate . . . with any movement having for its objective to convince the leaders of the Conservative Party that its rank and file are deeply dissatisfied with their inability to shake off 'the sleeping sickness.' "[52] Many of the diehards had already associated themselves with the movement for change within their party.[53]

Both the peers with Irish interests and those who were strong tariff-reformers were disgruntled about official Unionist policy long before 1911,[54] but during the first years of the Liberal government they had little reason to complain about their leadership's attitude toward Liberal legislation. Several of the most controversial Liberal bills were rejected or mutilated by the House of Lords with the full approval of Balfour and Lansdowne.[55] The majority of the diehards concentrated on uniting to resist the Liberals rather than on divisive issues within the Unionist party. Salisbury and Selborne attempted to heal the wounds of the protectionist controversy, and even Lord Halsbury, a staunch tariff-reformer and by no means a man of moderate opinions, sought to smooth over differences between the various wings of his party.[56] This short-lived quest for unity failed to resolve the problems of the Unionist leadership. The effort to paper over differences reached greater proportions after the introduction of the budget of 1909 under the pressure of a direct attack by the Liberals on upper-class economic interests. It was at this time that many former Balfourite moderates, including some future diehards, shifted their allegiance to tariff reform as the best way to defeat socialism. The Duke of Northumberland feared that

the only effect of a continued wrangle over Free Trade versus Tariff Reform will be to make us utterly powerless to withstand it. Standing as I do aloof from both parties, I can only say that I hope we shall sink our differences and combine upon the much more important issue . . . The only feasible course is to side with the bigger battalions, which I rather think the Tariff Reformers are . . . The whole thing seems to me to be merely one of expediency, whereas Socialism involves moral principle of the very highest importance. [57]

Thus the new-found party unity was heavily weighted toward the protectionist side of the party split, leaving the leadership, which was mainly middle-of-the-road, partially isolated from much of its following. In 1909, when Balfour officially accepted a measure of tariff reform as Unionist policy, the problem seemed to be somewhat eased. However, at Albert Hall on November 29, 1910, Balfour pledged that any protectionist legislation would be submitted to a referendum before being passed into law by a Unionist government.[58] This "referendum pledge" infuriated tariff-reformers and made clear the fact that the leadership was prepared to accept unity under the tariff-reform banner only temporarily and for opportunistic reasons.[59] Faced with the threat of the budget and the abolition of the veto power of the Lords, the diehards could not publicly quarrel with their leadership during 1909-1910. However, the fact that tariff-reformers dominated the party except in the top leadership may have further exacerbated feelings and contributed to the diehard tariff-reformers' belief that they represented the largest proportion of the population. The facade of unity, representing as it did an increased number of tariff-reformers, perhaps heightened the frustration of the diehards with the hesitant Balfour and Lansdowne.

Lloyd George's 1909 budget proposals were designed to meet the costs of new social legislation and greater naval building programs. The chancellor of the Exchequer wished to raise the rates for death and estate duties somewhat, and to increase income tax revenue by introducing a distinction between earned and unearned income, taxing the latter more heavily, and adding a supertax on all incomes above £5000. Most controversial and bitterly resented by the landed aristocracy, however, were three proposed taxes on land: a 20 percent tax on the unearned increment, a capital tax on the value of undeveloped lands and minerals, and a reversion duty on the increased value of leases whenever they were terminated.[60] Tariff-reformers in general were incensed by the budget, which they regarded as an attempt to raise revenue by more traditional means than their protectionist proposals. They were determined to defeat it to prove that tariff reform was the only answer to the need for increased revenue. The landed aristocracy was enraged by the taxes on land. These new burdens were aimed particularly at urban landlords, among whom several of the diehards were prominent.[61] Purely agricultural land had been exempted from the new duties, but not from the land valuation for which the budget also provided. This valuation, and the implication of the new land taxes, aroused the fears of both landed aristocracy and gentry.[62] In late May and June the Budget Protest League, headed by Walter Long, was formed, and talk of rejection of the budget by the Lords began to spread.

The future diehard peers were quick to discuss the possibility of throwing out the budget and were loud in their resentment of Lloyd George's proposals.[63] Fabian Ware, editor of the diehards' favorite newspaper, the *Morning Post,* and a close confidant of Lady Bathurst, summarized some of the main objections to and the implications of the budget:

it seems to me a *political* budget in the sense that it endeavours to effect financially all the worst political things *that we feared that this Govt. might do.* In their attempt to ruin the *classes* they hate . . . they are . . . ruining the *nation.* Capital will go out of this country more quickly than ever . . . This means more unemployed here & less money for the Navy etc. They mean confiscation of landed property . . . As far as landowners in rural districts are concerned the situation is really serious. Not only have the industrial classes . . . no sympathy with agriculture but they have been made to believe for years that they can get all their food cheaper & better from abroad & that our Navy is invincible & that an agricultural population is of no value . . . *Of course* every member of the Govt. knows better but they are playing the same shameful unscrupulous game that they played with old age pensions & in addition are appealing to the worst & most dangerous of class jealousies. [64]

Lord Halsbury expressed the meaning of the budget in simpler terms: "It means, of course, that everyone who has nothing, and deserves to have nothing because he would not work, has a right to take away something from his neighbour, who has something because he worked, while the other has been idle and lazy."[65]

Despite the diehards' universal detestation of the budget, there was some hesitation, for fear that throwing it out in the Lords might smack too much of self-interest. Lord Stanmore, one of the few free-trade diehards and hence a peer who had no ax to grind for tariff reform, was at first inclined to allow the budget to pass, in order to avoid giving the Liberals an issue with which to "mislead the mob of ignorant voters who now elect our Parliaments." But after reading the bill, Stanmore concluded that unless the Lords opposed the land clauses, "we shall forfeit our own self-respect and the respect of the country, and we shall be swept away as mere cumberers of the ground with the common assent of all parties."[66] Lord Milner, one of the most ardent diehard tariff-reformers, expressed similar early doubts about the course to follow. He concluded, like Stanmore, that the budget should be thrown out in order to maintain the dignity of the Lords, but admitted that if he were assured that rejection of the budget would strengthen the hand of the Liberal government, he might disregard the prestige of the peers. However, in August, he registered annoyance that Balfour and Lansdowne were not providing a more vigorous lead.[67] Lord Northcote held even stronger reservations about drastic action as late as October 1909, urging that the best course would be to state extreme disapproval and reserve the right to modify the budget's provisions when the party was restored to power: "Our fire-eaters will be furious, & will threaten never to work for the Party again; but time must bring them to heel."[68] Lord Northcote's moderate counsel was ignored, of course, and even those diehards who originally doubted (and these were not a great proportion of the diehard peers) almost universally voted against the despised "People's Budget," with the full approval of their Unionist party leaders.

The diehards were prominent in the debate on the 1909 Finance Bill in the House of Lords. Their speeches revealed a growing dissatisfaction with traditional political channels and indicated a willingness to take radical conservative action. Along with other Conservative peers, they objected to the budget on the grounds that it was socialistic, that it represented blatant discrimination against landowners as opposed to other wealthy men, and that it was the result, not of the will of the people, but — in Willoughby de Broke's words — of "the tyranny of that

small knot of Cabinet Ministers who have managed somehow to gain
the mastery over their colleagues, and to get the control for the time
being of the House of Commons."[69] This accusation, which was frequently reiterated, reflected the diehards' distrust of the growing
power of centralized party organizations and the cabinet. In a speech
described as "delightfully breezy," Willoughby de Broke expressed the
diehard intention to defy established procedure and law if these did not
suit their purposes: "though I have a very great respect for the Constitution, I do not believe the average elector cares the least bit about the
Constitution, provided he gets what he wants. He very rightly recog-
nizes that the Constitution of this country was made for England, and
not England for the Constitution." Some of the older diehards, such as
Halsbury and Norfolk, were more concerned in the debate with justify-
ing the rejection of the Finance Bill in constitutional terms. There was
a consensus among the future diehards that extreme steps were to be
sanctioned and that traditional modes of parliamentary behavior were
to be thrown aside if circumstances warranted.[70]

The dissolution of Parliament after the Lords voted down the budget was followed by the so-called "Peers' Campaign," organized mainly
by Curzon, in which the diehards played a leading and enthusiastic
part.[71] They attacked the tyranny of the Liberals, the dangers of the
budget and of an uncontrolled House of Commons, the Irish threat,
and the hostility of the Liberals to tariff reform. The Unionists made
large gains in January and held their ground in December 1910, but
the majority which the diehards sought did not materialize.[72] In the
meantime, their political attitude grew increasingly intransigent and
extreme. Stanhope feared possible violence and saw a parallel in the
situation which illustrated the diehard concern as to the extremity of
the crisis: "Have you grasped the historical analogy — 8th May 1641
Commons voted that they should not be dissolved except by their own
consent, Oct. the Irish Rebellion & 50,000 Irish were killed, 1642 Civil
War in England!"[73] Like most of the diehards, Stanhope was rather
matter-of-fact in his expectation of rebellion or other extreme action.
The diehards, especially the large proportion of them who had Irish
interests or were long-standing tariff-reformers, had by the end of
1910 come to accept any radical political moves as entirely justified
and as the result of long thought and experience. For most of them,
opposition to the Parliament Bill and defiance of their own Unionist

leadership was not the fruit of instinctive reaction but rather of a considered intent, based on a good deal of political activity, to take radical and absolutely clear action to restore an older framework of order.

During the years surrounding the constitutional crisis there was much discussion by the peers about the possibilities of a reform of the House of Lords and of instituting a referendum to decide certain important issues. The diehards were deeply involved in these discussions, though they frequently disagreed in their conclusions. An analysis of their views on both questions reveals their beliefs about trends in politics in general during the period before the vote on the Parliament Bill.[74]

They were divided on the question of House of Lords reform, although they were agreed that the Upper Chamber should remain strong. The Duke of Bedford, for example, advocated a purely elective system for recruitment to the Lords, while Willoughby de Broke and Bathurst opposed any change at all. Bathurst argued in May 1911 that "this House is the best possible House which could be devised by human beings as a Second Chamber for this country," while Bedford announced that he attached "no great importance to retaining a shred of the hereditary principle."[75] Lord Ampthill in 1907 admitted that a popular demand existed for changes in the Lords and supported the compromise stance of Lord Newton's Unionist reforms, that there should be some elective and some hereditary elements in the new House. "The hereditary principle is one which obtains throughout the whole universe. It holds sway in every single relation of our social life."[76] Other diehards stoutly defended the hereditary House unsullied by an elective portion. Somerset and Halsbury sent a circular letter to the peers in March 1910, urging them to reject the Earl of Rosebery's scheme for reform and to take their stand for an assembly " 'marked by birth alone.' "[77] Both Willoughby de Broke and Bathurst argued for the maintenance of the hereditary principle and against any tampering with the constitution, because, according to Bathurst, "if we once admit it is possible to tamper with our Constitution we do not know where it will stop."[78] Willoughby de Broke cited not only tradition — "a very ancient fabric gradually knitted together through the ages" — but also animal husbandry in his defense of the unreformed House of Lords: "I have been brought up in the midst of stock-breeding of all kinds all my life, and I am prepared to defend the hereditary principle . . . whether the principle is applied to Peers or . . . to fox-hounds."[79]

Despite wide differences of opinion over the wisdom of reforming the House of Lords, the diehards shared certain basic assumptions which they revealed during debates on the issue. They believed in the importance of a powerful Second Chamber to balance the House of Commons. Those who favored an elective element urged that only this reform would win the confidence of the people and thus strengthen the position of the Lords.[80] Ampthill argued that it was "necessary to bring the Second Chamber into more intimate association with the electorate than in the past in order to counteract the growing tendencies of Cabinet autocracy and House of Commons despotism."[81] No diehard wished to weaken the House of Lords in any way. As the Duke of Somerset argued, a strong Upper House provided the "only safeguard . . . against ill-considered legislation by the House of Commons and tyrannical unjust measures" of a Liberal government which had become the tool of the Irish Nationalists and Labour.[82]

The diehards were also united in debates on House of Lords reform in their distrust of democracy, and especially of the modern party system. The degree of vehemence on this issue varied, but not the basic sentiment. It was another aspect of the diehards' increasing alienation from trends in the political system. Distaste for the modern tightly knit organization of political parties, whether Liberal or Unionist, was expressed publicly and privately. It was not simply an electioneering cry or a political tactic, though it was without doubt sparked by the frustration which the diehards had felt for years about the policies of governments and parties. Dislike of both parties and of the House of Commons, the traditional forum of British government, was an expression of the diehards' adherence to radical rightist attitudes about the course of history and the necessity for drastic action and rapid change in the methods of politics.

The Duke of Northumberland was constantly lamenting the successes of democracy, which he defined as "simply that kind of Government which prevails in one form or another in the decay of a State."[83] He believed that the Commons had "deteriorated steadily ever since the Reform Bill of 1867, and it has deteriorated with still more celerity ever since the Reform Bill of 1884 . . . I speak of the powers of the House, and of the way it transacts its business, and of its independence."[84] The cabinet, he frequently stated, had gathered far too much power unto itself, assisted by the growth of party organizations. It dominated the legislature, and thus the country, in an almost "autocratic" manner, and never more so than under a Unionist prime minister who could count on the votes of the House of Lords.[85] Northumberland, like many of the diehards, was a staunch supporter of the independence of legislators, adopting the "Whig" view of representation propounded by Edmund Burke and in rapid decline by the late nineteenth century.[86]

The diehards were in general extremely critical of political parties and their leadership during the debates on reform of the House of Lords. The Duke of Somerset "was utterly disgusted with Lansdowne's [House of Lords reform] bill — he out-radicals the radicals & gives the whole situation away . . . It is too miserably wicked & weak."[87] Disgust with the Unionist party was nearly as great among the diehards as their hatred of the Liberals. Several diehards regarded the Lords reform bill which Lansdowne introduced in 1911 as a stratagem to gain more votes. Lord Bathurst blamed the "Conservative Parliamentary candidates [who] said, 'Now is our opportunity to sweep the country at the next election by advocating a scheme for the reform of the Upper House.' They therefore proceeded to put great pressure on our Parliamentary leaders, who adopted the policy." It was precisely this opportunistic policy on the part of the Conservative party that the diehards had deplored for years. They had pleaded for consistent principles, even if some innovations were involved. The diehards also claimed during the debate on Lansdowne's bill that the Commons no longer represented the people, but only the party organizations responsible for electing the members. This criticism was directed at least as much against the Unionists as against the Liberals. Lord Raglan considered Lansdowne's Reconstitution Bill

the apotheosis of the Conservative Agents' policy. The Unionist Party has suffered most bitterly from . . . the Conservative Agents' policy. I believe nobody knows less about the feelings of the country than the average Member of Parliament . . . because he sees the feelings of the people of the country . . . through the eyes of his agent and his committee, who are . . . extreme men, and naturally have a wild desire to snatch a few votes from the other side. Therefore they say to the Member, 'You say something pleasant about female suffrage, and you will pinch ten votes from the other side.' The thing is done; but you never get the ten votes, and you only disgust your own supporters.[88]

Discussion of the referendum began in earnest with the onset of the constitutional crisis in 1909. The concept was not new; it had been much discussed in Conservative circles for decades. The diehards and other Conservatives had proposed it long before as a possible means to settle disputes between the Lords and the Commons. As early as 1895, the Earl of Meath had stated that most peers would not be inclined to oppose the House of Commons indefinitely, that "the vast majority would only regard themselves as justified in opposition so long as the subject in dispute, uncomplicated by side issues, had not been clearly submitted to the electorate for the expression of its calm and deliberate opinion."[89] In 1907 the Earl of Selborne, always the most enthusiastic supporter of the referendum among the diehards, predicted in a letter to Lord Salisbury that there might soon be a conflict between the House of Lords and the people: "We cannot get away from the fact that in default of a revolution, if the people are mad or wrong-headed, in the long run their madness or wrong-headedness must prevail." He suggested that the responsibility be thrown "directly on them by the introduction of a referendum." Salisbury responded that the "Referendum is very attractive. I feel it is a great plunge but we are in extraordinary difficulties and we perhaps must not shrink from cold water."[90]

Distrust of the Commons and the Unionist party, combined with the deadlock between the Houses of Parliament, led many of the diehards to adopt the referendum as their solution to current problems. The referendum combined two tactics: a radical break from the tradition of the independence and nearly unfettered power of the legislature, and the ancient aristocratic stratagem of appealing to the supposedly loyal "people" over the heads of legislators and the middle classes. In early March 1911, Lord Balfour of Burleigh introduced his Reference to the People Bill, which provided that upon disagreement between the two Houses of Parliament, the measure in dispute, on the demand of either House, be submitted to a referendum. The bill was dropped after the first reading.[91]

Debates on the issue of the reform of the House of Lords brought frequent discussion of the referendum either as an alternative to or an element of comprehensive reform. The Duke of Bedford, Lords Colchester, Halifax, and Willoughby de Broke all spoke in the Lords in favor of a referendum, claiming that the Upper House should have the right to refer a question to the people before a bill became law.[92] The Earl of Selborne regarded the referendum as a crucial aspect of any reform of the Lords. He argued that the people would never accept a mere change in the membership of the House of Lords without an accompanying provision to refer legislation to the voters in case of disagreement between the two Houses. The referendum, Selborne claimed, provided the best method of settling differences between the peers and the Commons. "It is notorious that it is impossible at a General Election to isolate any particular issue. Theoretically therefore the Referendum is not merely a sound but it is the only solution." He proposed numerous safeguards, including a provision that there could be at most one referendum per year and that a government could not be forced to resign as the result of a defeat on a referendum.[93] Lord Salisbury agreed with Selborne's basic proposals. Asserting that the Commons was not the exact counterpart of the people, he espoused the idea of the referendum because "a Second Chamber . . . ought to be able to refer all drastic measures to the people unless it is quite certain that the people approve of them."[94]

The potential popularity of the referendum was another advantage of the innovation in the eyes of the diehards. It was "tactically far the best [policy] . . . It is consistent with what we have always said. The idea is perfectly simple. It exhibits trust in the people in its strongest and most undiluted form."[95] Others agreed with Selborne's analysis, including Salisbury's brother, Lord Hugh Cecil, who thought it "very plain . . . that the H. of L. ought to select the introduction of a referendum into the Parlt. Bill as the issue upon which to fight."[96]

The exasperation of the diehards with the Unionist leadership increased during the period between the budget debates of 1909 and the Parliament Bill vote of August 1911. The extreme tariff-reformers, led by the Bathursts and the *Morning Post,* were especially critical of Balfour and Lansdowne. The newspaper advocated firm resistance to the Liberals, and its editorial tone became more shrill after the Unionists failed to gain a majority in the January 1910 election and the Lloyd George budget passed both houses. Fabian Ware reported later in March:

The Tariff Reformers in the House are in a state of very healthy discontent, and I almost believe that Balfour will be forced to take the bold line, but of course things will never be right until the chariot comes for him, and this is beginning to be more and more the opinion among even those Tariff Reformers whom he has kept quiet with vague promises during these last five years. [97]

Although Lord Robert Cecil rightly identified the attitude of the *Morning Post* and the more extreme among its readers as "contempt for conservatism as such,"[98] even more moderate Unionist peers were by this time becoming greatly worried about Balfour's "extraordinary reluctance, or rather disinclination, to fulfill the ordinary functions of a leader."[99] Anxiety about the lack of direction of the Unionist party grew sharper while the Constitutional Conference, called in the summer of 1910 in an attempt to find a solution to the conflict between the Lords and the Commons, was in progress. There was concern about what terms the Unionist leadership might reach with the Liberals to avoid a direct confrontation on the issue of abolishing the Lords' veto: "A real quintessential Die-hard, although he may not say so, never entirely trusts his leaders not to sell the pass behind his back."[100]

In October and November, 1910, some of the diehards and others founded the "Reveille Movement" in an effort "to rouse the Unionist party without forsaking Unionist principle." The movement stood for tariff reform, national security, and "the constructive side of Unionism."[101] It was designed to strengthen the resolve of the Unionist leadership to resist the Liberals and to put pressure on the leaders to maintain their stated adherence to tariff reform. Most observers interpreted the movement as an assault on the Unionist leadership. This motive was denied by the founders, Willoughby de Broke and Page Croft, a Unionist M.P., and the leadership evidently accepted their disclaimer. In October Lord Lansdowne expressed at least qualified approval of the "Reveille" group:

> I need not tell you that I recognise the importance of doing all that can be done to rouse enthusiasm for Unionist principles . . .
> I am glad to know that you are working in consultation with the managers of the party, and that you have [chief whip Sir Alexander Acland] Hood's approval of your plan of campaign . . .
> It was perhaps a little unfortunate that your object should . . . have been misapprehended, and that the "Reveille" should have been interpreted as an attack upon the party leaders whose hands you really desire to strengthen. [102]

There could be no doubt, however, that the movement was an expression, if not of outright rebellion, at least of dissatisfaction with the leadership.

Hostility to Balfour grew even more vehement after he pledged at the end of November to submit the tariff reform question to a referendum, in response to Liberal challenges. This infuriated the extreme

tariff-reformers among the diehards, although it did give them a new
weapon. Richard Jebb, a writer on land issues for the *Morning Post,*
reported to Lady Bathurst that he was "not sure . . . that we have not
been making headway against AJB [Balfour] this time. We are not
attacking him but the Referendum, which makes all the difference
qua 'spite.' " The *Morning Post* and Lady Bathurst adopted a strong
anti-leadership line. Occasionally even H. A. Gwynne's editorials
failed to satisfy her impatience for Balfour's fall, and she urged him to
be even harsher than usual:

> I want to say boldly, we have done with such leaders. They have been the bane &
> ruin of the Unionist Party for 10 years . . . They are utterly discredited in the country
> & no amount of brilliant speeches will atone for cowardice, indecision, and utter lack
> of principle . . . The Policy of the M[orning] P[ost] is to give Balfour his due when, by
> accident, he is prodded into doing the right thing but when his true self appears, the
> Freetrader & intriguing compromiser, the man who doesn't want office and doesn't
> want any other to take his place, Balfour who would give votes to women, Balfour who
> refuses to pledge himself to National Service, the true Balfour in fact, then the Morn-
> ing Post must go for him . . . There can be no question of following such a leader.

Gwynne responded to the formidable proprietress in early August just
as the Parliament Bill debates were about to begin in the House of
Lords. He had hopes of victory in the division and exhorted Lady
Bathurst: "Always remember that the defeat of the Bill means the
political death of A.J.B. therefore, the struggle has to be kept up with
full strength."[103] It was Lady Bathurst's hope that the main effect of
the struggle over the Lords' veto powers would be the ouster of the old
leadership and the triumph of tariff reform within the Unionist party.

What was vital for Lady Bathurst, however, was not necessarily so
for the majority of the diehard peers. Roy Jenkins nevertheless assumed
that it was, that the distinguishing quality common to all the diehards
was their disgust with the existing leadership of their party, and that
the "real purpose" of the revolt "was to put new men at the head of the
Unionist Party."[104] This seems an excessively Machiavellian interpreta-
tion. There can be no doubt that most of the diehards were impatient
with their leadership and that they universally abhorred the stand for
abstention taken by Balfour and Lansdowne on the Parliament Bill
issue. However, Jenkins appears to confuse effect with cause. There is a
great deal of evidence of the diehards' distaste for the Liberal government and the Parliament Bill. There is more than enough such evidence, when coupled with general worries about social and political

trends and alienation from the traditional methods and practices of British politics, to account for their determination to resist the Parliament Bill.

Many of the diehards hoped to persuade their parliamentary leaders rather than remove them. The diehards expressed hostility for Balfour and Lansdowne, but most of them recognized that these men were probably the best suited to fill their positions, if only they would modify their opinions and take decisive action. Lord Willoughby de Broke, despite his profound dissatisfaction with his leaders, described the four Unionists, including Balfour and Lansdowne, who negotiated with the Liberals in the Constitutional Conference, as "the very Four Best we have."[105] Lord Roberts lamented both the general lack of faith in Balfour and the fact that Balfour and Lansdowne were not stronger leaders. Recognition of Balfour's skills was coupled with annoyance at his lack of a definite lead. Even when impatience with the Conservative central office was at its height, in January and December, 1910, some diehards spoke of reforming it with Balfour's aid and not against his wishes. Lord Stanhope, for one, had "learnt much about the Central Office which little Bobs [Lord Roberts] spent the weekend in inciting me to organize a revolt against in order to improve. I think I see how to do it but it is drastic & needs a good man — the authority & backing of A. J. B. & the bosses."[106]

Even as the battle over the Lords' veto drew near in the summer of 1911, many diehards hoped to fight under the official banner and expressed sadness at having to go against their leadership on the issue. Letters between several of the diehards in the months before the vote do not reveal a calculated desire to use the controversy to rid the Unionists of Balfour and company. George Wyndham learned from Lord Scarbrough in June that the decision had been made to recruit peers who would "fight to the end, even if the leadership counsel surrender."[107] This resolution evinced distrust of the leadership and a willingness to defy it if necessary, but offered no indication that the purpose of the revolt was to destroy that leadership. Lord Northcote promised to support the fight against the Parliament Bill if it was "approved of by our responsible leaders."[108] Willoughby de Broke noted in his memoirs that "the actual 'ditcher' [another name for the diehards] movement was only conceived within three weeks of the final struggle in the Lords."[109] It was then that Northcote changed his mind and wrote to Selborne that he would vote against the bill, despite the fact that "Alice [Lady Northcote] . . . is a hedger [a Unionist who supported abstention in the Parliament Bill division], not a ditcher, which is a further complication."[110]

Some diehards, recognizing it as a dramatic step, voted against their leadership only with the greatest reluctance. Several would have preferred to fight under their regular leaders, even those with whom they had disagreed. On July 9 Lord Plymouth pledged himself to resist the abolition of the Lords' veto, and "to act with anyone, (*I hope with Lansdowne*) who will lead us unflinchingly in adhering to our present position."[111] Lord Roberts wrote to both Curzon and Lansdowne that he regretted opposing them on the issue, and that "the warmth of the Speeches made by Unionists holding different views will soon be forgotten."[112] As late as July 10 even Willoughby de Broke spoke of stiffening Lansdowne's resolve rather than of undermining his position. He suggested to Halsbury that

we might have some resolution ready to sign or pass with a view of its being forwarded to Lord Lansdowne, *in order to strengthen his hands.*

The situation seems to have crystalized into insistence upon, or abandonment of his amendment to the Bill. I understand that forces are at work urging him to abandon the position he has taken up; and I think you will agree with me that we should try to influence him in the opposite direction; though I cannot seriously contemplate his withdrawal at the eleventh hour. [113]

On July 19 he was still willing to accept the leadership's help: "If Midleton, Curzon & Co. place themselves at the head of the fighting phalanx all will be well, though they must never be allowed to take any credit for it if they are proved to have advocated surrender."[114]

Even after the leadership decided to advocate surrender on the veto issue, in the face of Liberal threats to create peers, most of the diehards continued to disavow any plan to unseat Balfour and Lansdowne. Lord Halsbury was astonished to read "in a vile journal . . . that it was part of a conspiracy against my noble friend and against the distinguished leader in the other House to obtain from them the leadership forsooth!" Of course, there were those, such as Lady Bathurst, who wished to use the veto crisis to remove Balfour. However, most of the diehards voted against the Parliament Bill primarily because they were violently and genuinely opposed to it. This is not to deny that they were impatient with their leadership. After Balfour and Lansdowne counseled abstention on the Parliament Bill, most of the diehards wished to see new leaders for the Unionist party. Hostility was not the reason for their vote, although their feeling of alienation strengthened their purpose to act as they did. By 1911 the diehards had become accustomed to disagreeing with their chiefs. Some continued to profess loyalty to Lansdowne even during the Parliament Bill debate. The Duke of Marlborough defended their attitude as "not one of disloyalty to Lord Lansdowne but an attitude of conviction on our part." "In a matter of this kind loyalty to Party leaders bears no relation whatever to the magnitude of the present issue."[115] Hostility to the Parliament Bill, not the very real frustration with Balfour and Lansdowne, was the diehards' primary motivation.

They believed that the country faced disaster if the veto power of the House of Lords was abolished. They constantly stressed the restraining influence of a Second Chamber and the danger of a single chamber controlled by a democratic electorate subject to the whims of the moment. The Earl of Meath had warned as early as 1895 that "a single omnipotent popular assembly . . . might by a bare majority take an irretrievable step . . . entailing wide-spread misery, or even shaking, if not destroying, the foundations of the social fabric."[116] The diehards were sure that the Parliament Bill would lead to what Halsbury termed "the uncontrolled autocracy of the House of Commons . . . partially concealed by the existence of a sham House of Lords."[117]

An unrestrained, popularly elected house, according to the diehards, would destroy the traditional order and the established laws of society, would pass Home Rule, and further disrupt and weaken the empire by thwarting tariff reform and neglecting defense. The Earl of Selborne predicted in 1909 some of these consequences of a battle between the two houses. If the Unionists won the election he would join Balfour, if asked, in a cabinet whose most important tasks would be the passage of tariff reform and the application of a "remedy to the constitutional deadlock." In Selborne's view, the solution to the latter problem was the referendum. Such a remedy was absolutely essential:

If we do not find the remedy, the Home-Rule, Pro-Boer Little-England-Socialist party will one day surely return to power . . . They will request the King to create enough Peers to pass an "Emasculation of the House of Lords & Establishment of the House of Commons as a Single Chamber Tyranny Bill."

If the King refuses, we shall see the formation of an avowed republican party. If he yields, well, Exit Anglia. It would then be in the power of a House of Commons possessing a majority as bad or worse than the present . . . to disrupt the Empire.

Some people may say 'impossible' — I say that there is no depth of malignant lunacy to which such a majority, if constitutionally uncontrolled, would not sink.

Chamberlain evidently agreed with this apocalyptic vision, as he urged
resistance to the last by the diehards against the Parliament Bill.[118]
The Duke of Northumberland held similar fears for the future of private property under a single chamber government. He had warned the
Lords in May that their house represented "the property, the wealth,
of the country—that property which it is necessary to preserve, and
which . . . the tendency of all democracies is to attack, and which the
end of all democracies is to annihilate."[119]

The diehards also believed that the Parliament Bill was the result of
party politics rather than an expression of the will of the people. The
bill had been introduced by the Liberals, in thrall to the Irish Nationalists on whom their majority depended, to satisfy internal party considerations, and not for the good of the nation. Willoughby de Broke
wrote in the *National Review* that it was "a purely partisan contrivance
to enable the Radicals to maintain their Parliamentary position by
passing Home Rule for Ireland, as well as other experiments, without
an appeal to the electors."[120] He stated in the Lords that the Tories
would never oppose social welfare legislation, but only such measures
as Home Rule, Welsh disestablishment, and one-man one-vote.[121]
The diehards stated frequently that the people of the country were
really behind their efforts, despite Unionist defeat at the polls, and
that the true battle was between the cabinet, which controlled the
Commons through party machinery and the patronage it exercised,
and the people, rather than between the peers and the people.[122]

The drastic results of the passage of the Parliament Act justified, in
the diehards' opinion, determined resistance. Lord Stanmore, who dis-
claimed any description of himself as an "extremist," protested that
"revolutionary attempts can only be effectively met by strong measures
and strong men. I had rather see the Constitutional precedents slightly
strained than the Constitution itself overthrown through too scrupu-
lous a regard for etiquette."[123] Lord Mowbray advocated abandoning
traditional social intercourse, as well as ignoring parliamentary cour-
tesy and precedent. He applauded Lord Hugh Cecil's justification of
howling down the prime minister in the Commons during the debates:

Anything to bring home to our fellow countrymen, many of whom appear to be apathetic and weak-minded to the last degree, some appreciation of what is going on . . .
    Being rather logically minded I look upon public enemies as private foes and long
since determined never to set foot in the house of a Radical or Socialist or to see either
in my house . . . If we all did the like it might help to bring things home to those of the
other side who have something (and many of them have much) to lose.[124]

The diehards justified resistance to the Parliament Bill on the grounds of both honor and political expediency. They argued that the emasculation of the Upper Chamber would render the house as ridiculous as a Liberal mass creation of peers. But the opposition on their part would fulfill Unionist political principles and would serve as a warning to the country at large that drastic changes were occurring. Lord Stanhope, fearful of Liberal measures, was "convinced that the people of this country have never grasped that a revolution is in progress . . . The only way to bring it home to them is, if the Government desire revolution, by making them carry that revolution by revolutionary methods and by no other."[125] A defiant vote of the diehard peers would be a dramatic protest. It would negate any Liberal argument that the peers had concurred in their own political demise and would at the same time be useful if the Unionist party, at some future date restored to power, were then to repeal the bill. Lord Roberts anticipated that "by doing its duty the House of Lords may not be able to prevent the Parliament Bill from being carried, but it may awaken the nation to the real nature of the revolution which is in progress, check its further course, and make possible its reversal in the near future."[126] Resistance to the Parliament Bill was also justified by the necessity of keeping up the morale of the members of the Unionist party in the country. They would feel abandoned by the Lords and would subsequently be disinclined to rally to the cause if their party would not even make a struggle for its own principles.[127]

After the shadow cabinet meeting (the diehard peers Salisbury, Selborne, and Halsbury were members) of July 21, at which Balfour, Lansdowne, and Curzon all argued for surrender in the face of Liberal threats to create peers in order to pass the Parliament Bill, organization of a revolt began in earnest. Willoughby de Broke and others had already been canvassing for support of the diehard position. A committee was formed, with Halsbury as chairman, and F. E. Smith and Willoughby de Broke as secretaries, with members of the Lords and Commons working together. On July 25 Halsbury, Selborne, Salisbury, Mayo, Lovat, and Willoughby de Broke sent out a circular letter urging opposition to the bill and demanding another election. A banquet was held on the twenty-sixth, and meetings were held at the Duke of Westminster's and Lord Leith's London houses.[128]

In the few days before the debates of August 9 and 10 Willoughby de Broke, organizing the resistance, received a constant stream of answers to his letters requesting support. Several peers acted as canvassers for specific groups, either of friends or of peers living close to their country seats. Lords Ebury, Bathurst, Ampthill, Raglan, Saltoun, and Rothes were among these active participants in the organization, sending the names of those prepared to resist to Willoughby de Broke.[129] The diehards were especially anxious to gain the support of the Duke of Norfolk and of those who would follow the premier duke. Norfolk intended to abstain from the division, as was Unionist official policy, unless some Unionists decided to vote for the bill so as to avoid the creation of peers which would follow on a diehard victory. If renegade Unionists voted for the Liberal side, he would divide with the diehards.[130] George Wyndham thought that the government could be defeated in the Lords only if the whips were "ready to launch 'Lansdownites' — who will act with *Norfolk* — so soon as one Unionist peer votes *with* the Government, or if the K's [King's] secretaries do so . . . The immediate necessity is to collect 'Norfolkites' who will vote if one Unionist peer votes with the Government."[131] Viscount Halifax was one of the waverers who was believed to be a follower of Norfolk.[132]

On August 10, however, the diehards suffered defeat. Only eight peers came into their camp unexpectedly, while thirty-seven Unionists voted for the government, along with the two archbishops and eleven bishops. Twelve peers who were counted on to vote with the diehards, including the dukes of Abercorn and Sutherland, "Ran Out," in Willoughby de Broke's phrase, while five expected diehards were too ill to come. Of those who "Ran In," along with the Duke of Norfolk, only Halifax and Fingall, and perhaps the Bishop of Bangor, could be considered "Norfolkites," so that a major hope of the diehard organizers went largely unfulfilled.[133]

The diehards' effort to prevent the abolition of the veto power of the House of Lords ended in failure. They had fought to the end, defying their leadership, to avoid this result. The dramatic nature of their actions, and the extreme language in which their opposition to the Parliament Bill was frequently couched, should not be allowed to obscure the essential character of their political methods and goals. Their support of a lost cause and the spectacular nature of their failure led both contemporaries and later historians to emphasize the traditional and reactionary nature of the diehard peers. Some observers have interpreted the stand against the Parliament Bill as symbolic of the ultimate disinclination or inability of the landed aristocracy to adapt itself to changes in British society. On the contrary — these men, drawn overwhelmingly from the landed aristocracy, demanded considerable changes both in the political system and in the Unionist party. Far from being blind reactionaries, they attempted with some success to adapt themselves to alterations in economics and finance, local government, and the national social and political situation. They called for drastic measures — national service, tariff reform, and the referendum — to cope with international and internal perils. The diehards were selective, not total, in their resistance to change. On some issues, however, they were adamant, and these included many of the Liberals' most cherished goals. The diehards recognized that without the veto powers of the House of Lords their ability to influence the course of events would be greatly diminished. A series of electoral defeats, their hatred of Liberal legislation, and years of frustration with and alienation from the Unionist leadership, prepared the diehard peers to defy the Liberal government, their own political leadership, and the will of the House of Commons. Radical conservatives rather than simple reactionaries, they were ready to go against traditions of British parliamentary behavior and to demand sweeping transformations in government and public policy in order to achieve their goal of preserving as far as possible an older way of life and politics.

7 / The Diehards and the Tory Revolt

Many of the diehard peers continued to be active in national political affairs in the period following the passage of the Parliament Act. The abolition of the veto power of the House of Lords, in their opinion, left the country exposed to the radical legislation of the Liberal party, which was captive to the wishes of its Irish Nationalist and Labour allies. The Liberal measure which dominated political activity for the three years prior to the Great War was Irish Home Rule, but both Welsh disestablishment and the "land campaign" were also areas of profound concern to the diehards. A large number of these peers, among the most politically active of the House of Lords, regarded it as their duty to oppose these policies strenuously and to insure that the Unionist party was unflinchingly loyal to conservative ideals. Motivated by these goals, the diehards became deeply involved in the controversies surrounding the Unionist leadership and policies. The diehards' belief in the justice of their cause led them to ever more extreme behavior. In the resistance to Home Rule for Ireland, the nation was being treated to the spectacle of members of the British aristocracy, along with other supposed conservatives, encouraging armed defiance of the government and generally behaving in a manner "essentially un-English."[1] It is clear, however, that the extreme and radical behavior of the diehard peers had grown out of years of alienation from the direction of political and social affairs.

Immediately following the August 10 division on the Parliament Act, discussion began among the diehards about a means "to keep together men who are prepared to fight questions to the bitter end."[2] Willoughby de Broke received a steady stream of letters from his fellow diehards expressing this sentiment, as well as congratulations for having preserved, as they saw it, the Unionist party from the dishonor of abject surrender.[3] The organization of diehard peers was conceived as a device to put pressure on Unionist leaders to remain true to conservative principles and also to propagate a new, more aggressive and militant type of conservatism which would enable Unionists to compete successfully against the Liberals.[4] Many of the diehards felt that they had won a moral victory which might be turned to good practical account if they could remain a group united to put fight into the Conservative cause. "We have now got all the men on our side both in and out of Parliament that are worth having. We must keep them going."[5]

There were great difficulties in this effort to keep the diehards together. Although these peers had united on the basis of one overriding issue, the Parliament Bill, they had had various motives for doing so. Prior to 1911 they had not been a unified faction. All despised the Liberal program and felt alienated to some degree from the Unionist leadership, yet they were not agreed on such fundamental issues as tariff reform, Irish land legislation, House of Lords reform, or social legislation. Nor were they all equally active in politics. Lord Lovat, one of the leading organizers of the diehard opposition to the Parliament Bill, recognized the problems involved in molding a coherent and permanent group along the lines suggested by Willoughby de Broke.

We have done some good in the House by gathering together those who are prepared to fight for principle as opposed to those who are engaged in the hunt after expediency. I am not clear, however, *how far* it will be advisable to attempt to keep that lot together for future use. You must remember that the body of peers who went into the Lobby with Halsbury have to be divided up into those who went there either from the motive of ultra-Conservatism or those who went there with a view to reforming the House of Lords . . . A body of men who are divided on essentials and who are only united in their determination to sit tight against Court and Cabal; Church and Curzon, cannot hold together once the fight which froze them together is over. . . . I am with you in thinking that we should have a re-union of our stalwarts in October, but it should be a re-union to prepare for future emergencies rather than a re-union to make pacts or to take action against the 37 [Unionist] cranks and jackasses who went into the Lobby against us. [6]

Lovat's analysis of the diehards' reasons for opposition to the Parliament Bill was, however, overly simplistic. The Duke of Northumberland warned against asking the Marquess of Salisbury or the Earl of Selborne to become officers of an on-going diehard organization because, as past and potential ministers, they might feel a degree of loyalty to the Unionist leadership which would be incompatible with their roles as strenuous upholders of principle against tactical compromise.[7] Selborne himself saw tariff reform as the great stumbling block in the way of a workable diehard combination.[8]

The diehards disagreed about the form an organization should take. It was a mark of the radical lengths to which some of them were prepared to go that for a brief moment they entertained the idea of forming an entirely new party, outside the confines of the Unionist party. To a large extent this proposal was based on a distrust of the current leadership of the Unionist party and a disinclination to follow it in the future. On August 17 Lord Willoughby de Broke presented Selborne with the idea of a new party, noting that the membership had lost confidence in Balfour and Lansdowne and would no longer follow them. The alternative courses of action were either to capture the official Unionist organization for the diehards or to found an independent group: "Why not be first in the field, start a separate organization for a time anyhow, and put forward your own programme? How about meetings at the Albert Hall and Free Trade Hall in Manchester in October before the Nat. Union meeting?"[9] Lord Selborne replied that he had "slaved for six years making the organization" of the Liberal Unionist Party after 1886 and that it was extraordinarily difficult to make a new political party. He insisted that the diehards did not have to resort to such extremes because they could "capture the party and Unionist machine lock, stock & barrel." Selborne agreed on a meeting in early October, before the National Union convention, to plan diehard strategy.[10] He worked hard to prevent secession and to turn the energies of the dissident peers toward capturing the Unionist party. Reporting to Austen Chamberlain, Selborne said that the meeting in October would "prevent some of our friends from doing anything foolish" and mold those who disagreed with the party leadership into a group which could "speak with one voice on all the important questions of current politics."[11]

Willoughby de Broke and other diehard peers readily fell in with Selborne's suggestion that a meeting of the "no-surrender" group be held in order to form an organization to work within the party. Both peers and commoners were included in the invitations to meet on October 12, 1911, at the 1900 Club.[12] Lord Lovat, after questioning some leading Unionists, warned that this group should not be too rigid in its views lest it alienate many Conservatives. He wanted "a flexible combine of sorts to stiffen our Party," but not a formal grouping.[13] This principle of non-exclusivity was agreed upon even by those diehards who wished to form a club for the propagation of their ideas. Lord Milner summarized his views:

1. That it is desirable that the Diehards should remain a working body, acting together 'separate but not hostile' (this need not necessarily include every one of those who cooperated last session, nor exclude others joining.)

2. That it is further desirable that they should strike a common note and have an agreed general line of Policy.
    The main features of that policy should be
      (a) Tariff Reform.
      (b) Imperial Unity.
      (c) Defence.
      (d) Social Uplifting.
      (e) A sound Constitution.
      (f) A real United Kingdom. [14]

Selborne reported that the meeting would be private and would include about fifty members of the Lords and Commons. Its purpose was "to avoid anything like a split in the party and yet to keep the ditchers together as a club within the party which others of the party, who were not ditchers, can join." The club would stiffen the Unionist resolve to resist Liberal measures and prepare for the "reconstruction of the constitution after the government have done destroying it, to do the study & education for this subject for the party which the T.R.L. has done for the tariff." In short, it was to be the "tip of the party spear" on all controversial matters. [15]

On October 12 the diehards and their supporters decided to form the "Halsbury Club," despite objections of those like Salisbury who believed that to identify the club with the nominal leader of the diehard revolt would exacerbate old wounds and prevent the adherence of men who had not voted against the Parliament Bill. [16] The first meeting took place on November 6, and the members unanimously resolved to cooperate with Unionists "in defence of Unionist principles & tender to Mr. Balfour & Lord Lansdowne the assurance of their loyal support in the coming struggle." [17] The executive committee included Lords Milner and Lovat among the diehards, and the chairman was Lord Selborne. [18] Committees were quickly formed to discuss questions of imperial defense and reform of the House of Lords, and diehards such as Willoughby de Broke, Milner, Selborne, Plymouth, Northumberland, and Marlborough took part. [19] Complicated schemes for the reconstruction of the House of Lords were worked out, with an emphasis on a strong, elective second chamber.

The contemporary and historical notoriety of the Halsbury Club was and is based, however, not on its programs but on the belief that it was an instrument for attacking the leadership of A. J. Balfour. [20] The vast majority of the diehards and other members of the club were certainly distressed with both Balfour and Lansdowne, but the desire to oust them immediately after the Parliament Act division was far from universal. Selborne, the chairman, and Lord Robert Cecil, for example, wished to use the organization to keep the leadership in line with what they defined as true conservative principles and to change that leadership only if that effort failed. Lord Robert professed to believe that all the club members shared this attitude and told his brother, Lord Salisbury, who had just dissociated himself from the group, that "the idea is to induce them to lead better."[21] Leo Maxse proposed to submit to the National Union Conference a resolution thanking the diehards for their actions, but this was regarded as a severe slap at the Unionist leadership. Such a move would promote discord, whereas the primary goal, in the opinion of several of the diehards, should be a strong and united Unionist party. It would perhaps be more worthwhile to impress the leaders with the force of the "no surrender" sentiment by working "to secure the election of a 'diehard' as Chairman of the Nat'l Union for the coming year."[22] Some Halsbury Club members, disturbed when Balfour resigned from the Unionist leadership on November 8, sympathized with George Wyndham's emotional letter to Balfour, calling him "that sole star of fortitude and radiance in the night-fall that has overtaken our country."[23]

On the other hand, while some members of the club may have preferred to keep the old leadership and change its attitudes, most of them believed that the time had come to oust Balfour. Northumberland was typical of many who were ready to drop the old leadership quickly if it did not immediately begin to take firm stands. "If my leaders assent to those principles & act upon them I will be loyal to them but if they won't I have no hesitation about taking a line of my own."[24] The more extreme tariff-reform members of the club were firmly convinced that the moment had come to drive out both Balfour and Lansdowne. "The time has come to strike hard . . . This is no intrigue. But there can be no doubt that most people want a new Party. They simply won't work for Balfour and Lansdowne again. I won't," wrote Willoughby de Broke.[25] Maxse's resolution that the National Union thank the diehards won warm support from many of these peers, as did his "BMG" ("Balfour Must Go") campaign in the *National Review*. Lord Stanhope approved the leadership change as "a blessed transformation" but urged Maxse not to withdraw his motion too soon after Balfour's resignation, "as it will look as if it was merely meant as an attack on A.J.B. & not on all the hedgers [those Unionists who abstained from the Parliament Bill division]. Having got him out we naturally do not wish to appear *personal*."[27] On the issue of the immediate ouster, the diehards were somewhat divided. There is no doubt, however, that their general feeling was that the leadership must at least conform to diehard opinion or the majority of those peers would unite to further the political destruction of that leadership. Drastic measures were felt to be in order if political trends were not to the diehard peers' liking.

The somewhat ambivalent tone of the Halsbury Club and the diehards toward the Unionist leadership was reflected in conflicting opinions among the leadership group about their intentions. It was not universally perceived, even by those presumably most sensitive to the direction of political breezes, that much of the club was dedicated to Balfour's ouster. The organization was certainly taken as a serious threat within top Unionist circles. In mid-October 1911, Lord Midleton, formerly secretary of War in Balfour's cabinet, warned that "unless something is done, 3/4 of the [Unionist] party will drift into the Halsbury Club."[28] Perhaps most interesting, however, is that Arthur Steel-Maitland, principal agent for the Unionist party, believed that the Halsbury Club, although not very desirable from the point of view of party discipline, was not determined to remove Balfour. He stressed to Halsbury that the "shadow cabinet" was the place to bring up differences about policy and that a permanent group founded for no specific purpose would waste energy and money and would cause organizational trouble.[30] Halsbury had assured him that the club was not antagonistic to Balfour's leadership, that it had been founded "to keep alive the fighting spirit," but that there was no particular program. As a result of this correspondence, Steel-Maitland reported to Balfour that he was "convinced that it is *not* hostile, but that it is muddle-headed. There is no question that Austen, of course, and Lord Halsbury, Lord Selborne, George Wyndham, & Willoughby etc & other no surrender principals are very anxious to show their loyalty to you."[31] These startlingly naive remarks from an old political professional may have been the result of the genuine and, to the onlooker, perhaps confusing divisions of opinion about the leadership which actually existed within the Halsbury Club and of the conciliatory public statements made by the club as a whole. It was also a testimony to the political skill of those diehard and other members of the club who wished fervently for the ouster of Balfour, at least from the day of the division on the Parliament Act.

In the short-lived battle for the Unionist leadership which followed Balfour's resignation on November 8, 1911, the majority of the diehards supported Austen Chamberlain. This was especially true of the strong tariff-reformers in their ranks. They did not wish to go back to the old Toryism represented by the other initial contender for the leadership, Walter Long. Long was an opponent of tariff reform and of diehard resistance to the Parliament Bill. The diehards, in the main members of the landed aristocracy, were not willing to support a man who might have been considered one of their own, both politically and socially. Instead they rallied around the essentially middle-class Chamberlain on practical grounds: the diehards believed Joseph and Austen Chamberlain were men who could lead them to victory.[32] While they longed for the supposed stability of former times, they demanded new policies to cope with new social and political problems. They believed that Austen Chamberlain and the imperial programs for which he stood were essential to restore the internal stability of England and to preserve its strength.

Several of the diehards maintained close contact with Austen Chamberlain and assisted his cause. Lord Plymouth had helped him financially in his East Worcestershire constituency in 1910. Lord Selborne and others kept Chamberlain posted on the early stages of the Halsbury Club. In the matter of the potential split, Selborne expressed the hope that he had "steered in a way" which Chamberlain would approve. Lord Malmesbury urged Chamberlain to provide the strong lead which Unionists desperately required to overcome "the apathy and discontent" which pervaded the party organization: "Your name is on every lip among our eminent Statesmen — *not only* for your own distinguished services, but for your father's sake — ." Even after Chamberlain and Long withdrew from the Unionist party battle in favor of Andrew Bonar Law, some diehards continued to express their preference for Chamberlain. Just after Chamberlain stepped out of contention, Willoughby de Broke acknowledged "the privilege of working with you . . . I had hoped you would be leader in the House of Commons."[33] In the months ahead, however, the blunt tactics of Bonar Law on most issues pleased the diehard peers. Even Gwynne, the editor of the *Morning Post,* who had supported Chamberlain, soon came "to believe from the chagrin of the Radicals that we have blundered on the right man."[34]

During the three years before the Great War the stormiest political controversy was that over Home Rule for Ireland. The Unionists' most powerful weapon against Irish independence had been fatally weakened with the passage of the Parliament Act. In 1912 Asquith introduced the third Home Rule Bill which, however, offered no special measures regarding primarily Protestant Ulster. The diehards and other Unionists bitterly opposed the bill and threw it out. In the new circumstances created by the Parliament Act, however, a veto in the Lords could be only a temporary measure as long as the Liberals and their allies held the majority in the Commons. One goal of the Unionists was thus to force another general election as a means of thwarting Home Rule.[35]

Several of the diehards were among the most ardent anti-Home Rulers. Some of them, as Irish landowners, opposed Home Rule at least in part out of economic self-interest. Others, such as Willoughby de Broke, owned no Irish land but were deeply dedicated to the idea of empire and were troubled by the plight of the Irish loyalists. In addition, the diehards' concern for the safety and the strength of England led them to argue that an independent Ireland would be a strategic liability in the event of a European war.[36] In July 1913 Willoughby de Broke warned the Liberal ministers that "we do not propose to allow on our most vulnerable flank a separate existence to a nation whose very leaders have constantly declared war upon this country."[37] He and other Unionists recognized also that the Irish issue could be used to great effect to embarrass and harass their Liberal foes. Willoughby de Broke went so far as to suggest in 1912 that the House of Lords might even conspire to allow the Home Rule Bill to pass. By opposing the bill, the House of Lords ran the risk of "turning itself into a tool for the purpose of working the Parliament Act so as to conform to the Radical plan of campaign. If we were to let it through now, it would place Asquith & Co. in the position of having to face the music forthwith, and we might force a General Election before they had time to abolish the plural voting."[38] Needless to say, this particular strategy claimed few adherents among English Unionists and Irish loyalists, and Willoughby de Broke himself quickly reverted to staunch opposition to the bill.

The diehards continued to distrust their Unionist leadership, even after Balfour's resignation. They feared that the leadership would work out an arrangement with the Liberal party which would grant the substance of Home Rule. Both Bonar Law and Lord Lansdowne anticipated another diehard revolt if there were a compromise over Ireland.[39] Willoughby de Broke warned in July that the House of Lords would oppose Home Rule even if it were approved by the Unionist party in the House of Commons: "We have proved on a great occasion . . . that the House of Lords is no mere appanage of the Carlton Club, and that when feeling really runs high this assembly is an independent assembly."[40] In September he told Robert Cecil that compromise would be fatal to the Unionists' credibility with the voters, and would not prevent further strife in Ireland. A conference on Ireland, Willoughby de Broke thought, might be successful if diehards represented their party and if a solution could be worked out which would salvage the Union. "We cannot trust those opposition leaders who have already given away the Constitution, and countenanced the Parliament Act. We will never let them out of our sight again if we can help it . . . If our friends think that we are going to help the Rads. out of another difficulty, I don't believe we shall ever see office again."[41] In January 1914, Lord Ampthill reported that many Unionists feared that their leadership might be "trapped into some unprincipled and disastrous 'compromise,'" and pledged himself ready to resist "anything so fatuous and fatal." Lord Leconfield urged that "we must not give way but I do not trust our leaders a yard and they will do so for certain unless we can stop them."[42] The diehards' resistance to Home Rule was characterized by the same insistence on principle, as opposed to political tactics, which had dominated their thinking on many of the other issues of the early twentieth century.

The Irish crisis of 1912-1914 provided the most striking example of the radical lengths to which the diehards were willing to go in order to achieve their goals. During this period many of the diehard peers pledged to resist the authority of Parliament. Irish diehard peers were among those landowners who commanded the Ulster Volunteer Force and who supported it by financial and other aid.[43] During the debates on the Parliament Bill, diehards had spoken in ominous terms of the consequences of forcing a Home Rule bill through a weakened Upper House. Lord Farnham, speaking as "an Ulster man," warned that such a measure would "end in plunging a part of the United Kingdom into a state of turmoil, strife, and bloodshed, if not indeed an actual state of civil war."[44] In January 1913 Farnham was more explicit, threatening that if Home Rule passed, "we shall use to our utmost the time that is at our disposal in preparing for eventualities which might occur should they attempt to force this Bill upon us."[45] The Duke of Bedford, who was not himself an Irish landowner, was of the opinion "that the fact that the Home Rule Bill will be carried this Parlmt [1912] without the sanction of the country and while the constitution is in suspense justifies extreme measures."[46] He did not rule out violence as a means of political action in regard to Ireland and other social issues. On March 5, 1914, Bedford wrote in support of Willoughby de Broke's National Service Bill, which provided for compulsory service on the part of the middle and upper classes. The duke said he would vote for the bill, "but I don't think it would be prudent for me to speak in support of arming and training the classes against the masses. I am strongly in favour of so doing, I quite admit."[47] This extraordinarily frank sentiment is an expression of the generally extreme temper of the diehard peers in the months before the outbreak of the Great War. The Irish question was just one occasion for the display of this readiness to resort to revolutionary and drastic measures, made especially attractive because it involved the defense of the empire, an attack on the Liberals, and the protection of property.

Many of the diehard peers committed themselves to violent resistance to Home Rule, or at least to the threat of violence, in the hope of forcing a general election. Years of frustration with political trends, coupled with the exasperating failure to regain control of the House of Commons, contributed to a feeling of desperation and crisis. These immediate political pressures acted upon men who had been exposed throughout their formative years to an increasing emphasis on muscularity, manliness, and the importance of the military and armed might. Extreme and dogged resistance, even violent denial of the sovereignty of Parliament, appeared to many diehards and other Unionists to be an alternative to what they perceived as the disastrous policies of the Liberals.

In March 1912 the "British League for the Support of Ulster and the Union" was formed under the chairmanship of Lord Willoughby de Broke.[48] This group dedicated itself to the exclusion of Protestant Ulster from any scheme for Home Rule and was vehemently opposed to Home Rule in general. The talk of armed resistance was partly a ploy to persuade the government to submit to a general election. When Lord Robert Cecil, a staunch anti-Home Ruler, confided to

Willoughby de Broke his worries about the consequences of civil war in Ireland, the latter replied that he was actually trying to avoid violence: "Those who are acting with me think that the stronger the forces arrayed against Home Rule the more likely the government are to avoid the extreme touch, and to appeal to the constituencies." The ultimatums given the government by the "British League" were to call an election or to fight Englishmen as well as Irish loyalists. On July 14, 1913, Willoughby de Broke addressed the House of Lords and informed the Liberal ministers that what all decent men "wish to see is that this matter would be fairly fought to a finish. They would sooner see it fought to a finish at a General Election, but if that means of settlement is denied to us, then we must fall back on the only other means at our disposal."[49]

There seems to be no doubt, despite Liberal professions of disbelief at the time, that many of the diehard peers and others who had pledged to resist Home Rule were in fact ready to resort to violence.[50] Both public announcements and private correspondence mentioned the possibility of armed conflict and of civil war. In the *Morning Post* of November 8, 1913, the British League called on Englishmen to "prepare to reinforce the ranks of men who are going to risk their lives for the integrity of the Empire . . . We want men who have been trained to bear arms, and who have been accustomed both to command and to obey."[51] These sentiments were echoed in private letters. Lord Roberts complimented Bonar Law in 1912 on a speech against Home Rule, stating categorically that "Ireland is not going to be separated from Great Britain. The strange thing is that any Unionist should have believed that such a thing was possible, and should have actually contemplated submitting to a Law passed by a disloyal Coalition."[52] Lord Stanhope volunteered to help if armed resistance was confined to Ulster and "provided Germany is quiet & civil war in Ireland does not mean as I expect Germany's long awaited opportunity. . . You cannot stop civil war & anarchy even by the threat of national destruction."[53] It is significant that, despite Stanhope's qualifications about the German threat, he, as well as others, seriously contemplated plunging England and Ireland into "civil war and anarchy" in order to pursue their objectives.

Lord Milner, the influential diehard pro-consul, organized support for resistance to Home Rule. In March 1913 he began collecting signatures to a "British Covenant," a declaration modelled after the Irish covenant for which Sir Edward Carson campaigned, pledging to resist or to support resistance to Home Rule. The first signatories included Rudyard Kipling, A. V. Dicey, Sir Edward Elgar, Lord Balfour of Burleigh, and several of the diehards.[54] Milner wrote that he was fully in agreement with "a very large body, who feel that the crisis altogether transcends anything in their previous experience, and calls for action, wh. is different, *not only in degree, but in kind,* from what is appropriate to ordinary political controversies."[55] Milner had earlier made it clear that if the government tried to coerce Ulstermen into Home Rule, "we could not allow them to be coerced without doing something to help them more than *talking.*"[56]

Unionist extremism in opposition to Home Rule continued into 1914, and diehard peers were among those calling most strenuously for drastic measures. During January and February, Bonar Law and other Unionists seriously discussed the possibility of amending the annual Mutiny Act to prevent the Liberal government from using the army against Ulster. Halsbury, Willoughby de Broke, Selborne, and the Cecils were among those who considered this course of action but abandoned the idea after the Curragh incident in March showed that the officers of the army in Ireland would refuse to act against Ulster.[57] Several of the diehards thoroughly expected civil war to break out if the Liberals implemented the Home Rule Bill. Lord Saltoun, suffering from the gout and writing from his Fraserburgh estate in January 1914, argued that the diehards and others who opposed the Liberals were perfectly justified in violent resistance because they would be fighting to preserve the constitution. In this letter from an eminently respectable Scottish peer, it is the matter-of-fact acceptance of bloodshed which is astonishing:

> We cannot be guilty of civil war, because we are maintaining the Constitution of the United Kingdom & Ireland as by law established & it is those who seek to destroy that constitution who will be guilty of civil war. A curious one it will be. Civil wars up to this have been against the Supreme Authority The King. This if it comes will be on our side for The King & Constitution and against the government of the Country.

Willoughby de Broke, Stanhope, Ampthill, and the Earl of Arran (who had not participated in the battle against the Parliament Bill) dispatched a letter to all peers on February 4 warning against any compromise on Home Rule. They charged that to pass the bill without submitting it to the electorate would be "an act of betrayal . . . The real alternative to Civil War is a Dissolution of Parliament." In the weeks which followed, Willoughby de Broke also directed the circulation of numerous letters opposing compromise with the Liberals and the Irish Nationalists until the "nation" was "consulted."[58]

Not all of the diehards were willing to resort to violence in the Irish loyalist cause, however. Some were willing to agree to the exclusion of Ulster from Home Rule as embodied in the Amending Bill introduced to the Lords and passed in mid-July with drastic alterations (Ulster to be permanently rather than temporarily excluded from Home Rule). The Duke of Northumberland opposed compromise on Home Rule but did not sanction armed resistance in Ulster: "I believe those who are preparing it are hatching a brood of chickens which will some day —and probably at no distant date—come very awkwardly home to roost in England." Ampthill, Stanhope, and Lovat, all of whom had previously expressed their willingness to fight, adopted a wait-and-see attitude after the introduction of the Amending Bill when it appeared that Ulster might be spared.[59] Willoughby de Broke remained dissatisfied: he could not agree to the exclusion of Ulster as a solution to the crisis. He argued in early July that the Nationalists would not accept such a proposal and that the Unionists would be abandoning the very principle which had given the party its name if they agreed to Home Rule for any part of Ireland.[60]

Perhaps the most extraordinary, backward-looking suggestion made during the Irish crisis in 1914 was Bathurst's proposal that the king should step in to solve the crisis by dismissing the prime minister, dissolving Parliament, and insisting, "there must be a general election before Home Rule is passed." Lord Bathurst advanced this notion to the Duke of Norfolk as an alternative to the civil war which he foresaw as a "disaster" but nonetheless the only alternative to a new government: "My idea is that you & two or three of the most influential peers . . . should beg H.M., if necessary on your knees, to be firm, and not allow the U.K. to be torn to pieces by the Nationalists who refuse to acknowledge either His M. or his flag." The premier duke declined to follow Bathurst's advice, feeling that such a course would be regarded as a party intrigue which was "very likely to bring about an openly Republican party."[61] Violence or a total disregard of constitutional practice were the options proposed in the Irish crisis by Lord Bathurst and by many of the diehards. Most opponents of Home Rule did not look to such antique methods as Bathurst's to stop the Liberals and rather preferred more direct action, even if it resulted in civil war. Some of the violent diehard rhetoric was an attempt to force the Liberals to call an election, but many of the diehards accepted the idea that if such demands for elections failed, armed force would be used against the legally constituted government of the United Kingdom. Those who opposed Home Rule at any cost, including a prominent group of diehards, were not merely bluffing, as the Liberals mistakenly believed. Private correspondence reveals that diehard peers (along with others) were prepared to spill blood to achieve their goals. This was the ultimate extension of the diehards' alienation from the political trends of the last three decades and a striking indication of their increasing willingness to resort to drastic, radical action if they believed it necessary. The outbreak of the Great War, in which diehards participated with courage and much sacrifice, diverted this potential revolutionary outburst from many of Britain's oldest and supposedly most conservative families.

During the four long years of war, political issues remained of great importance to many of the diehard peers. They continued to voice their distrust of the party machines and leaders. In October 1915, for example, Lord Milner suggested to Willoughby de Broke that they meet with patriotic members of the Labour party in order "to see whether there might not be some permanent basis of agreement between them and men like you and me, whom they do not regard as party men of the ordinary type."[62] This willingness to go outside regular party channels found its fullest expression for several diehards in the later years of the war with the short-lived foundation of a political party, separate from either the Unionists or the Liberals, called "A National Party to Promote Reform, Union and Defence."

Committed to complete victory and the maintenance of a powerful empire, the National party's ranks included a high proportion of enthusiastic tariff-reformers. In fact, the first meeting of the party took place at the Victoria Street offices of the Tariff Reform League on July 27, 1917, and the plan of organization, a central federation of district federations, was nearly identical to that of the league. Among the diehard peers who figured prominently on the letterhead and in the pamphlets of the new party were Lords Ampthill, Willoughby de Broke, the Bathursts, Ebury, Leconfield, Clifford of Chudleigh, Northesk, and the Duke of Somerset. Three of the seven proposed district federations were to be chaired by diehards. The program of the

National party stressed many of the principal elements of the diehard peers' attitudes toward national politics. Announcing the decision to "sever our connection with the *Unionist Party,*" it attacked the "discredited party caucus," charging that, "For years past the old party system has been nothing better than an organised mockery of the true spirit of the nation." The National party emphasized, as the diehards had, the importance of a union of all classes, of defense, and of the consolidation of the empire. Politics was not simply a contest between two groups of civilized men but rather "a matter of life and death."[63] Claiming that the old parties had "yielded to the influence of hidden funds," the National party pledged to publish its financial records. Only when all parties followed suit would "the government be free to adopt an honest British policy."[64]

Though the alternative of the National party failed to get much beyond the planning stage, it was an indication of the persistence of diehard attitudes through the Great War. Before the war Willoughby de Broke had stated the principles of a rejuvenated Toryism in a series of articles for the *National Review.* He felt that "conservatism as a National Policy has had no school of thought for a very long time," and hoped "to produce a few national ideas that everyone can understand and accept."[65] There was nothing particularly original about the results of Willoughby de Broke's efforts, as he would have been the first to admit. He constantly urged that the established conservative tradition should be the basis for Unionism and that the real problem was to get back to principles instead of playing the party game of compromise. In his articles he expressed faith that most Englishmen were "Tory by temperament and disposition."[66] He advocated "constructive social reform" allied to a respect for "Law, Order, Liberty, and Religion."[67] Rank was to mean something more than simply an accident of birth. "Service to the state," rather than lineage, should determine rank. "In the new Toryism, each man and woman will be known not by *who* they are, but by *what* they are."[68]

The diehards continued an established Tory tradition of periodically criticizing the party leadership for lacking vigor or for abandoning conservative principles. In 1846 the party had split over the repeal of the Corn Laws; Arthur Balfour, Randolph Churchill, and others had founded the "Fourth Party" in the early 1880s to advocate a more forceful stance by the Conservative leader of the Commons, Sir Stafford Northcote; and later in the nineteenth century, even the third

Marquess of Salisbury, for many years Conservative prime minister, had stated that if his party ever turned its back on the principles in which he believed, he would leave it without hesitation.[69] This concern with political ideals, and fear that the leadership might abandon them for pragmatic reasons, found powerful expression in the speeches and actions of the diehards. Willoughby de Broke complained that the increasingly strong party system gave added scope to the "masterful section" of both parties to manipulate politics for their own benefit and to ignore fundamental principles. He looked about him at the society and government of his day and saw only "a morass compounded of the accumulation of years of huckstering, wire-pulling and opportunism."[70]

The diehards, among the most politically active members of the Edwardian House of Lords, were determined to invigorate the Unionist party in order to make it an effective instrument of conservative policy. Recognizing as they did the dangers of the social and political trends of their times, they forged an alliance between new methods and traditional goals. Most of the diehards were relatively prosperous members of the aristocracy, who learned to adopt modern business techniques to strengthen the landed system. They were sensitive to political issues on both the national and the local level and were willing to fulfill the new demands of changing electoral conditions by campaigning actively to maintain their former easy dominance.

Far from being suspicious of any and all change in political affairs, the diehard peers were willing to go far along the road to radical change in certain aspects of British national life in order to preserve their position and to maintain British preeminence in the international arena. In their readiness to advocate innovation, the diehards might be termed radical conservatives. The "radical right" in America has been "characterized as radical because it desires to make far-reaching changes in American institutions, and because it seeks to eliminate from American political life those persons and institutions which threaten its values, or its economic interests."[71] There are certain important similarities in the political attitudes of these British and American groups, however widely varying their social and historical context. Like the American right, the diehards were not anxious simply to preserve the status quo. They wished in some instances to change conditions, sometimes in a drastic manner, in order to preserve what they saw as the quintessence of British life and politics.

The diehards were leading participants in the most controversial rightist political campaigns in the years before the Great War. The majority of them supported tariff reform, compulsory military service, a vastly strengthened army and navy, the introduction of a referendum system, and armed resistance to Home Rule for Ireland. Many of them sympathized with the demands for national efficiency which threatened normal British political practice. Their flexibility in turning to new methods was, however, firmly wedded to a strong commitment to the traditional conservative goals of aristocratic dominance and British imperial power. The diehards bitterly attacked their established Unionist leaders for declining to fight for military and imperial changes, and for their supposed abandonment of conservative doctrine.

At a time when the basic assumptions and conditions of British society and politics had been called into question, the diehards strove to remain at the top of the social hierarchy. Their insistence on taking seriously their customary roles and responsibilities led them to extreme measures and political notoriety. In order to maintain their position in the face of economic perils and democratic hostility, they participated enthusiastically and effectively in local and national affairs. By doing so, the diehards helped to preserve the influence of the landed aristocracy in British society and politics in the midst of a turbulent era.

Appendix, Notes, Bibliography, Index

Appendix: List of Diehards

Abbreviations

A.D.C.	Aide-de-Camp
A.S.C.	Army Service Corps
C.A.	County Alderman
C.C.	County Councillor
chm.	chairman
cmdr.	commander
comm.	in command of
comr.	commissioner
D.L.	Deputy Lieutenant
ed.	educated at
F.R.S.	Fellow Royal Society
F.S.A.	Fellow Society of Antiquaries
Gren. Guards	Grenadier Guards
J.P.	Justice of the Peace
K.G.	Knight of the Garter
L.C.C.	London County Council
L.I.	Light Infantry
m.	married
M.P.	Member of Parliament
O.M.	Order of Merit
P.C.	Privy Councillor
pres.	president
QC	Queen's Counsel
R.A.	Royal Artillery
Res.	Reserves
ret.	retired
R.F.A.	Royal Field Artillery
R.G.A.	Royal Garrison Artillery
R.H.A.	Royal Horse Artillery
R.N.	Royal Navy
R.V.	Rifle Volunteers
s.	succeeded
T.D.	Territorial Decoration
T.F.A.	Territorial Force Association
V.C.	Victoria Cross
Vol.	Volunteers
yeo.	yeomanry

List of Diehards

An asterisk (*) indicates a manuscript collection listed in the Bibliography.

Abingdon, Montague Arthur Bertie, 7th Earl of, b. 1836, s. 1884, d. 1928; ed. Eton; lt. col. Royal Berks militia, 1863-1880, hon. col. 1880; J.P. and D.L. Berks, J.P. Oxford; m. into Towneley family of Lancs, important mineral owners; 21,276 acres in Oxford, Berks, Bucks, Lancs and Yorks, with mineral revenues from last two counties

Abinger, Shelley Leopold Laurence Scarlett, 5th Baron, b. 1872, s. 1903, d. 1917; ed. Willington; capt. and hon. col. Beds regt.; J.P. Hants; hon. attaché, Stockholm, 1897-1899; 40,419 acres in Inverness and Surrey

Amherst, Hugh Amherst, 4th Earl, b. 1856, s. 1910, d. 1927; capt. Coldstream Guards; lt. col. 12th batt. West Kent vol. regt.; 7,633 acres in Kent, Warwick, Sussex, Essex

Ampthill, Sir Arthur Oliver Villiers Russell, 2nd Baron, b. 1869, s. 1884, d. 1935; ed. Eton and New College, Oxford; lt. col. 3rd batt. Beds regt.; chm. T.F.A., Beds; J.P. and D.L. Beds; priv. sec. to colonial sec. (J. Chamberlain), 1895; gov. of Madras, 1900-1906; interim viceroy and gov. gen. of India, 1904

Ashtown, Frederick Oliver Trench, 3rd Baron, b. 1868, s. 1880, d. 1946; ed. Eton and Magdalen College, Oxford; J.P. and D.L. Galway, J.P. Waterford; rep. peer, Ireland, 1908-1946; 43,643 acres in Yorks (W.R.), Limerick, Waterford, Galway, Tipperary, King's Co., Roscommon, Dublin, Westmeath

Atkinson, John Atkinson, Baron, b. 1844, s. 1905, d. 1932; barrister, King's Inns, Dublin, 1865; appointed QC 1880, bencher 1885; barrister, Inner Temple 1890, bencher 1906; M.P. for N. Londonderry, 1895-1905; solicitor gen. for Ireland, 1889-1892, attorney gen. 1892, 1895-1905; P.C. (Ireland) 1892, (England) 1905; lord of appeal in ordinary and life peer, 1905; represented the *Times* before the Parnell Commission, 1888

Bagot, Sir William Bagot, 4th Baron, b. 1857, s. 1887, d. 1932; capt. 3rd batt. South Staffs regt.; lt. col. Staffs imp. yeo.; J.P. and D.L. Staffs and Derby; A.D.C. to gov. gen. of Canada, 1879-1884; gentleman usher of the Privy Chamber, 1885-1887; lord-in-waiting (Conservative), 1896-1901; m. American; 30,543 acres in Staffs, Denbigh, Merioneth

Barrington, Walter Bulkeley Barrington, 9th Viscount, b. 1848, s. 1901, d. 1933; ed. Eton; lieut. Coldstream Guards, capt. Oxford militia; C.C., J.P. and D.L. Berks; J.P. Northants and Bucks; 6,387 acres in Berks, Yorks (W.R.), Northumberland

*Bathurst, Seymour Henry Bathurst, 7th Earl, b. 1864, s. 1892, d. 1943; ed. Eton and Christ Church, Oxford; hon. col. 5th batt. Glos regt.; C.C., J.P. and D.L. Glos; m. Hon. Lilias Borthwick, who inherited the *Morning Post* on the death of her father, Lord Glenesk; 13,663 acres in Glos and Derby

*Bedford, Sir Herbrand Arthur Russell, 11th Duke of, b. 1858, s. 1893, d. 1940; ed. Balliol College, Oxford; lieut. Grenadier Guards; lt. col. and hon. col. 3rd batt. Beds regt.; hon. col. 19th Middlesex R.V. and 3rd vol. batt. Beds regt.; Egyptian campaign, 1882; A.D.C. to gov. gen. of India, 1884-1888, to Edward VII, 1908; president, Beds T.F.A.; lord lt. Middlesex; chairman, Beds C.C.; J.P. and D.L. Beds; first mayor of Holborn, 1900; pres., Zoological Society of London, 1899;

trustee, British Museum, 1906; F.S.A. 1901; K.G. 1902; F.R.S. 1908; 86,335 acres in Beds, Devon, Cambridge, Northants, Dorset, Bucks, Hunts, Cornwall, Hants, Herts, Lincoln; large London property

Brabourne, Wyndham Wentworth Knatchbull-Hugessen, 3rd Baron, b. 1885, s. 1909, d. 1915 (killed in action); lieut. Grenadier Guards; 4,173 acres in Kent

*Bristol, Frederick William Fane Hervey, 4th Marquess of, b. 1863, s. 1907, d. 1951; ed. Tonbridge Grammar School; capt. and rear admiral, R.N.; M.P. for Bury St. Edmunds, 1906-1907; chm., West Suffolk C.C., 1914-1935; pres., Institute of Naval Architects, 1911-1916; 32,014 acres in Suffolk, Lincoln, Essex, Sussex

Bute, Sir John Crichton-Stuart, 4th Marquess of, b. 1881, s. 1900, d. 1947; ed. Harrow and Christ Church, Oxford; pres., Bute T.F.A.; lord lt. Bute, 1905; 116,668 acres in Glamorgan, Durham, Bedford, Brecon, Monmouth, Ayr, Bute, Wigtown

*Cathcart, Alan Cathcart, 4th Earl, b. 1856, s. 1905, d. 1911; ed. Eton; lieut. 6th Dragoon Guards and Scots Guards; J.P. and D.L. North Riding, Yorks; 5,554 acres in Yorks (N. and W.R.), Staffs, Renfrew

Churchill, Sir Victor Albert Francis Charles Spencer, 1st Viscount, b. 1864, s. 1886, d. 1934; lieut. Coldstream Guards; maj. Oxford yeo.; J.P. Oxford and Leicester; lord-in-waiting (Conservative), 1889-1892, 1895-1901, 1901-1905; master of buckhounds, 1900-1901; lord chamberlain, 1902; Conservative whip, House of Lords; chm., Great Western Railway and British Overseas Bank; 9,112 acres in Oxford and Wilts

*Clanricarde, Hubert George deBurgh-Canning, 2nd Marquess of, b. 1832, s. 1874, d. 1916; ed. Harrow; attaché, Turin, 2nd sec., Turin, 1862; M.P. for Galway, 1867-1871; 56,826 acres in Galway

Clanwilliam, Sir Arthur Vesey Meade, 5th Earl, b. 1873, s. 1907, d. 1953; Royal Horse Guards, capt. gen. Reserve of Officers; extra A.D.C. to viceroy of India; severely wounded in Boer War; D.L. Down; 3,584 acres in Co. Down

Clarendon, Sir Edward Hyde Villiers, 5th Earl of, b. 1846, s. 1870, d. 1914; ed. Harrow and Trinity College, Cambridge; hon. col. Herts yeo.; yeo. A.D.C. to Edward VII and George V from 1897; pres. and chm. Herts T.F.A.; M.P. for Brecon, 1869-1870; J.P. and D.L. Warwicks; lord lt. Herts from 1892; lord-in-waiting (Liberal Unionist), 1895-1900; lord chamberlain, 1900-1905; P.C.; 2,298 acres in Warwicks and Herts

*Clifford of Chudleigh, Lewis Henry Hugh Clifford, 9th Baron, b. 1851, s. 1880, d. 1916; ed. Stoneyhurst College, London Univ.; hon. col. 5th vol. batt. Devon regt.; col. T.F.A. from 1908; vice-chm. Devonshire T.F.A.; vol. A.D.C. to Edward VII from 1901; barrister, Inner Temple, 1882; J.P., D.L. and C.A. for Devon; chm. Quarter Sessions, Devon; Roman Catholic; 7,860 acres in Devon, Warwick, Somerset, Bucks, Cornwall

Clonbrock, Sir Luke Gerald Dillon, 4th Baron, b. 1834, s. 1893, d. 1917; ed. Eton and Balliol College, Oxford; 2nd sec., Vienna, 1862; sheriff, Co. Galway, 1865; private sec. to viceroy of Ireland, 1866-1868, 1874-1876; lord lt. of Galway, 1892; rep. peer of Ireland from 1895; P.C. (Ireland); chm., Irish Landowners' Convention; 29,550 acres in Galway

*Colchester, Reginald Charles Edward Abbot, 3rd Baron, b. 1842, s. 1867, d. 1919; ed. Eton and Christ Church, Oxford; pres., Union Society, 1863; barrister, Lincoln's Inn, 1867; fellow, All Souls' College, 1864-1869; priv. sec. to pres. of Board of

Trade and first lord of the Treasury; examiner in law and history at Oxford Univ.,
1869-1871; charity comr. 1880-1893; member of London School Board, 1891-1894;
F.S.A. 1875

Combermere, Sir Francis Lynch Willington Stapleton-Cotton, b. 1887, s. 1898, d.
1969; 13,679 acres in Cheshire, Salop, Lancs; also West Indies estates

Coventry, George William Coventry, 9th Earl of, b. 1838, s. 1843, d. 1930; ed. Eton
and Christ Church, Oxford; hon. col. 5th and 6th batts. Worcester regt.; lord lt.
Worcester from 1891; C.C. and D.L. Worcester; pres., Worcester T.F.A.; P.C.;
high steward of Tewkesbury; pres., Royal Agricultural Soc., 1899; capt. of Corps of
Gentlemen-at-Arms, 1877-1880, 1885-1886; master of the buckhounds, 1886-1892,
1895-1900; 14,419 acres in Worcs and Glos

Crawford and Balcarres, Sir James Ludovic Lindsay, 26th Earl of, b. 1847, s. 1880, d.
1913; ed. Eton and Trinity College, Cambridge; lieut. Grenadier Guards; hon. col.
5th batt. Manchester regt.; J.P. Lancs and Aberdeen; M.P. for Wigan, 1874-1880;
pres., Royal Astronomical Soc., 1878-1880; pres., Camden Soc., 1888; trustee of
British Museum, 1885; author of several astronomical and bibliographical works;
large mineral holdings; 13,480 acres in Aberdeen, Lancs, Carmarthen, Westmorland

DeFreyne, Arthur French, 4th Baron, b. 1855, s. 1868, d. 1913; ed. Downside and
Beaumont Colleges; Roman Catholic; former officer; hon. col. 5th batt. Connaught
Rangers; 38,788 acres in Roscommon, Sligo, Galway, Mayo

Denbigh, Rudolph Robert Basil Aloysius Augustine Feilding, 9th Earl of, b. 1859, s.
1892, d. 1939; ed. Oscott College and Military Academy, Woolwich; capt. Royal
Horse Artillery, serving in Egypt, 1882; A.D.C. to viceroy of Ireland, 1887; lt. col.
Hon. Artillery Comp., 1893; member of L.C.C. for the City, 1896-1898; lord-in-
waiting, 1897-1905; J.P., D.L. and C.C. for Warwick; appointed to staff, Great
War; col. in T.F.A. and A.D.C. to Edward VII; vice-chm. of City of London
T.F.A.; pres., Catholic Assoc. of England, from 1892; 3,218 acres in Leicester and
Flint

*Deramore, Sir Robert Wilfrid de Yarburgh-Bateson, 3rd Baron, b. 1865, s. 1893, d.
1936; major Yorks Hussars; Great War; J.P., D.L. and C.C. Yorks (E.R.); J.P.
Yorks (W.R.); J.P. and D.L. Co. Down; 26,373 acres in Yorks, Down, Limerick,
Londonderry, Antrim

*Devon, Sir Charles Pepys Courtenay, 14th Earl of, b. 1870, s. 1904, d. 1927; ed.
Rugby; capt. and hon. maj. 3rd batt. Somerset Light Infantry; J.P. Devon; inspec-
tor in Board of Agriculture, 1895-1904; 53,075 acres in Devon and Limerick

Digby, Edward Henry Trafalgar Digby, 10th Baron, b. 1846, s. 1889, d. 1920; ed.
Harrow; col. Coldstream Guards; hon. col. Dorset R.G.A. and 3rd batt. Dorset
regt.; J.P. and C.A. Dorset; M.P. for Dorset, 1876-1885; 39,505 acres in Dorset,
Warwick, King's Co., Queen's Co., and Co. Mayo

*Dynevor, Walter FitzUryan Rice, 7th Baron, b. 1873, s. 1911, d. 1956; ed. Eton and
Christ Church, Oxford; capt. Carmarthen Artillery; priv. sec. to sec. of state for
India, 1899-1903, and to first lord of Admiralty, 1903-1905; M.P. for Brighton,
1910-1911; asst. in Ministry of Munitions, 1916-1918; lord lt. Carmarthen; J.P.,
C.C. Carmarthen, 1919-1935; 10,728 acres in Carmarthen, Glamorgan, Oxford,
Wilts, Glos

Ebury, Robert Wellesley Grosvenor, 2nd Baron, b. 1834, s. 1893, d. 1918; ed. Harrow and King's College, London; capt. 1st Life Guards; capt. Cheshire yeo. cav.; M.P. (Liberal) for Westminster, 1865-1874; Liberal Unionist, 1886; property includes the Ebury estate in Pimlico; 2,723 acres in Herts and Middlesex

Erne, Sir John Henry Crichton, 4th Earl of, b. 1839, s. 1885, d. 1914; ed. Eton and Christ Church, Oxford; high sheriff of Fermanagh, 1864, of Donegal, 1867; lord lt. Fermanagh from 1885; chairman of Fermanagh C.C., 1899-1902, 1905, 1908; M.P. for Enniskillen, 1868-1880, for Fermanagh, 1880-1885; lord of the Treasury, 1876-1880; Conservative whip in the House of Commons, 1876-1885; P.C. (Ireland), 1902; Imperial Orange Grand Master; 40,365 acres in Fermanagh, Donegal, Mayo, Sligo

Erroll, Sir Charles Gore Hay, 20th Earl of, b. 1852, s. 1891, d. 1927; ed. Harrow; D.L. Aberdeen; hereditary lord high constable of Scotland; col. ret., lt. col. comm. Royal Horse Guards; hon. col. 5th batt. Gordon Highlanders; S. Africa, 1899-1901; brig. gen., 1900-1901; asst. adj. gen., War Office, 1901; A.D.C. to comdr.-in-chief from 1895; Great War as brig. gen.; lord-in-waiting (Conservative), 1903-1905; 8,264 acres in Aberdeen and Northumberland

Falkland, Byron Plantegenet Cary, 12th Viscount, b. 1845, s. 1886, d. 1922; ed. Cheltenham and Sandhurst; lt. col. 35th Foot; J.P. and D.L. Yorks; rep. peer (Scotland) from 1894; m. American; 3,011 acres in Yorks (N.R.)

Farnham, Sir Arthur Kenlis Maxwell, 11th Baron, b. 1879, s. 1900, d. 1957; lieut. 10th Hussars; S. Africa, 1899-1902; capt. N. Irish Horse yeo.; Great War; rep. peer (Ireland) from 1908; involved in gun-running for Ulster Volunteers during post-1911 crisis; 25,920 acres in Cavan

Fingall, Arthur James Francis Plunkett, 11th Earl of, b. 1859, s. 1881, d. 1929; maj. 7th batt. Prince of Wales's Leinster regt. during Great War; Roman Catholic; active in Irish Unionist Alliance; sheriff of Meath, 1881; state steward to lord lt. of Ireland, 1882-1885; master of horse to lord lt. of Ireland, 1905-1906; Liberal Unionist in 1886; P.C. (Ireland), 1892; 9,594 acres in Meath and Berks

*Fitzwilliam, William Charles de Meuron Westworth Fitzwilliam, 7th Earl, b. 1872, s. 1902, d. 1943; ed. Eton and Trinity College, Cambridge; capt. in army; maj. and brevet lt. col. West Riding R.H.A.; capt. and hon. maj. 3rd batt. Oxford L.I.; extra A.D.C. to the viceroy of India, 1893-1894; capt. in headquarter staff in S. African War; deputy asst. director headquarter staff in Great War; J.P. Yorks (W.R.); C.C., J.P. and D.L. Wicklow; M.P. (Liberal Unionist) for Wakefield, 1895-1902; treas., Liberal Unionist Assoc.; lord mayor of Sheffield, 1909-1910; alderman of Sheffield, 1910; 115,743 acres in Yorks (N.,E. and W.R.), Northants, Cambridge, Derby, Hunts, Lincs, Wicklow, Kildare, Wexford

Forester, Cecil Theodore Weld-Forester, 5th Baron, b. 1842, s. 1894, d. 1917; ed. Harrow and Trinity College, Cambridge; J.P. Kent; J.P., D.L. and C.C. Salop; M.P. for Wenlock, 1874-1885; mayor of Much Wenlock, 1898-1899; 15,615 acres in Salop and Staffs

Gormanston, Sir Jenico Edward Joseph Preston, 15th Viscount, b. 1879, s. 1907, d. 1925; lieut. Manchester regt.; capt. Royal Irish Fusiliers; Great War; J.P. and D.L. Meath; premier viscount of Ireland; 10,957 acres in Meath and Dublin

Halifax, Sir Charles Lindley Wood, 2nd Viscount, b. 1839, s. 1885, d. 1934; ed. Eton and Christ Church, Oxford; D.L. Yorks (W.R.); groom of the bedchamber to the Prince of Wales, 1862-1877; F.S.A., 1880; ecclesiastical comr. from 1886; pres.,

English Church Union from 1868; prominent High Churchman; 10,142 acres in Yorks (E. and W.R.)

*Halsbury, Sir Hardinge Stanley Giffard, 1st Earl of, b. 1823, s. 1885, d. 1923; ed. Merton College, Oxford; barrister, Inner Temple, 1850; QC and bencher, 1865; solicitor gen., 1875-1880; knighted 1875; M.P. for Launceston, 1877-1885; treas., Inner Temple, 1881; constable of Launceston Castle from 1883; P.C., 1885; lord chancellor, 1885-1886, 1886-1892, 1895-1905; F.R.S., 1887; pres., Royal Society of Literature from 1891; high steward, Oxford Univ. from 1896; F.S.A., 1900

Hardwicke, Charles Alexander Yorke, 8th Earl of, b. 1869, s. 1909, d. 1936; lieut. Army Motor Reserve; 19,382 acres in Cambs, Hants, Hunts, Suffolk, Herts

Harlech, George Ralph Charles Ormsby-Gore, 3rd Baron, b. 1855, s. 1904, d. 1938; ed. Eton and Sandhurst; capt. Coldstream Guards; chm., Salop T.F.A.; col. Salop. imp. yeo.; J.P., D.L., Salop and Leitrim; D.L. and lord lt. Merioneth; lord lt. Leitrim, from 1904; high sheriff Leitrim, 1885; M.P. for Oswestry, Salop, 1901-1904; constable, Harlech Castle, 1927-1938; 58,358 acres in Carnarvon, Merioneth, Salop, Montgomery, Denbigh, Berks, Sligo, Leitrim, Westmeath, Mayo, Roscommon

Holmpatrick, Hans Wellesley Hamilton, 2nd Baron, b. 1886, s. 1898, d. 1942; lieut. 16th Lancers; capt. Reserve of Officers; brig. maj. Cav. Brig. from 1917; Great War; senator of Southern Ireland; 6,889 acres in Dublin, Queen's Co., Down, Meath

Hood, Sir Grosvenor Arthur Alexander Hood, 5th Viscount, b. 1868, s. 1907, d. 1933; ed. Eton and Royal Military Academy, Woolwich; lt. col. comm. 7th batt. London regt.; maj. Gren. Guards; Ashanti, 1895-1896, and S. Africa, 1899-1902; 2,600 acres in Warwick, Northants, Bucks

Hothfield, Sir Henry James Tufton, 1st Baron, b. 1844, s. 1881, d. 1926; ed. Eton and Christ Church, Oxford; pres., Westmorland T.F.A.; hereditary high sheriff of Westmorland; vice-admiral of Coast of Cumberland and Westmorland; lord. lt. of Westmorland; lord-in-waiting, 1886; J.P. and D.L. Kent; mayor of Appleby, 1895-1896; created baron, 1881; received peerage from Gladstone, became a Unionist about 1890; 39,276 acres in Westmorland, Kent, Yorks (W.R.), Cumberland

Kensington, Hugh Edwardes, 6th Baron, b. 1873, s. 1900, d. 1938; ed. Eton; lieut. 15th Hussars; S. Africa, 1900; A.D.C. to Lt. Gen. Rundle, 1900-1901; Great War, col. Welsh Horse yeo.; J.P. Pembroke; large London estate; 7,471 acres in Pembroke, Radnor, Cardigan, Carmarthen

Kesteven, Sir John Henry Trollope, 2nd Baron, b. 1851, s. 1874, d. 1915; ed. Eton and Magdalen College, Cambridge; lt. col. comm. Lincoln yeo.; S. Africa imp. yeo. in 1900; chm., Lincoln T.F.A.; C.C. Lincoln; J.P. Peterborough; 10,500 acres in Lincoln and Northants

*Kilmaine, Sir John Edward Deane Browne, 5th Baron, b. 1878, s. 1907, d. 1946; ed. Magdalen College, Oxford; J.P. and D.L. Mayo; rep. peer (Ireland) from April, 1911; 14,665 acres in Mayo, Westmeath, Roscommon

Kinnoul, Archibald Fitzroy George Hay, 13th Earl of, b. 1855, s. 1897, d. 1916; lieut. Black Watch; served with Baker Pasha in Egypt as chief of staff; J.P. and D.L. Perth; 12,657 acres in Perth

Lauderdale, Sir Frederick Henry Maitland, 13th Earl of, b. 1840, s. 1884, d. 1924;

capt. 8th Hussars; lt. col. Bengal Staff Corp.; capt. Lothian and Berwicks yeo. cav.; political agent for foreign dept. of govt. of India, 1869-1889; rep. peer (Scotland), 1889-1920; lord lt. of Berwick, 1889-1901; D.L. Haddington and Berwick; 25,512 acres in Berwick, Roxburgh, Haddington

*Leconfield, Charles Henry Wyndham, 3rd Baron, b. 1872, s. 1901, d. 1952; lieut. 1st Life Guards; S. African War and Great War; military member Sussex T.F.A.; D.L. Sussex; 109,935 acres in Sussex, Yorks, Cumberland, Clare, Limerick, Tipperary

*Leeds, Sir George Godolphin Osborne, 10th Duke of, b. 1862, s. 1895, d. 1927; ed. Eton and Trinity College, Cambridge; lieut. Yorks Hussars; hon. cmdr. R.N. Vol. Res.; Great War; M.P. for Brixton, 1887-1895; treas. of H.M. Household, 1895-1896; asst. sec. to sec. of state for the Colonies, 1887-1888; J.P. Yorks (N.R.); member of L.C.C.; 24,237 acres in Yorks (N. and W.R.), Cornwall, Bucks, Cambridge, Middlesex

Leith of Fyvie, Alexander John Forbes-Leith, 1st Baron, b. 1847, s. 1905, d. 1925; ed. Berlin, St.Cyr; royal navy, 1860-1872; J.P. and D.L. Aberdeen; began business career as sec. and mgr. of the Missouri Furnace Co. at St. Louis, 1885; pres., Joliet Steel Co. and (1890) Illinois Steel Co.; an organizer of the Federal Steel Co., and United States Steel Corp.; m. American (St. Louis); raised to peerage, 1905

Leitrim, Charles Clements, 5th Earl of, b. 1879, s. 1892, d. 1952; ed. Eton and Christ Church, Oxford; lieut. 9th Lancers; S. Africa, 1899-1902; Great War, major 11th batt. R. Inneskilling Fusiliers; priv. sec. to sec. of state for the Colonies, 1917; lieut. of Co. Londonderry; involved in gun-running for the Ulster Volunteers during post-1911 crisis; 56,852 acres in Donegal and Leitrim

Limerick, William Henry Edmond deVere Sheaffe Pery, 4th Earl of, b. 1863, s. 1896, d. 1929; ed. Eton; lieut. 4th batt. Rifle Brig.; capt. and hon. maj. Royal Munster Fusiliers; 5,709 acres in Limerick, Clare, Cork

Llandaff of Hereford, Henry Matthews, Viscount, b. 1826, s. 1895, d. 1913; ed. Univ. of Paris and Univ. College, London; barrister, Lincoln's Inn, 1850; QC, 1868; member of senate of Univ. of London, 1885-1901; sec. of state for Home Department, 1886-1892; P.C. 1886; M.P. for Dungarvan, 1868-1874, and for East Div. of Birmingham, 1886-1895

Londesborough, Sir William Francis Henry Denison, 2nd Earl of, b. 1864, s. 1900, d. 1917; hon. col. 5th batt. East Yorks regt.; lieut. Yorks yeo. cav.; D.L. Yorks (E.R.); vice-admiral of Yorks; 52,655 acres in Yorks

Loudoun, Charles Edward Hastings Abney-Hastings, 11th Earl of, b. 1855, s. 1874, d. 1920; lieut. Leicester yeo. cav.; D.L. Ayr; 32,910 acres in Ayr, Leicester, Derby, Yorks (W.R.)

Lovat, Sir Simon Joseph Fraser, 14th Baron, b. 1871, s. 1887, d. 1933; lieut. 1st Life Guards; raised Lovat's Scouts for S. African War, in which he served 1900-1902; Great War, temp. maj. gen. comm. 4th Mounted Div.; chm., Inverness T.F.A.; A.D.C. to Edward VII; D.L. Inverness; 181,791 acres in Inverness

Lovelace, Lionel Fortescue King, 3rd Earl of, b. 1865, s. 1906, d. 1929; ed. Eton and Sandhurst; capt. and adj. 9th Lancers; Great War, maj. Northumberland Fusiliers; J.P. and D.L. Surrey; 18,481 acres in Surrey, Leicester, Somerset, Warwick, Devon

Malmesbury, James Edward Harris, 5th Earl of, b. 1872, s. 1899, d. 1950; ed. Christ Church, Oxford, capt. 3rd (militia) batt. Hants; lieut. Hants yeo. cav.; D.L., J.P.

and C.A., Hants; member of L.C.C. (Stepney div.) 1904-1905; asst. priv. sec. (un-paid) to under-sec. of state for the Colonies (1901); Great War, maj. 3rd batt. Hants regt. and staff officer; lord-in-waiting, 1922-1924; chm., Hants C.C., 1927; pres., County Councils Assn. of England and Wales, 1931; 5,446 acres in Hants, Wilts, Dorset

Mar, John Francis Erskine Goodeve-Erskine, 33rd Earl of, b. 1836, s. 1866, d. 1930; ed. Queen's College, Cambridge; premier earl of Scotland; complicated legal battle regarding the earldom of Mar, 1875-1885; rep. peer (Scotland), 1886-1922

Marlborough, Sir Charles Richard John Spencer-Churchill, 9th Duke of, b. 1871, s. 1892, d. 1934; ed. Winchester and Trinity College, Cambridge; hon. col. 3rd batt. Oxford and Bucks L.I.; lt. col. Oxford Hussars; staff capt. imp. yeo., South Africa, 1900; Great War, lt. col. gen. staff; military member Oxford T.F.A.; C.C. Wood-stock; mayor of Woodstock, 1907-1908; P.C., 1894; paymaster gen. 1899-1902; asst. mil. sec. to Lord Roberts, 1900; under-sec. of state for the Colonies, 1903-1905; m. Consuelo Vanderbilt, 1896, she obtained divorce, 1921; convert to Roman Catholicism; 23,511 acres in Oxford, Wilts, Berks

Massy, John Thomas William Massy, 6th Baron, b. 1835, s. 1874, d. 1926; J.P. and D.L. Leitrim and Limerick; sheriff Leitrim, 1863, and Limerick, 1873; rep. peer (Ireland) from 1876; 33,003 acres in Limerick and Leitrim

Meath, Sir Reginald Brabazon, 12th Earl of, b. 1841, s. 1887, d. 1929; ed. Eton; 2nd sec. diplomatic service; militia A.D.C. to Victoria 1883-1901, and to Edward VII 1901; P.C. (Ireland), 1887; J.P. and D.L. Wicklow; J.P. Dublin; lord lt. county and city of Dublin; chancellor of Royal Univ. of Ireland, 1902-1905; alderman of L.C.C. 1889-1892, 1898-1901; founded Empire Day and the Hospital Saturday Fund; participated in a wide variety of philanthropic and patriotic activities; 15,448 acres in Wicklow, Dublin, Hereford

Merthyr, Sir William Thomas Lewis, 1st Baron, b. 1837, s. 1911, d. 1914; J.P., D.L. and C.A. Glamorgan; J.P. Brecon; high sheriff, Brecon, 1884; knighted, 1885; created baronet, 1896; created Baron Merthyr, 1911; pres., Institute of Mining Engineers, Mining Assoc. of Great Britain, South Wales Institute of Engineers; vice-pres., Iron and Steel Institute, Institute of Mechanical Engineers; founder and chm. Monmouth and South Wales Coal Assoc., South Wales Sliding Scale Committee, and South Wales Miners Provident Fund; member of royal commissions on Coal Supplies, on Trade Disputes and Trade Combinations, on shipping, mining and labor questions; member of J. Chamberlain's tariff reform commissions; agent for Marquess of Bute

*Milner, Sir Frederick George Milner, Viscount, b. 1854, s. 1901, d. 1925; ed. St. Peter's and Tübingen, King's College, London Univ., Balliol College, Oxford; fel-low, New College, Oxford, 1876; pres., Oxford Union Society; barrister, Inner Temple, 1881; sub-editor, *Pall Mall Gazette,* 1882-1885; priv. sec. to chancellor of the Exchequer, 1887-1889; under-sec. for finance in Egypt, 1889-1892; chm., Board of Inland Revenue, 1892-1897; gov., Cape of Good Hope, 1897-1901; high comr. for S. Africa, 1897-1905; P.C., 1901; gov., Transvaal and Orange River Colony, 1901-1905; member of war cabinet and minister without portfolio, 1916-1918; sec. of state for War, 1918-1919; sec. of state for Colonies, 1919-1921

Monkswell, Robert Alfred Hardcastle Collier, 3rd Baron, b. 1875, s. 1909, d. 1964; ed. Eton and Trinity College, Cambridge; entered Foreign Office, 1895; 3rd sec. in dipl. service, 1902-1905; 2nd sec., 1905; clerk in Foreign Office, 1905-1910; Great War

*Morley, Edmund Robert Parker, 4th Earl of, b. 1877, s. 1905, d. 1951; ed. Eton and Trinity College, Cambridge; Great War, capt. 1st Royal Devon yeo. and staff lieut.; J.P. and C.A. Devon; pres., Port of Plymouth chamber of commerce from 1905; 4,238 acres in Devon

*Mowbray, Segrave, and Stourton, Charles Botolph Joseph Stourton, 24th Baron, b. 1867, s. 1893, d. 1936; ed. Woburn Park School; premier baron of England; lieut. 3rd batt. E. Yorks regt. (militia); Great War; J.P. and D.L. Yorks (W.R.); 5,097 acres in Yorks (W.R.)

Muskerry, Sir Hamilton Matthew Tilson Fitzmaurice Deane-Morgan, 4th Baron, b. 1854, s. 1868, d. 1929; served in R.N.; rep. peer (Ireland) from 1892; spokesman for merchant seamen in the House of Lords; 15,227 acres in Wexford, Limerick, Tipperary, Carlow, Waterford, Kilkenny, Cork

Newcastle, Henry Pelham Archibald Douglas Pelham-Clinton, 7th Duke of, b. 1864, s. 1879, d. 1928; ed. Eton and Magdalen College, Oxford; D.L. Notts; member of London School Board (City), 1894-1897; 35,547 acres in Notts, Derby, Yorks (W.R.), Lincoln

*Norfolk, Sir Henry Fitzalan-Howard, 15th Duke of, b. 1847, s. 1860, d. 1917; premier duke; lt. col. and hon. col. comm. 4th batt. Royal Sussex regt.; pres. and chm., Sussex T.F.A.; lord lt. Sussex from 1905; J.P. and C.C. for West Sussex; S. Africa, 1900; postmaster-gen., 1895-1900; mayor of Sheffield, 1895-1897; mayor of Arundel, 1902-1903; first mayor of Westminster, 1900; P.C.; pres., Catholic Union of Great Britain, and chief lay spokesman for English Catholics; chm., Royal Commission on Militia and Volunteer Forces, 1903; 49,866 acres in Yorks (W.R.), Sussex, Norfolk, Surrey, Derby, Suffolk, Staffs, Notts

*Northcote, Sir Henry Stafford Northcote, Baron, b. 1846, s. 1900, d. 1911; ed. Eton and Merton College, Oxford; clerk, Foreign Office, 1868-1871; attached to Marquess of Ripon's mission to arrange Alabama Treaty, 1871; sec. to comrs. under Treaty of Washington, 1871-1873; priv. sec. to Lord Salisbury, Constantinople embassy, 1876-1877, and to chancellor of Exchequer, 1877-1880; M.P. for Exeter, 1880-1899; financial sec. to War Office, 1885-1886; surveyor gen. of Ordnance, 1886-1887; charity comr., 1891-1892; gov. gen. of Bombay, 1900-1903; gov. gen. of Australia, 1903-1908; created Baron Northcote, 1900

Northesk, David John Carnegie, 10th Earl of, b. 1865, s. 1891, d. 1921; ed. Eton; D.L. and J.P. Angus; maj. and hon. lt. col. 3rd batt. Glos regt.; A.D.C. to gov. of Victoria, 1889-1891, 1892-1895; Great War; rep. peer (Scotland) from 1900; 7,735 acres in Angus, Hants, Staffs

Northumberland, Sir Henry George Percy, 7th Duke of, b. 1846, s. 1899, d. 1918; ed. Christ Church, Oxford; M.P. for North Northumberland, 1868-1885; summoned to Parliament in his father's barony as Lord Lovaine, 1887; treas. of the Household, 1874-1875; P.C. 1874; militia A.D.C. to Victoria 1892, to Edward VII 1901; pres., Royal Institute, 1899; trustee, British Museum, 1900; F.R.S. 1900; lord. lt. of

Northumberland; chm., Northumberland C.C.; pres., Northumberland T.F.A. from 1909; J.P. Surrey; member of senate of Univ. of Durham, 1909; 186,397 acres in Northumberland, Surrey, Middlesex, Durham

*Plymouth, Robert George Windsor-Clive, 1st Earl of, b. 1857, s. 1869, d. 1923; ed. Eton and St. John's College, Cambridge; D.L. Worcester and Salop; lord lt. of Glamorgan from 1890; P.C., 1891; pres., Glamorgan T.F.A.; paymaster-gen., 1891-1892; mayor of Cardiff, 1895-1896; chief comr. of works, 1902-1905; trustee, National Gallery; chairman of Trustees, Tate Gallery; high steward of Cambridge Univ. from 1919; hon. col. Glamorgan yeo., Glamorgan R.G.A., 3rd batt. the Welsh regt., and 8th batt. Worcester regt.; created Earl of Plymouth, 1905; s. grandmother as 14th Baron Windsor, 1869; 37,454 acres in Glamorgan, Salop, Worcester, Flint, Hereford

Portsmouth, Newton Wallop, 6th Earl of, b. 1856, s. 1891, d. 1917; ed. Balliol College, Oxford; pres., Oxford Union Society, 1877; J.P., D.L. and C.A. Hants; D.L. Wexford; J.P. Devon; M.P. for Barnstaple, 1880-1885, and for North Devon, 1885-1891; ecclesiastical comr. for England from 1909; under-sec. of state for War and civil member, Army Council, 1905-1908; a Liberal until 1886, then a Unionist until 1905, when he accepted office in the Liberal government of Henry Campbell-Bannerman; 46,984 acres in Hants, Devon, Somerset, Wexford

Radnor, Sir Jacob Pleydell-Bouverie, 6th Earl of, b. 1868, s. 1900, d. 1930; ed. Harrow and Trinity College, Cambridge; lt. col. comm. 4th batt. Wilts regt.; chm., Wilts T.F.A.; S. Africa, 1900; asst. priv. sec. to pres. of Board of Agriculture, 1890-1892; chm., Royal Commission on the Care and Control of the Feeble-Minded, 1904-1908; lord lt. of Wilts, 1925; M.P. for S. Wilts, 1892-1900; 24,870 acres in Wilts, Berks, Kent, Glos

Raglan, George FitzRoy Henry Somerset, 3rd Baron, b. 1857, s. 1884, d. 1921; ed. Eton and Sandhurst; J.P. and D.L. Monmouth; gov. of Isle of Man, 1902-1919; under-sec. of state for War, 1900-1902; capt. Grenadier Guards; Afghan War, 1879-1880; lt. col. and hon. col. Royal Monmouth regt. (militia); A.D.C. to gov. of Bombay, 1880-1883; pres., Society of Genealogists; first pres., National Service League

Ranfurly, Sir Uchter John Mark Knox, 5th Earl of, b. 1856, s. 1875, d. 1933; ed. Harrow and Trinity College, Cambridge; lord-in-waiting, 1895-1897; gov. of New Zealand, 1897-1904; P.C. (Ireland), 1905; director of Ambulance dept., 1915-1919; member, Ulster Unionist Party Standing Committee; founder and pres., Ulster Loyalist Anti-Repeal Union, 1886; 10,153 acres in Tyrone and Fermanagh

Rayleigh, John William Strutt, 3rd Baron, b. 1842, s. 1873, d. 1919; ed. Harrow and Trinity College, Cambridge; F.R.S., 1873; Cavendish Professor of Experimental Physics, 1879-1884; pres., Brit. Assoc., 1884; sec., Royal Soc., 1885-1896; prof. of Natural Philosophy, Royal Inst.; pres., Royal Society, 1905-1908; O.M., 1902; Nobel Prize for Physics, 1905; chancellor of Cambridge Univ., 1908; pres., Society for Psychical Research, 1919; lord lt. of Essex, 1892-1901; 8,632 acres in Essex

*Roberts, Sir Frederick Sleigh Roberts, 1st Earl, b. 1832, s. 1892, d. 1914; ed. Eton, Sandhurst and Addiscombe; field marshall in the army; comdr.-in-chief in India, 1885-1893, in Ireland, 1895-99, in S. Africa, 1899-1900; comdr.-in-chief of the

army from 1900 to the abolition of that office in 1904; P.C., 1895; O.M., 1902;
V.C., 1858; pres. and leading spirit, National Service League
Rosmead, Sir Hercules Arthur Temple Robinson, 2nd Baron, b. 1866, s. 1897, d.
1933; ed. Eton; lieut. Royal Irish Fusiliers, 1889-1898; maj. and hon. lt. col. 5th
batt. Royal Fus.; S. Africa, 1888, 1900; maj. 6th batt. Lancs Fus. (militia), 1900-
1906
Rosslyn, Sir James Francis Harry St. Clair-Erskine, 5th Earl of, b. 1869, s. 1890, d.
1939; ed. Eton and Magdalen College, Oxford; lieut. 3rd batt. Northants regt.
(militia), 1886-1890; 2nd lieut. Royal Horse Guards, 1890; capt. Fife Light Horse
Vol., 1890-1897; served with Thorneycroft's Mounted Infantry in S. Africa and was
war correspondent (*Daily Mail*), 1900; bankrupt, 1897; maj. King's Royal Rifle
Corps, 1915-1917; J.P. and D.L., Fife; 3,310 acres in Fife and Midlothian
Rothes, Norman Evelyn Leslie, 19th Earl of, b. 1877, s. 1893, d. 1927; ed. Eton; lieut.
4th batt. Devon regt. (militia), 1896-1899; 2nd lieut. 6th vol. batt. Black Watch,
1908; lt. col. Highland Cyclist batt.; capt. Fife R.F.A.; J.P., Fife; 3,562 acres in Fife
St. Levan, Sir John Townshend St. Aubyn, 2nd Baron, b. 1857, s. 1908, d. 1940; ed.
Eton and Trinity College, Cambridge; Gren. Guards; A.D.C. to various commanding generals in Egypt, Sudan, etc., and to gov. of Hong Kong, 1889-1890; military
sec. to gov. gen. of Canada, 1892-1893; comm. Gren. Guards, 1904-1908 (brig.
gen.); D.L. and J.P. Cornwall; 6,555 acres in Cornwall and Devon
*Salisbury, James Edward Hubert Gascoyne-Cecil, 4th Marquess of, b. 1861, s. 1903,
d. 1947; ed. Eton and Univ. College, Oxford; lt. col. 4th batt. Beds regt. (militia);
S. Africa, 1900; A.D.C. to Edward VII, 1903; J.P., D.L. and chm. of Quarter Sessions, Herts; M.P. for North East Lancs, 1885-1892, for Rochester, 1893-1903;
under-sec. of state for Foreign Affairs, 1900-1903; lord privy seal, 1903-1905 and
1924-1929; pres., Board of Trade, 1905; lord pres. of Council, 1922-1924; chancellor of Duchy of Lancs, 1922-1923; leader of House of Lords, 1924-1929; 20,202
acres in Herts, Dorset, Lancs, Essex, Middlesex, Beds, Norfolk, Wilts
Saltoun, Alexander William Frederick Fraser, 18th Baron, b. 1851, s. 1886, d. 1933;
ed. Eton; lt. col. Gren. Guards; maj. 3rd batt. Gordon Highlanders; J.P. and D.L.
Aberdeen; rep. peer (Scotland), 1890-1933; 10,762 acres in Aberdeen
Sandys, Michael Edwin Marcus Sandys, 5th Baron, b. 1855, s. 1904, d. 1948; J.P.
Worcester; member London Stock Exchange; 2,585 acres in Worcester
*Scarbrough, Sir Aldred Frederick George Beresford Lumley, 10th Earl of, b. 1857,
s. 1884, d. 1948; ed. Eton; lieut. 7th Hussars; col. Yorks Dragoons; hon. col. Yorks
Dragoons; col. A.S.C. (T.D.); S. Africa, 1900; A.D.C. to Edward VII, 1902; direc-
tor-gen. terr. and vol. forces, 1917-1921; lord lt. Yorks (W.R.), 1892-1904; 21,698
acres in Lincoln, Yorks (W.R.), Durham
*Selborne, Sir William Waldegrave Palmer, 2nd Earl of, b. 1859, s. 1895, d. 1942; ed.
Winchester and Univ. College, Oxford; asst. priv. sec. to chancellor of Exchequer,
1882-1885; M.P. for East Hants, 1885-1892, for West Edinburgh, 1892-1895;
under-sec. for Colonies, 1885-1900; first lord of Admiralty, 1900-1905; P.C., 1900;
gov. of Transvaal and Orange River Colonies, and high comr. of S. Africa, 1905-
1910; pres., Board of Agriculture, 1915-1916
Sempill, Sir John Forbes-Sempill, 18th Baron, b. 1863, s. 1905, d. 1934; ed. Eton;

entered militia, 1883; served in various army regiments until 1904 (retired as capt. Black Watch); S. Africa with Lovat's Scouts, 1901-1902; Great War as comdr. 8th batt. Black Watch; severely wounded, 1915; J.P. and D.L. Aberdeen; chm., Aberdeen T.F.A.; rep. peer (Scotland), 1910-1934; 9,347 acres in Aberdeen

Shrewsbury, Sir Charles Henry John Chetwynd-Talbot, 20th Earl of, b. 1860, s. 1877, d. 1921; ed. Eton; premier earl of England; hereditary high steward of Ireland; 35,729 acres in Staffs, Chester, Worcester, Salop, Derby, Glamorgan, Northants, Berks, Oxford

Sinclair, Charles William St. Clair, 15th Baron, b. 1831, s. 1880, d. 1922; ed. Sandhurst; Crimea, Indian Mutiny, and New Zealand war, 1861-1862; col. 57th regt.; J.P. and D.L. Berwick; rep. peer (Scotland), 1885-1922; 4,346 acres in Roxburgh, Berwick, Haddington

*Somerset, Sir Algernon St. Maur, 15th Duke of, b. 1846, s. 1894, d. 1923; ed., [R.N. training ship] *Britannia;* ranched for some time in Western America; lieut. 60th Rifles; col. 1st Wilts Rifle Vol.; J.P. Leicester and Wilts; pres., Navy League and Dr. Barnardo's Homes; 25,387 acres in Devon, Somerset, Wilts, Lincoln, Bucks, Cambridge, Norfolk, Dorset

*Sondes, Lewis Arthur Milles, 3rd Earl, b. 1866, s. 1907, d. 1941; capt. 16th Lancers; lt. col. comm. 3rd batt. Yorks L.I.; S. Africa, 1900-1901; 19,096 acres in Kent and Norfolk

Southampton, Charles Henry Fitzroy, 4th Baron, b. 1867, s. 1872, d. 1958; ed. Eton and Sandhurst; capt. 10th Hussars; maj. 4th batt. Yorks regt., Great War; D.L. Warwick; J.P. Yorks; 6,861 acres in Northants and Bucks

*Stanhope, James Richard Stanhope, 7th Earl, b. 1880, s. 1905, d. 1967; ed. Eton and Magdalen College, Oxford; capt. Gren. Guards; S. Africa, 1902; Great War as capt. Gren. Guards, then as maj. and lt. col.; L.C.C. (Lewisham), 1910-1913; parl. sec. War Office, 1918-1919; chm., Joint Substitution Board, 1923-1924; civil lord of the Admiralty, 1924-1929; P.C., 1929; trustee, National Portrait Gallery, 1930; parl. and fin. sec. to Admiralty, 1931; under-sec. of state for War and vice-pres. of Army Council, 1931-1934; under-sec. of state for Foreign Affairs, 1934-1936; member of council of Duchy of Lancs, 1935-1937; first comr. of Works, with seat in Cabinet, 1936-1937; pres., Board of Education, 1937-1938; first lord of the Admiralty, 1938-1939; leader of House of Lords, 1938-1940; lord pres. of the council, 1939-1940; chm., Standing Com. on Museum and Galleries, 1941-1948; 14,241 acres in Kent, Devon, Derby

*Stanmore, Sir Arthur Hamilton-Gordon, 1st Baron, b. 1829, s. 1893, d. 1912; ed. Trinity College, Cambridge; asst. priv. sec. to his father, the 4th Earl of Aberdeen, when Prime Minister, 1852-1855; M.P. (Liberal) for Beverly, 1854-1857; lt. col. 2nd batt. Aberdeen R.V.; J.P. and D.L. Aberdeen and Berks; gov. of New Brunswick, 1861-1866, Trinidad, 1866-1870, Mauritius, 1871-1874; first gov. of Fiji, 1875-1880; first high comr. for the Western Pacific, 1877-1880; gov. of New Zealand, 1880-1882, Ceylon, 1883-1890; chm., Bank of Mauritius; pres., Ceylon Assoc. in London; author of several books; created baron 1893; 3,021 acres in Banff

Strathmore and Kinghorne, Claude George Bowes-Lyon, 14th Earl of, b. 1855, s. 1904, d. 1944; ed. Eton; lieut. 2nd Life Guards; pres., Angus T.F.A.; J.P. and C.C. Herts; D.L. Dundee; lord lt. Angus; 24,686 acres in Angus, Perth, Sussex, Herts

Templetown, Henry Edward Montague Dorington Clotworthy Upton, 4th Viscount, b. 1853, s. 1890, d. 1939; ed. Wimbledon School and Sandhurst; lieut. 60th Rifles; J.P. and D.L. Antrim; rep. peer (Ireland) from 1894; chm., Ulster Loyalist Anti-Repeal Union; organized Unionist Clubs Council, 1893; authority on dairy farming; 24,769 acres in Antrim and Monaghan

Tollemache, Bentley Lyonel John Tollemache, 3rd Baron, b. 1883, s. 1904, d. 1955; ed. Eton; capt. 3rd batt. Cheshire regt.; S. Africa, 1902, and Great War; J.P. and D.L. Cheshire; 35,726 acres in Cheshire, Suffolk, Denbigh, Flint

Vaux of Harrowden, Hubert George Charles Mostyn, 7th Baron, b. 1860, s. 1883, d. 1935; ed. St. Mary's College and Trinity College, Cambridge; J.P. and D.L. Northants; diplomatic service, 1883-1899; Roman Catholic; bought back Great Harrowden Hall, Northants, 1895; 4,323 acres in Westmeath, Kilkenny, Meath

Vivian, Sir George Erespigny Brabazon Vivian, 4th Baron, b. 1878, s. 1893, d. 1940; ed. Eton; lieut. 17th Lancers; S. Africa, 1901; maj. Res. of Officers; Great War, chief of staff to mission to Belgian Army, 1917; chm., Cornwall T.F.A. from 1931; 8,269 acres in Cornwall, Anglesey, Flint, Denbigh

Waldegrave, Sir William Frederick Waldegrave, 9th Earl, b. 1851, s. 1859, d. 1930; ed. Eton and Trinity College, Cambridge; lt. col. 9th vol. batt. King's Royal Rifle Corps; hon. col. Somerset vol. regt.; lord-in-waiting, 1886-1892, 1895-1896; chief Conservative whip in House of Lords, 1896-1911; capt. of Yeomen of the Guard, 1896-1905; P.C., 1897; lunacy comr., 1899; vice-pres., National Rifle Assoc.; J.P. Somerset, Westminster, Middlesex; C.A. Somerset; 15,425 acres in Sussex, Somerset, Essex, Yorks (E.R.), Middlesex, Louth, Carlow

Westminster, Sir Hugh Richard Arthur Grosvenor, 2nd Duke of, b. 1879, s. 1899, d. 1953; ed. Eton; A.D.C. to gov. Milner, Cape of Good Hope, 1899; A.D.C. to Lord Roberts, 1900-1901; 2nd lieut. Royal Horse Guards, 1900-1901; Great War; lord lt. Cheshire, 1907-1920, pres., Cheshire T.F.A.; 32,655 acres in Cheshire, Flint, Denbigh, Bucks, Dorset, Wilts; large London estate

Wicklow, Ralph Francis Howard, 7th Earl of, b. 1877, s. 1891, d. 1946; ed. Eton and Sandhurst; 2nd Life Guards in S. Africa; lt. col. South Irish Horse, 1909-1922; Great War; J.P. and D.L. Wicklow; rep. peer (Ireland), 1905-1946; senator, Southern Ireland, 1921-1928; 28,713 acres in Wicklow, Donegal, Westmeath

*Willoughby de Broke, Richard Greville Verney, 19th Baron, b. 1869, s. 1902, d. 1923; ed. Eton and New College, Oxford; maj. Warwick yeo. cav.; Great War; M.P. for Rugby Div. of Warwick, 1895-1900; J.P. and D.L. Warwick; pres., Imperial Maritime League; chm., British League for the Support of Ulster and the Union; 18,145 acres in Warwick, Lincoln, Northants, Somerset, Staffs, Anglesey, Leicester

Winchester, Henry William Montagu Paulet, 16th Marquess of, b. 1862, s. 1899, d. 1962; capt. Hants imp. yeo.; pres., Hants T.F.A., 1907-1917; Great War, maj. 13th batt., the Rifle Brig.; premier marquess of England; lord lt. of Hants, 1904-1917; chm., Hants C.C., 1905-1909; 4,797 acres in Hants

Wynford, Philip George Best, 6th Baron, b. 1871, s. 1904, d. 1940; ed. Wellington and Woolwich; capt. R.H.A.; maj. Dorset yeo.; lt. col. R.A., Great War; J.P. Dorset; 3,460 acres in Dorset, Essex, Kent

Notes

Abbreviations

CCC	Christ Church College Library, Oxford
CRO	County Record Office
Hansard	*Parliamentary Debates*
HH	Hatfield House
H.L.R.O.	House of Lords Record Office
L.J.	*Journals of the House of Lords*
P.P.	*Parliamentary Papers*
PRO	Public Record Office
RO	Record Office

Chapter 1: The Diehards and the Myth of the "Backwoodsmen"

1. The widespread nature of the "backwoodsman" image can be illustrated by a sampling of comments by both contemporaries and later historians. In the first full-length study of the constitutional crisis, Harry Jones, a Liberal, wrote: "In November, 1909, the 'backwoodsmen' came to town in large numbers, some of them redolent of the countryside, bucolic in aspect, many of them wearing the early Victorian stock, and in their antique dress and old-fashioned manners recalling a bygone generation" (*Liberalism and the House of Lords* [London, 1912], pp. 151-152). The Earl Winterton, an active young Unionist M.P. at the time of the Parliament Bill, wrote in his memoirs of the "famous mass attack of the backwoodsmen," many of whom "had never even been in the Chamber, except to take the oath" (*Pre-War* [London, 1932], p. 177). The Viscountess Barrington, wife of the diehard Viscount Barrington, referred to the younger peers who voted against the Parliament Bill as "diehards" who "had not set foot in the House until that time" (Charlotte, Viscountess Barrington, *Through Eighty Years* [London, 1936], p. 171). These comments have been accepted by modern historians such as George Dangerfield, who wrote of the diehards as a "horde of hereditary nobodies," who "lived an obscure and doubtless a useful existence on their country estates" but were "old-fashioned and useless" in the national scheme of things (*The Strange Death of Liberal England* [New York, 1935], pp. 22, 42, 43). Finally, Roy Jenkins, the author of the most thorough study of the constitutional crisis of 1909-1911, again identifies the majority of the diehards with the familiar and faintly ridiculous figures of the "backwoodsmen," who were "inexperienced and unsagacious" and who seldom attended the House of Lords (*Mr. Balfour's Poodle* [London, 1954], p. 171).

2. *Parliamentary Debates,* House of Lords, 5th ser. (1909-   ), vol. 8, col. 408 (15 May 1911). Cited hereafter as 5 *Hansard* (Lords) 8: 408 (15 May 1911).

3. *Sessional Papers* (Lords), 1910, no. 13: "Temporal Peers," p. 3.

4. Statistics for the diehards were obtained from the daily attendance lists included in the *Journals of the House of Lords* (hereafter cited as *L.J.*) for 1902 and 1906. The diehard figures for 1909 were compiled from a detailed attendance list pre-

pared for the Earl of Onslow (Guildford Muniment Room, memorandum marked
"Confidential," 27 April 1910, Onslow Archive, 173/19/33). Statistics for the whole
House of Lords were taken from *Sessional Papers* (Lords), 1910, n.13: "Temporal
Peers," p.3. The eligibility of peers to sit in the House of Lords was determined by
reference to *Burke's Peerage and Baronetage* (London, 1911). Figures for both the
diehards and the whole House exclude those who had no title, had not yet succeeded to
a title, or had not been elected to a representative peerage they would hold in 1911.

5. Jenkins, *Balfour's Poodle,* p. 171.

6. Lord Dynevor, *My Reminiscences* (Carmarthen, 1937), p. 47.

7. Statistics obtained from the lists of the membership of individual committees
in *L.J.* for 1902, 1904, 1906, and 1908.

8. P. A. Bromhead, *The House of Lords and Contemporary Politics, 1911-1957*
(London, 1958), pp. 34-35.

9. Raw data obtained from indexes to 5 *Hansard* (Lords) for the years 1911-1913.

10. Ibid., 8: 562 (17 May 1911).

11. *Times,* 11 June 1929.

12. Northcote Papers, 30/56/1; Joseph Chamberlain Papers; H. S. Northcote to
Selborne, 10 January 1902, Selborne Papers, 197/62.

13. J. G. Lockhart, *Charles Lindley Viscount Halifax,* Part One, *1839-1885* (London, 1935), p. 173; Norfolk to Salisbury, 1889, Salisbury Papers, CCC, Class E.

14. See the 12th Earl of Meath, *Memories of the Nineteenth Century* (London,
1923), *Memories of the Twentieth Century* (London, 1924), and *The Diaries of Mary,
Countess of Meath* (2 vols., London, 1928-1929), and Sir Francis Lindley, *Lord Lovat*
(London, 1935), pp. 82, 126.

15. Atkinson, Bristol, Clanricarde, Clarendon, Crawford and Balcarres, Digby,
Dynevor, Ebury, Erne, Fitzwilliam, Forester, Halsbury, Harlech, Leeds, Llandaff,
Northcote, Northumberland, Portsmouth, Radnor, Salisbury, Selborne, Stanmore,
and Willoughby de Broke.

16. Clonbrock, Colchester, Dynevor, Malmesbury, Radnor, Ampthill and Leeds.

17. Dynevor, *Reminiscences,* p. 23.

18. Clarendon, Coventry, Denbigh, Erroll, Churchill, Ranfurly, Norfolk, Bagot
and Leeds held court offices.

19. Ashtown, Farnham, Kilmaine, Massy, Muskerry, Templetown, and Wicklow.

20. Clanricarde, Clonbrock, Erne, DeFreyne, Farnham, Gormanston, Holmpatrick, Kilmaine, Leitrim, Limerick, Massy, Muskerry, Ranfurly, Templetown,
Vaux of Harrowden, and Wicklow held nearly all their land in Ireland, as did a total
of sixty peers eligible to sit in the Lords in 1911 (John Bateman, *The Great Landowners of Great Britain and Ireland* [4th ed., London, 1883]).

21. *Times,* 11 September 1913; 4 *Hansard* (Commons) 101: 708-709 (23 January
1902).

22. L. P. Curtis, Jr., *Coercion and Conciliation in Ireland* (Princeton, 1963), pp.
134, 255-258.

23. For Erne, Ranfurly and Templetown, see John F. Harbinson, *The Ulster
Unionist Party, 1882-1973* (Belfast, 1973), pp. 19, 24; Patrick Buckland, *Irish Unionism;* II, *Ulster Unionism and the Origins of Northern Ireland, 1886-1922* (Dublin,
1973), pp. 9, 16. For Ashtown, see *Times,* 25 March 1946; 4 *Hansard* (Commons) 180:
1616 (15 August 1907), and 181: 478 (20 August 1907). For Clonbrock: *Estates Gazette,* 3 October 1908; for Meath: Earl of Dunraven, *Past Times and Pastimes,* II
(London, 1922), p. 9. For Ranfurly and Fingall: 5th Earl of Ranfurly to 3rd Marquess
of Salisbury, 30 January 1893, Salisbury Papers, CCC, Class E, and Elizabeth, Coun-

tess of Fingall, *Seventy Years Young, Memories* (London, 1937), p. 150. For Atkinson: *Times,* 14 March 1932; for Farnham and Leitrim: A. T. Q. Stewart, *The Ulster Crisis* (London, 1967), pp. 93, 103.

24. National Union of Conservative and Constitutional Associations, *Annual Conference Program,* 1911.

25. Julian Amery, *The Life of Joseph Chamberlain,* VI: *Joseph Chamberlain and the Tariff Reform Campaign, 1903-1968* (London, 1969), pp. 579-590; Liberal Unionist Association, *Memoranda,* n.s., vol. 6, no. 3 (March 1909), p. 98.

26. Even non-attendance did not necessarily imply lack of knowledge concerning serious problems (although the diehard attendance record compared favorably with that of the House of Lords as a whole). For instance, Lord Rayleigh seldom appeared in the Upper Chamber — he was a distinguished scientist and a Nobel Laureate for the discovery of argon (4th Baron Rayleigh, *Life of John William Strutt Third Baron Rayleigh* [London, 1924]). Lord Bathurst came to Westminster somewhat more often, but could hardly be considered a prominent politician. However, his wife owned the *Morning Post,* the most important right-wing newspaper of the day, and both Lord and Lady Bathurst were in constant contact with its editor and with the latest political maneuvers and events (see uncatalogued papers of the 7th Earl and Countess Bathurst, Cirencester). The 2nd Duke of Westminster also voted against the Parliament Bill. By the criterion of attendance in the Lords, he should be described as a "backwoodsman," for he attended a total of only five times in the sessions of 1902, 1904, 1906, and 1908. In most discussions he would be included among the supposed group of impoverished country noblemen isolated from national political affairs before the constitutional crisis. In reality Westminster was one of Britain's wealthiest men. His enormous financial interests involved him in national affairs and with prominent people whether or not he wished to take his seat in Parliament. See Michael Harrison, *Lord of London* (London, 1966), and Gervas Huxley, *Victorian Duke, The Life of Hugh Lupus Grosvenor First Duke of Westminster* (London, 1967).

Chapter 2: The "Lordliest Life on Earth"

1. Adam Badeau, *Aristocracy in England* (London, 1886), pp. 147-148; Hilaire Belloc, *Mr. Clutterbuck's Election* (London, 1908), p. 73; John Galsworthy, *The Island Pharisees* (New York and London, 1908), p. 65; Henry James, "The Velvet Glove," in *The Finer Grain* (London, 1910), pp. 3, 6; Viscount Churchill, *All My Sins Remembered* (London, 1964), p. 15; Earl of Warwick and Brooke, *Memories of Sixty Years* (London, 1917), p. vi; Robert Gathorne-Hardy, ed., *Memoirs of Lady Ottoline Morrell: A Study in Friendship, 1873-1915* (New York, 1964), p. 39; Lord Willoughby de Broke, ed., *The Sport of Our Ancestors* (London, 1921), pp. 18, 19.

2. Lord Willoughby de Broke, *The Passing Years* (London, 1924), pp. 1-2.

3. Lord David Cecil, *Melbourne* (London, 1965), pp. 1-14.

4. Frances, Countess of Warwick, *Discretions* (New York, 1931), p. 41; Earl of Rosslyn, *My Gamble With Life* (London, 1928), p. 175.

5. Eustace Percy, *Some Memories* (London, 1958), pp. 10-11; L. E. Jones, *Victorian Boyhood* (London, 1965), pp. 36, 37, 40.

6. C. R. L. Fletcher, *Edmond Warre* (London, 1922), p. 172.

7. Selborne to Wolmer, 2 October 1870 (Selborne Papers, 96/19), and 15 February 1880 (Papers of Roundell Palmer, 1st Earl of Selborne, MS. 1879-f. 133).

8. *Debrett's Peerage, Baronetage, Knightage and Companionage* (London, 1912), p. xl; Winefride Elwes, *The Feilding Album* (London, 1950), p. 131; E. C. F.

Collier, ed., *A Victorian Diarist: Extracts from the Journals of Mary, Lady Monkswell, 1873-1895* (London, 1944), p. 155.

9. Stanhope to his mother, 24 June 1905, Stanhope Papers, U1590, 1217, Kent R.O.

10. Shrewsbury and Talbot to Lady Castlereagh, 2 January 1905, Londonderry Papers, D/Lo/C670 (43).

11. Meath, *Diaries,* II, 94-96.

12. Rosslyn, *Gamble,* p. 22.

13. Willoughby de Broke to A. Bontwood, 1 November 1914, Willoughby de Broke Papers, H.L.R.O., Hist. Coll. 142, WB 11/3.

14. *Rugby and Kineton Advertiser,* 11 July 1914.

15. F. M. L. Thompson, *English Landed Society in the Nineteenth Century* (London, 1963), pp. 76-78. See also, for example, Meath, *Twentieth Century,* pp. 133, 154; Rosslyn, *Gamble,* p. 40; Lindley, *Lovat,* p. 50; Dynevor, *Reminiscences,* p. 15; 4th Baron Rayleigh, *Life of John William Strutt Third Baron Rayleigh* (London, 1924), pp. 148-149; Helen, Countess-Dowager of Radnor, *From a Great-Grandmother's Armchair* (London, 1928), p. 142; Aubrey Newman, *The Stanhopes of Chevening, A Family Biography* (London, 1969), p. 334.

16. Willoughby de Broke, *Passing Years,* p. 100; Sir Max Beerbohm, "London Revisited," in *Mainly on the Air* (New York, 1947), pp. 5-6.

17. Consuelo Vanderbilt Balsan, *The Glitter and the Gold* (London, 1952), p. 133.

18. Arthur Ponsonby, *The Decline of Aristocracy* (London, 1912), pp. 16-17; Sir W. S. Gilbert, *The Savoy Operas* (London, 1926), p. 108.

19. George W. E. Russell, *Seeing and Hearing* (London, 1907), p. 355; Lady Dorothy Nevill, *Under Five Reigns,* ed. Ralph Nevill (London, 1910), p. 140.

20. Ralph Pumphrey, "The Introduction of Industrialists into the British Peerage: A Study in Adaptation of a Social Institution," *American Historical Review,* 65 (1959), 8, 11.

21. Ralph Nevill, ed., *The Reminiscences of Lady Dorothy Nevill* (London, 1906), pp. 104-105; Meath, *Nineteenth Century,* pp. 88-89.

22. Selborne to Lady Selborne, 18, 15, and 24 August 1910, Selborne Papers, 101/192, 199.

23. Russell, *Seeing,* p. 324.

24. See Charlotte, Viscountess Barrington, *Through Eighty Years* (London, 1936), pp. 194-195, and Mary, Countess of Lovelace, *Ralph Earl of Lovelace, A Memoir* (London, 1920), pp. 24-28.

25. John Galsworthy, *The Country House* (New York, 1914), p. 138.

26. For a superb record of county society in the early twentieth century, see three visiting books belonging to Miss Violet Peek (second daughter of Sir Cuthbert Peek, Bart.), of Rousdon, Devon, 1904-1913, Peek of Rousdon Papers, 1405M/ff. 1-3, Devon R.O.

27. Beatrice Webb, *My Apprenticeship* (London, 1926), pp. 48-49.

28. F. H. Cripps was perhaps an extreme example of the hunting undergraduate while at Oxford: "My life at Oxford consisted of hunting most Mondays with the Rothschild stag Hounds; the drag hounds on Tuesday; always a special train on Wednesday to hunt from Chipping Norton with the Heythrop; Thursday, a special to the Warwickshire in the Shuckburgh Vale country; Friday, the drag hounds; Saturday, some shooting — and a well earned rest on the Sabbath" (F. H. Cripps, *Life's a Gamble* [London, 1957], p. 38). Henry Chaplin offered to resign his mastership of the hounds

in the 1870s if someone could be found to hunt six days per week (The Marchioness of Londonderry, *Henry Chaplin: A Memoir* [London, 1926], p. 218).

29. Churchill, *Sins Remembered,* p. 19.

30. Willoughby de Broke to L. J. Maxse, 5 November 1913, L. J. Maxse Papers, 466-P206.

31. G. F. Underhill, et al., *The Master of Hounds* (London, 1903), p. 142. Die-hards who were masters of one or more packs of fox-hounds included Lords Fitzwilliam, Leconfield, Willoughby de Broke, Bathurst, Coventry, Southampton, Fingall, Wicklow, and the Duke of Westminster. George Wyndham wrote to his father in 1902 describing Westminster's Eaton Hall seat: "The whole place has been turned into a glorified embodiment of a boy's holidays . . . He enjoys it all from morning to night and gives unbounded satisfaction to a horse-loving community" (J. W. Mackail and Guy Wyndham, *Life and Letters of George Wyndham,* II [London, n.d.], pp. 440-41). See also William Scarth Dixon, *Fox-Hunting in the Twentieth Century* (London, 1925), pp. 129, 161-162, 164, 201, 243; George Cornwallis-West, *Edwardian Hey-Days* (London and New York, 1930), p. 88; *Times,* 9 December 1958, 13 November 1920; clipping from supplement to *Country Sport,* 30 October 1897, "Hounds and their Masters—Season 1897-8," from leather-bound volume of unbound letters, vol. IX, "M. F. H.," Bathurst Papers, Cirencester Park.

32. Willoughby de Broke, *Fox,* p. 8.

33. Draft, Bathurst to Wemyss, 2 and 8 March, 1897, vol. IX, "M. F. H.," Bathurst Papers, Cirencester.

34. Wilfred Scawen Blunt, *My Diaries,* II (London, 1920), 361.

35. Willoughby de Broke, *Sport,* p. 44.

Chapter 3: Land and Wealth

1. "The Needs of Rural England," *Quarterly Review,* 197 (1903), 544.

2. Anthony Trollope, *The Duke's Children* (New York, 1909), p. 202.

3. Rosslyn, *Gamble,* pp. 82, 111, 113, 115, 118, 147, 157, 159, 235, 271.

4. W. Bence Jones, "Landowning as a Business," *Nineteenth Century,* 11 (1882), 254.

5. Christabel S. Orwin and Edith H. Whetham, *History of British Agriculture, 1846-1914* (London, 1964), p. 242; T. W. Fletcher, "The Great Depression of English Agriculture," *Economic History Review,* 2nd ser., 13 (1960-1961), 423.

6. Orwin and Whetham, *Agriculture,* p. 267; P. J. Perry, ed., *British Agriculture, 1875-1914* (London, 1973), p. xxv; Thompson, *Landed Society,* p. 310.

7. 1897 *P.P.* 15 (*Reports,* vol. 1, C8540), Final report of the Royal Commission on Agriculture, pp. 23-24; Thompson, *Landed Society,* p. 310; H. A. Rhee, *The Rent of Agricultural Land in England and Wales* (London 1949), p. 37.

8. 1895 *P.P.* 16 (*Reports,* vol. 3, C7671), "Report on the County of Lincolnshire," pp. 53, 55; Rider Haggard, *Rural England* (London, 1906), I, 364; 1895 *P.P.* 17 (*Reports,* vol. 4, C7764), "Report on the County of Dorset," pp. 14, 12; Thompson, *Landed Society,* p. 312; comparison of 1880 and 1911 rental of Derbyshire estate, November 1911, Stanhope Papers, U1590, no. 1016; Rental 6 and Rental 1887-1912, Allerton Park Papers; West Sussex Record Office, letter book, p. 489; uncatalogued papers of the 3rd Lord Leconfield, 2885.

9. Fletcher, "Depression," p. 429.

10. Sir William Gavin, *Ninety Years of Family Farming* (London, 1967), pp. 83, 86, 98; Rayleigh, *Third Baron Rayleigh,* p. 186; Blanche E. C. Dugdale, *Family*

Homespun (London: John Murray, [1940], 162. Rayleigh, the discoverer of argon, was very much the landed aristocrat: "his roots were planted in the land as firmly as those of any other English squire. The country was his home, not, as so often with learned men, his holiday resort."

11. Anthony Trollope, *The Way We Live Now* (New York, 1950), p. 44.

12. 1893 *P.P.* 41 (*Reports,* vol. 26, C6980), "Final Report of the Royal Commission on Mining Royalties," p. 4; J. T. Ward, "West Riding Landowners and Mining in the Nineteenth Century," *Yorkshire Bulletin of Economic and Social Research,* 15 (1963), 62.

13. J. T. Ward, "Landowners and Mining," in J. T. Ward and R. G. Wilson, eds., *Land and Industry* (London, 1971), pp. 68, 108; 1919 *P.P.* 12 (*Reports,* vol. 5, Cmd. 360), p. 655.

14. 1919 *P.P.* 12 (*Reports,* vol. 5, Cmd. 360), "Reports and Minutes of Evidence on the Second Stage of the Inquiry," pp. 625-626, 630.

15. Stewards Papers, Wentworth Woodhouse Muniments, Stw 31, A 1616.

16. Childe & Rowand, civil and mining engineers, to Bromet & Sons, solicitors, 1880-1910, Allerton Park Papers.

17. Ward, "West Riding Landowners," p.69; Scarbrough to Salisbury, 14 December 1889, Salisbury Papers CCC, Class E; *Times,* 5 March 1945; interview with the 12th Earl of Scarbrough, 10 October 1974.

18. Ward, "Landowners and Mining," pp. 96-97; *Times,* 1 February 1913.

19. *Times,* 31 May 1928; Ward, "Landowners and Mining," p. 75; *Estates Gazette,* 13 July 1912; Bathurst Papers, Gloucester CRO, D2525/47.

20. Frank Banfield, *The Great Landlords of London* (London, 1888), frontispiece map; Huxley, *Victorian Duke,* p. 134.

21. Bedford Estates annual reports, 1889 and 1898; F. H. W. Sheppard, ed., *Survey of London,* XXXVI, *The Parish of St. Paul Covent Garden* (London, 1970), pp. 48, 50-51; *Estates Gazette,* 3 January 1914.

22. *Estates Gazette,* 3 January 1903.

23. Ibid., 3 January 1920, and 1 January 1921.

24. *Complete Peerage,* XII, pt. 2, p. 544.

25. David Spring, "The English Landed Estate in the Age of Coal and Iron: 1830-1880," *Journal of Economic History,* 11 (1951), 9; Spring, "Landowners and Industrialism," in Ward and Wilson, *Land and Industry,* pp. 42, 43.

26. 1886 *P.P.* 56 (A.P., vol. 19, C221), "Return of Market Rights and Tolls," p. 34; Arundel Castle MSS., S 362, S 363.

27. T. H. S. Escott, *England: Its People, Polity, and Pursuits* (London, 1881), p. 29; *Estates Gazette,* 3 January 1920.

28. 4 *Hansard* (Lords) 186: 1392-1393 (25 March 1908).

29. Spring, "Landowners and Industrialism," pp. 43-44.

30. 1886 *P.P.* 56 (*A.P.,* vol. 19, No. 221), "Return of Market Rights," p. 34.

31. 1884-85 *P.P.* 31 (*Reports,* vol. 18, C4547), "Third Report of Her Majesty's Commissioners for Inquiring into the Housing of the Working Classes: Ireland," pp. 10, 29.

32. *Estates Gazette,* 4 January 1908.

33. Data collected from *Burke's Peerage.*

34. James Laver, *Edwardian Promenade* (Boston, 1958), p. 26; and see also Balsan, *Glitter.*

35. *Burke's Peerage; Complete Peerage;* Collier, *Victorian Diarist,* p. 167.

36. Wharncliffe to F. W. F. Hervey, 14 October 1896, Hervey Papers, 941/71/4.

37. Meath, *Diaries,* I, 89.

38. Fingall, *Seventy Years Young,* pp. 81, 95.

39. Escott, *England,* pp. 280-281; W. H. Mallock, *The Old Order Changes* (London, 1887), pp. 140-141; Hilaire Belloc, *Emmanuel Burden* (London, 1904); Elie Halévy, *A History of the English People in the Nineteenth Century,* V, *Imperialism and the Rise of Labour* (New York, 1961), p. 295; Thompson, *Landed Society,* p. 307; Spring, "Landowners and Industrialism," pp. 52-53. Historians have generally assumed that, with the decline of agricultural rents, increasing numbers of landowners invested in ever larger quantities of shares with important social consequences. "A new spirit was coming over the landed gentry. . . . Landlords no longer lived in the country to make their money, they visited the country to spend it." Two more recent authorities, F. M. L. Thompson and David Spring, believe that much more work is needed on the subject.

40. Evelyn Waugh, *Noblesse Oblige,* p. 71.

41. Thompson, *Landed Society,* pp. 306, 307.

42. *Complete Peerage,* V, app. C, pp. 836-839; *Directory of Directors,* 1911.

43. Ibid. Thirteen diehards were directors of railways and of insurance or assurance companies. Fifteen were involved in ventures overseas.

44. Churchill, *Sins Remembered,* p. 47.

45. Shrewsbury and Talbot to Lady Castlereagh, n.d. [1903?], Londonderry Papers, D/Lo/C679 (33).

46. Laver, *Promenade,* pp. 168-169; *Times,* 3 October 1939.

47. *Morning Post,* 6 January 1910.

48. *Times,* 28 August 1914.

49. A. M. W. Stirling, *Fyvie Castle, Its Lairds and Their Times* (London, 1928), pp. 384-385, 389-390, 392, 398.

50. Blanche E. C. Dugdale, *Family Homespun* (London, 1940), pp. 161-162.

51. Fingall, *Seventy Years Young,* pp. 222-223.

52. Conclusions concerning investments are necessarily tentative, given the limited number of surviving estate papers and the political nature of public statements by the diehards on this subject. Wills and inventories of estates, for both the diehards and their predecessors, available in Scotland and Ireland, are sometimes useful but contain nothing about the important question of the dates when investments were made. The date is especially significant when, as is usually the case where wills of the diehards are concerned, the document dates from after World War I. Wills and inventories also omit information about investments which were transferred to the younger generation before the death of the head of the family.

53. Michelmore to Somerset, 14 September 1914, Michelmore, Loveys & Carter, Totnes Papers, Berry Pomeroy Estate Letter Books, 867B/ES 23/23, p. 358.

54. "Investments to 1892," 23 February 1892, Wentworth Woodhouse Muniments, T84; "Statement for the information of the Hon. W. H. W. Fitzwilliam as Executor," November 1907, ibid., T89.

55. Bedford Estates annual reports, 1898, 1899; abstract, 1903; Bedford Estates abstract, 1911, p. 8; sub-agent Henry Whitcomb to Leconfield, 5 April 1909, letter book 1900-1910, p. 484; uncatalogued papers of the 3rd Lord Leconfield, Petworth House Archives, 2885; Salisbury Papers CCC, Class L.

56. W. Forrest to Nicholl, Manisty & Company, 28 May 1913, Letter book 1913, p. 354, Plymouth Estate Papers, D/D Pl 291.

57. Handwritten summary of Dynevor sale, 1911 (no date, probably 1912), Dynevor Muniments, box 137-1; list of stock, April 1909, Sondes Addn. Papers, E 43/3;

Bathurst to R. Anderson, 8 November 1883, Bathurst Papers, D2525/54, Gloucester CRO; Rosslyn, *Gamble,* pp. 61, 103.

58. *Western Times,* Exeter, 24 December 1909, quoting Lord Portsmouth.

59. 1912-13 *P.P.* 47 (*Reports,* vol. 38, Cd.6031), "Departmental Committee on Tenant Farmers and Sales of Estates, Minutes, 1912-13," p. 73.

60. Vouchers for investment by trustees, Kilmaine Papers, 9; list of investments, December 1907; estimate by Lord Kilmaine of probable income for future, 22 January 1908; inventory of the estate of the 4th Lord Clonbrock, 1917, Irish RO; "The Marquis of Clanricarde deceased. Accounts for 2-1/2 years to 12th October 1918, and report thereon," Harewood Accounts, 120 (307).

61. Inventory of the estate of the 10th Earl of Northesk, 1921, Scottish RO: inventory of the Aberdeen Sheriff Court of the 18th Lord Saltoun, 1933.

62. Fingall, *Seventy Years Young,* p. 189.

63. Inventory of the personal estate of the 11th Earl of Fingall, 1929, Irish RO.

64. Charles Milnes Gaskell, "The Country Gentleman," *Nineteenth Century,* 12 (1882), 461; Haggard, *Rural England,* II, 522; 5 *Hansard* (Lords) 11: 347-348 (7 March 1912).

65. Bedford, *Great Agricultural Estate,* pp. 1-2, 6, 10-11, 48-56, 68-69, 75. Bedford's statistics have proven to be substantially accurate when compared to similar statistics for rental and expenditure in the annual reports at the Bedford Estates Office, London, and with the Thorney Estate Rentals included in Russell Papers, Acc. 3029, R5/4139/4158/4173, Bedfordshire CRO.

66. George W. E. Russell, "Land and Lodging Houses (A colloquy with the Duke of Bedford)," *Nineteenth Century,* 42 (1897), 384.

67. R. C. K. Ensor, *England 1870-1914* (London, 1936), pp. 217, 218n; 1912-13 *P.P.* 47 (*Reports,* vol. 38, Cd.6031), "Departmental Committee on Tenant Farmers and Sales of Estates, Minutes, 1912-13," p. 37.

68. Percy to Salisbury, 8 August 1894, Salisbury Papers CCC, Class E.

69. See opinion of solicitor, Mr. C. T. Simpson, as to how Finance Act of 1894, regarding estate duty, would affect Fitzwilliam settlements, 1894, Wentworth Woodhouse Muniments, T86; Messrs. Warrens to Dynevor, 18 December 1904, Dynevor Muniments, box 137-7; Henry Nicholl to Bristol, 23 July 1908, Hervey Papers 941/71/11; Josiah Wedgwood, *The Economics of Inheritance* (London, 1929), p. 21; inventory of the 18th Lord Saltoun, 1933, Aberdeen Sheriff Court.

70. "Statement," November 1907, Wentworth Woodhouse Muniments, T89; draft letter, 3 October 1920, Dynevor to Mineral Owners Association, Dynevor Muniments, box 137-50.

71. A. R. Farrer to Sondes, 7 June 1909, Sondes Addn. Papers E43/4; Stanhope to his mother, 28 and 30 May 1907, Stanhope Papers U1590, 1217.

72. See F. M. L. Thompson, "The Land Market in the Nineteenth Century," in *Essays in Agrarian History,* ed. W. E. Minchinton (Newton Abbot, Devon, 1968), II; Thompson, *Landed Society,* pp. 318-319.

73. 1912-13 *P.P.* 47 (*Reports,* vol. 38, Cd.6030), "Departmental Committee on Tenant Farmers and Sales of Estates," p. 5.

74. Statistics from *Estates Gazette,* 1911-1913.

75. Statistics from Bateman's *Great Landowners.*

76. *Complete Peerage,* XII, pt. 1, p. 138, n.b. See various articles in *Stratford-upon-Avon Herald* for the period.

77. *Complete Peerage,* III, 209; Churchill, *Sins Remembered,* p. 45.

78. For Londesborough, see *Estates Gazette,* 11 February and 30 December 1905,

1 January 1910, 17 June and 30 December 1911, and other reports; for Portsmouth, ibid., 1902-1915, passim; for Willoughby de Broke, ibid., 29 December 1906; for Westminster, ibid., 19 November and 10 December 1910; for Harlech, Shrewsbury, Sondes, and Abingdon, ibid., 16 and 23 September, and 30 December 1911; for Somerset, Marlborough, Malmesbury and St. Levan, ibid., 1912-1915, passim.

79. Thompson, *Landed Society,* p. 322; *Estates Gazette,* 20 February 1909; 17 and 24 June 1911; 8 July 1911; 26 July 1913.

80. 1912-13 *P.P.* 47 (*Reports,* vol. 38, Cd.6031), "Departmental Committee on Tenant Farmers and Sales of Estates, Minutes," p. 10.

81. Bedford Estates abstracts, 1900-1909, 1911.

82. M. J. Greener to L. Palairet, 27 May 1910, Courtenay of Powderham Papers, 1508M (Devon) E.C. XXI.

83. Smyth-Richards to Stanhope, 2 September 1909, and 28 January 1910; Stanhope to Smyth-Richards (farewell letter to tenants), n.d., Stanhope Papers, U1590, add. 323/6.

84. "Memorandum by Viscount Halifax," August 1887, and "The Devon Estates," 30 January 1892, Courtenay of Powderham Papers, 1508M Devon Add. EL 1/14, 21.

85. 4 *Hansard* (Commons) 157: 1140 (22 May 1906); "Statement," November 1907, Wentworth Woodhouse Muniments, T89.

86. 4 *Hansard* (Commons) 197: 1242 (1 December 1908); material on Irish sales, 1898, Stanhope Papers, U1590, Add. 355/2; see the Bibliography for "Returns of Advances under the Purchase of Land (Ireland) Acts" of 1891 and 1903, in the *Parliamentary Papers,* 1892-1919 passim.

87. *Freeman's Journal,* 24 November 1904, Kilmaine to the editor, Kilmaine Papers 10M; 4 *Hansard* (Lords) 126: 1268-1269 (3 August 1903); 4 *Hansard* (Commons) 183: 415 (17 February 1908); Kilmaine to his son, 7 August 1907, Kilmaine Papers, 10T.

88. See "Returns of Advances," 1892-1919 *P.P.* passim (n.86, above); *Tyrone Courier,* September 1909.

89. Curtis, *Coercion and Conciliation,* pp. 256-258.

90. 1915 *P.P.* "Returns of Advances." No record of any sales by Ashtown and Erne in the pre-war period; inventory of the estates of the 4th Lord Muskerry, 1929, of the 15th Viscount Gormanston, 1925, Irish RO.

91. For example, Lord Milner, *Estates Gazette,* 29 December 1906; for Lord Fitzwilliam, Irish RO.

92. Bathurst to R. Anderson, 8 August 1879, Bathurst Papers, D2525/54; "investments to 1892," 23 February 1892, Wentworth Woodhouse Muniments, T84 and "statement," November 1907, T89; "Clanrikarde . . . Accounts," Earl of Harewood's Archives, Harewood Accounts, 120 (307).

93. F. M. L. Thompson, "The End of a Great Estate," *Economic History Review,* 2nd ser., 8 (1955-1956), 36-52; David Spring, "English Landownership in the Nineteenth Century: A Critical Note," *Economic History Review,* 2nd ser., 9 (1956-1957), 472-484.

94. Sir Osbert Sitwell, *Left Hand, Right Hand!* (Boston, 1944), pp. 86, 159.

95. Lockhart, *Viscount Halifax,* II, 2; Lindley, *Lord Lovat,* p. 49.

96. *Times,* 31 May 1928; Bateman, *Great Landowners,* p. 331; Thompson, *Landed Society,* p. 286.

97. Countess-Dowager of Radnor, *Armchair,* pp. 142-43.

98. Memorandum on estates by Stanhope, n.d. [1895?], Stanhope Papers, U1590, Add. 212.

99. Morley's journal, 1880, 1884, Morley Papers, Add. MS. 48,291, ff. 22-23, 83, 64-65, 72-75; ibid., 48,292: f. 32 (1888).

100. Shrewsbury and Talbot to Lady Castlereagh, n.d. (ca. 1900), Londonderry Papers, D/Lo/C679 (33).

101. "We went to London in the winter of 1893, because our agent had again ordered us to economise. So Killeen was let" (Fingall, *Seventy Years Young,* p. 213).

102. Unpublished memoir by the 19th Lord Saltoun, " 'Twixt Mormond and the Sea," pp. 5-6.

103. "Memorandum by Viscount Halifax," August 1887, Courtenay of Powderham Papers, 1508M/Devon Add. EL 1/14; "The Devon Estates," 30 January 1892, ibid.

104. "The coal syndicate are getting on with their boring at Chilham—time will show what is there." F. Neame to Sondes, 19 April 1911, Sondes Addn. Papers, E 39/4; Farrer to Sondes, 8 and 10 March 1909, and 20 December 1909, ibid., E43/2 and 3; statement of charges on the Kent and Norfolk estates, 1907 with alterations to 1912, ibid., F4.

105. F. W. F. Hervey to Lord John Hervey, 26 July 1899, Hervey Papers, 941/71/5; two drafts of heads of agreement, 1897, ibid., 941/71/4; F. W. F. Hervey to Lady Augusta Hervey, 15 May 1897, ibid., 941/67/6; F. W. Pixley of Jackson, Pixley & Co. (solicitors) to F. W. F. Hervey and the 3rd Marquess of Bristol, 28 May 1903, ibid., 941/71/8.

106. F. W. F. Hervey to Lord John Hervey, 11 January 1900, ibid., 941/71/7.

107. Thompson, *English Landed Society,* p. 314.

Chapter 4: Local Government and Politics

1. Mrs. Humphry Ward, *Marcella* (New York and London, 1894), p. 105.

2. Thompson, *Landed Society,* p. 23.

3. Professor Thompson has detected this close interrelationship between local and national affairs in certain areas: "stability in the counties seemed, to the aristocracy, to make possible concessions and compromises on other fronts without incurring mortal risks to the deference society. When, in some heavily industrialized counties, this stability was threatened by insubordination from urban and industrial elements, we find that the aristocracy felt they had reached the edge of the precipice, and that the time had come to abandon compromises and efforts to accommodate the forces of change" (Thompson, *Landed Society,* p. 23). For two contemporary Liberal views, see E. N. Bennett, *Problems of Village Life* (London, 1913), and F. E. Green, *The Tyranny of the Countryside* (London, 1913). Recent work on the subject includes Pelling, *Social Geography;* Richard W. Davis, *Political Change and Continuity, 1760-1885, A Buckinghamshire Study* (Newton Abbot, 1972); Janet Howarth, "The Liberal Revival in Northamptonshire, 1880-1895: A Case Study in Late Nineteenth Century Elections," *Historical Journal,* 12 (1969), 78-118; and J. M. Lee, *Social Leaders and Public Persons* (Oxford, 1963).

4. Earl of Meath, "Reasonable Patriotism," *Nineteenth Century,* 39 (1896), 297.

5. See, for example, Balsan, *Glitter,* p. 119; Barrington, *Through Eighty Years,* p. 229; John, Duke of Bedford, ed., *The Flying Duchess* (London, 1968), p. 56.

6. William Forrest to P. H. Coward, 21 April 1913, and to Rev. W. Popham, 28 April 1913, Plymouth Estate Papers, letter book 1913, D/D P1-291, pp. 13 and 54; other letters for same year.

7. Michelmore to Somerset, 17 August 1901, Michelmore, Loveys & Carter, Totnes Papers, Berry Pomeroy Estate letter books, 867B/ES23/19, p. 410.

8. Two lists of "bounties, charities, & pensions, etc.," February 1886 and early

1894, Earl of Scarbrough Papers (uncatalogued); bound vol. "Accounts," Bathurst Papers, Cirencester.

9. Derbyshire Estate subscriptions, Stanhope Papers U1590, no. 415.

10. Bedford Estates annual reports, 1889, 1898, and abstract books, 1903, 1911, Bedford Papers. In the late nineteenth century some peers began keeping more careful records of their charitable contributions. They distributed money where they believed it would do the most good for both master and man, and not as indiscriminate benevolence. The 3rd Marquess of Bute was typical in this respect. His "far-reaching charities were regulated . . . by strictly business-like methods. Every appeal for help which reached him was carefully sifted and inquired into through the almoner." (Sir David Hunter Blair, *John Patrick, Third Marquess of Bute, K.T.* [London, 1921], p. 182n.)

11. Statistics derived from Bateman, *Great Landowners.*

12. Thompson, *Landed Society,* p. 288; C. H. E. Zangerl, "The Social Composition of the County Magistracy in England and Wales, 1831-1887," *Journal of British Studies,* 11 (1971), 116, 125.

13. J. M. Lee, "Parliament and the Appointment of Magistrates, The Origin of Advisory Committees," *Parliamentary Affairs,* 7 (1959), 90.

14. 1910 *P.P.* 37 (*Reports,* vol. 31, Cd.5250), "Report of the Royal Commission on the Selection of Justices of the Peace," pp. 8, 4-5.

15. Sir W. Hayward to Cranborne, 22 July 1898, Salisbury Papers HH, S4/36/48.

16. Herbert Eccles to Cranborne, 14 March 1892, ibid., S4/10/162.

17. Roberts to Norfolk, 23 December 1901, Arundel Castle MSS., ACM-S501(f).

18. Clarendon to Cranborne, 27 April 1897, Salisbury Papers HH, S4 papers, quarter sessions.

19. Applications volume, 1867-1885, Seymour of Berry Pomeroy Papers, box 17, 19, Magistrates, 1392M/19-20: Clifford of Chudleigh to Somerset, 20 July 1885; Morley to Somerset, 8 April and 30 March 1885.

20. Morley to Clifford, 26 March 1903, Clifford of Chudleigh Papers, ser. 1, box 3-7.

21. Lee, "Parliament and Magistrates," *Parliamentary Affairs,* 7 (1959), 92-93.

22. See, for example, letter book, W. Forrest to T. W. Lewis, 22 May 1913, Plymouth Estate Papers, D/D Pl, 291, p. 303; ibid., Forrest to several prominent men in Pontypridd division, 7 June 1913, pp. 270ff; ibid., Forrest to Colonel J. E. Vaughan, 8 June 1913, and to General Tyler, 7 June 1913, pp. 447 and 466; ibid., Forrest to several prominent men in the Pontypridd division, 20 May 1913, pp. 270ff.

23. Ebrington to Clifford, 8 November 1904, and many other letters on the same subject from April 1904, Clifford of Chudleigh Papers, ser. 1, box 3-7.

24. 3 *Hansard* (Lords) 329: 929, 930, 933, 926 (31 July 1888).

25. Arthur Gordon [Lord Stanmore] to Selborne, 9 November 1888, Stanmore Papers, Add. MS. 49,219: 212-213.

26. Selborne to Gordon, 6 December 1888, Papers of Roundell Palmer (First Earl of Selborne), MS. 1874f, 198-199.

27. 4 *Hansard* (Lords) 20: 1580 (25 January 1894).

28. Ibid., 1572.

29. 4 *Hansard* (Lords) 21: 69 (5 February 1894).

30. J. M. Lee, *Social Leaders and Public Persons: A Study of County Government in Cheshire since 1888* (Oxford, 1963), pp. 14-15; Dunbabin, "Expectations," *Historical Journal,* 8 (1965), 370.

31. Charles E. Barker, "The New Councils," *County Council Magazine,* 1 (1889), 1-2.

32. Dunbabin, "Expectations," *Historical Journal,* 8 (1965), 358. In 1907, for ex-

ample, the *County Council and Agricultural Record* (April 1907, p. 136) noted that "the small number of contests in each county is quite remarkable, very few reaching double figures," and that even in contests the old members were generally returned.

33. 5 *Hansard* (Lords) 5: 324 (16 March 1910).

34. *Burke's Peerage, Complete Peerage*. The Marquess of Bute, the Earl of Rosslyn, and Lords Leith, Lovat, and Sempill belonged to county councils in Scotland. Lord Merthyr was a county alderman for Glamorgan, Wales. The Earl Fitzwilliam sat on the Wicklow Council and the Earl of Erne chaired the Fermanagh Council for several years. The remaining diehard councillors and aldermen sat on councils all over England, with no one area predominating.

The inclusion of so many of the county councillors and aldermen in *Walford's* is remarkable, especially considering the small number of the so-called "county families," the wide electorate, and the large number of seats in the councils. Almost 50 percent of the county aldermen on average could be found in *Walford's*. The term "country gentlemen" as defined there is generally applied to the larger landowners or men with notable careers in the church, civil service, or the military. Men were not usually admitted to this august company by *Walford's* during the first generation on the basis of wealth alone. It is a much more select group than the magistrates.

Twenty of the county councils obtained less than one-fifth of their members from the "county families," but there was no correlation between this fact and that of the diehards' places of residence or landholding. In fact, in only one of these twenty councils (including seventeen counties) — the West Riding — was there a high concentration of diehard peers. Warwickshire, one of these twenty county councils, was the home county of Willoughby de Broke, who expressed such satisfaction with developments in local government. Experiences varied from council to council, but had no relation to the composition of the diehards. (Walford, *The County Councils and Municipal Corporations Companion,* 1911).

35. T. B. Forwood to Cranborne, 19 October 1894, Salisbury Papers HH, S4/16/90.

36. *Wilts and Gloucestershire Standard,* 29 December 1888.

37. Ibid., 20 and 23 February 1895.

38. Notes for speech by C. P. Hall, County Council election poster, 1895, "List of ways in which voters say they will vote," and Hall to W. R. Lawrence, 19 February 1898, and Bedford's notation on letter, 22 February 1898, Russell Papers, Acc. 3029, Rus G/D 1.

39. *Bedfordshire Times,* 25 March 1910.

40. *Stratford-upon-Avon Herald,* 18 January 1889.

41. Ibid., 4, 18, and 25 January 1889.

42. Ibid., 29 January; 5 and 12 February; 4, 11, and 18 March 1892; 22 February 1901.

43. *Rugby and Kineton Advertiser,* 8 November 1913.

44. Richard Heath, "The Rural Revolution," *Contemporary Review,* 67 (1895), 182.

45. F. E. Green, *The Tyranny of the Countryside* (London, 1913), pp. 29-30, 197; W. D. M., "The Peasants' Charter," *Local Government Review,* 1 (1910), 286.

46. Hall to Mr. Wing, 22 February 1895, Russell Papers, Acc. 3029, Rus G/D 1.

47. *Wilts and Gloucestershire Standard,* 22 December 1894.

48. Clarendon to Salisbury, 8 December 1894, Salisbury Papers CCC, Class E.

49. Ampthill to Maxse, 20 February 1909, Maxse Papers, 445-W265.

50. *Stratford-upon-Avon Herald,* 7 December 1894.

51. *Stratford-upon-Avon Herald,* 10 March 1899, and 8 March 1901; *Rugby and Kineton Advertiser,* 13 December 1913.

52. *Stratford-upon-Avon Herald,* 10 March 1899.

53. 1919 *P.P.* 12 (*Reports,* vol. 5) Coal Industry Commission, vol. II, *Reports and Minutes of Evidence on the Second Stage of the Inquiry,* p. 656.

54. Lord Ernle, *Whippingham to Westminster* (London, 1938), p. 213; *Bedfordshire Times,* 29 April 1910.

55. Annual Report, 1889, p. 221, Bedford Papers.

56. *Kelly's Directory of Bedfordshire,* 1910.

57. *Kelly's Directory of Birmingham,* 1905; *Worcestershire Advertiser and Agricultural Gazette,* 23 January 1909. John Hill, land agent to another Worcestershire diehard, the Earl of Coventry, served as Chairman of the Upton-on-Severn Rural District Council. Lord Coventry's brother, Canon H. W. Coventry, was an active magistrate of the Upton-on-Severn petty sessions.

58. *Kelly's Directory of Monmouthshire,* 1910; 1894 *P.P.* 36 (*Reports,* vol. 21, C7439), Royal Commission on Land in Wales and Monmouthshire. *Minutes of Evidence,* pp. 170-171.

59. *Kelly's Directory of Birmingham,* 1908.

60. Among other examples: the Kent land agents for two diehards, Lords Hothfield and Brabourne, were chairmen of their local parish councils. Lord Ebury's Moor Park, Hertfordshire, estate agent was a member of the Rickmansworth Urban District Council. William Bell, the Duke of Northumberland's Alnwick agent, sat on the Alnwick Urban District Council, and Lord Londesborough's agent was a member of the Scarborough Rural District Council. Lord Digby and his brothers were magistrates for Dorset, and one brother was chairman of the Cerne Rural District Council. Lord Rayleigh's brother and estate agent, the Hon. Charles Hedley Strutt, was a county alderman, chairman of quarter sessions, and a member of the parliament for Essex for several years. Henry Milles, younger brother of Lord Sondes, served as a magistrate and a county councillor for Kent, the family's home county. Lord Denbigh's estate agent, John Cave, was a county councillor for Warwickshire. Both Lord Forester and his son, the Hon. George Forester, were members of the Shropshire County Council. George also represented his family's interests on the Wenlock Borough Council, the Wenlock Education Committee, the Barrow Sanitary Committee, as an active magistrate, and as a councillor on the Wenlock Corporation. The agents of the Duke of Marlborough, the Earl of Malmesbury and the Viscount Halifax were all clerks of their local district councils. Several other agents for the diehards were active magistrates in the areas of the diehards' estates, including agents to Hothfield, Strathmore, Somerset and Norfolk. Agents also represented their employers on innumerable local boards and committees. For example, in September 1905 Lord Devon nominated his agent to replace him as a member of the Teignmouth Harbour Commission. See *Kelly's Directory of Kent, Surrey and Sussex,* 1909; *of Essex,* 1909, 1910; *of Durham,* 1910; *of the North and East Riding of Yorkshire,* 1909; *of Hampshire,* 1907; *of Hertfordshire,* 1913; *of Berkshire,* 1907; *of the West Riding,* 1908; *of Devon,* 1910; also see *Scarborough Post,* 1 September 1909; *Walford's,* 1911, p. 782; *Stratford-upon-Avon Herald,* 4 March 1892; *Wellington Journal and Shrewsbury News,* 9 March 1907, and 23 January and 20 March, 1909. For Lord Devon, see Devon to the Teignmouth Harbour Commission, 26 September 1905, Courtenay of Powderdam Papers, 1508M (Devon), E.C. XIX.

61. *Wilts and Gloucestershire Standard,* 20 February 1892, and 14 April 1894.

62. Ibid., 6 October 1906.

63. Ibid., 5 May 1894 and 16 March 1895.

64. *Rugby Advertiser,* 21 January 1899.

65. *Stratford-upon-Avon Herald,* 8 and 22 March 1907.

66. Ibid., 14 July 1905, and 17 January 1914.

67. Ibid., 30 December 1904, 14 July 1905, and 17 January 1914; *Rugby and Kineton Advertiser,* 13 December 1913.

68. *Royal National Directory of Scotland,* 1907; *Macdonald's Scottish Directory and Gazetteer, County Supplement,* 1909-10; *Bute County Directory,* 1909-10; *Royal National Directory of Scotland,* 1907. Ralston's relative, Gavin Ralston, was also a local magistrate and the chairman of the Glamis Parish Council. Robert Hendrie, agent for the Earl of Loudoun, served as a magistrate and as chairman of his local school board. Lord Ninian Crichton-Stuart, the brother of the 4th Marquess of Bute, was a county councillor for Fife. Factors for Lords Bute and Saltoun were members of local governing bodies.

69. *Inverness County Directory,* 1907; *Northern Chronicle,* Inverness, 3 February and 3 March 1909; *Oswestry and Border Counties Advertiser,* 13 January 1909. The Hon. William Ormsby-Gore, son of the 3rd Lord Harlech, sat on the Oswestry, Wales, Board of Guardians.

70. *Kelly's Directory of Ireland,* 1905; *Bray and South Dublin Herald,* 23 January 1909. In Ireland, land agents for Lords Ranfurly, Devon, Leconfield, Clanricarde, Portsmouth, Fitzwilliam, and Meath were magistrates. The Earl of Devon's county Limerick agent, Captain Richbull Curling, J.P., was a town commissioner for Newcastle West, and the Earl of Ranfurly's factor, Hunt W. Chambre, served as a member of both the Dungannon Urban District Council and the local Rural District Council.

71. *Burke's Peerage.* Between 1832 and the passage of the Reform Act of 1867, the families of the diehard peers were represented in the House of Commons by seventy-five family members. This total declined to sixty between 1868 and 1885, and to forty-nine from 1885 to 1918. Even in the post-World War I era, diehard families managed to send twenty-nine of their members to the Commons.

72. Bateman, *Great Landowners;* Pelling, *Social Geography;* Neal Blewett, *The Peers, the Parties and the People* (London, 1972), pp. 16, 18, 41, 386; Michael Kinnear, *The British Voter* (London, 1968), pp. 14-36. From the passage of the Third Reform Act in 1884 through the elections of 1910 the areas of strongest Conservative support in England lay in the southeast, the south, and the western Midlands, with certain extensions in western Lancashire and the rural areas of Yorkshire. Devon and Cornwall, the east Midlands, urban Yorkshire, Wales, and Scotland, especially in the north and east, were usually Liberal. All of Ireland except Ulster usually voted Nationalist throughout the period. There were fluctuations and shifts in this pattern, but the areas of Conservative or Liberal strength remained relatively the same. The diehards held a disproportionately large amount of land compared to other peers in only five of Pelling's eleven regions of England, and these five were varied in their political allegiance. The southeast was perhaps the most Conservative part of England, the north was generally Liberal, the central region and Yorkshire were politically divided, and the Devon and Cornwall region was usually, though not always, Liberal.

73. *Primrose League Gazette,* 1887-1912.

74. Notes on social activities, Stanhope Papers, U1590 Add. 104; Stanhope to his mother, 5 January 1910, ibid., 1217.

75. *Rugby Advertiser,* 1 January 1910.

76. Westminster to Gladstone, 13 July 1886, and Gladstone to Westminster, 14

July 1886, Gladstone Papers, B.L. Add. MS. 44,337, f. 385 and 44,387, f. 387; Limerick to Salisbury, 29 July 1890, Salisbury Papers CCC, Class E.

77. H. J. Hanham, *Elections and Party Management* (London, 1959), pp. 407, 410.

78. *Burke's Peerage; Conservative Year Book,* 1911.

79. Joseph Chamberlain to A. J. Balfour, November 30, 1904, Balfour Papers, B.L., Add.MS. 49,774, ff.57-58. Lords Malmesbury, Clifford, and Leconfield were among the other diehards who exercised influence in their local party organizations. Henry Page Croft recalled in his memoirs that it was Malmesbury, along with one or two other locally prominent men, who invited him in 1909 to contest the Christchurch, Hampshire, seat for the Unionists at the next election (H. Page Croft, *My Life of Strife* [London, 1948], pp. 45, 47). Lord Clifford was an important, active figure in the mid-Devon constituency (see Clifford of Chudleigh Papers, ser. 1, box 3-7). Lord Leconfield was the leading figure in the local Conservative Association and the Sussex Tariff Reform League. Earl Winterton attributed his selection as the candidate of the Horsham, Sussex Conservative Association to Lord Leconfield (Winterton, *Pre-War,* p. 1).

80. Wells to Hervey, 28 July 1904, and 3rd Marquess of Bristol to Hervey, 27 July 1904; Colonel Anderson to Hervey, n.d. (late August 1904), and n.d. (between 28 July and 6 August 1904); Lord Francis Hervey to F. W. F. Hervey, 21 September 1904; W. H. Folk to Hervey, 29 January 1906, Hervey Papers, 941/71/9.

81. See, for example, Salisbury Papers HH: J. Blundell Whyte, M.P., to Cranborne, 17 January 1892, S4/10/23-26; A. Rowden to Cranborne, 25 March 1892, S4/10/182; other letters on local politics in early 1890s, S4/10 and S4/11 and others.

82. Van Raalte to Cranborne, 7 December 1902, ibid., S4/50/109.

83. Colonel Churchill to Salisbury, 9 January 1908, ibid., S4/63/15.

84. Croft to Salisbury, 22 October 1906, ibid., S4/59/21; reply, copy letter Salisbury to Croft, 22 October 1906, S4/59/22.

85. Salisbury to Selborne, 26 April 1907, Selborne Papers, 5/151-152.

86. Smith to Salisbury, 16 and 22 August 1909, S4/66/14-15, 16-17; Salisbury to Lord Robert Cecil, 16 April 1909, Cecil of Chelwood Papers, Add. MS. 51,085, ff. 24-27.

87. Sir John Rolleston to Salisbury, 6 December 1909, Salisbury Papers HH, S4/66/148, 154.

88. *Rugby Advertiser,* 18 February 1893.

89. Willoughby de Broke, *Passing Years,* p. 167.

90. See *Rugby Advertiser,* 25 March and 19 August 1893, 16 February and 16 March 1895.

91. Willoughby de Broke, *Sport,* p. 5.

Chapter 5: The Armed Forces and the Empire

1. *Rugby Advertiser,* 19 January 1909.

2. Earl of Selborne, "The Case for Woman's Suffrage," *National Review,* 57 (1911), 256; ibid., Lord Ebury, "A Commentary on 'The Case for Woman's Suffrage,' " pp. 431-432.

3. Edward C. Mack, *Public Schools and British Opinion since 1860* (New York, 1942), pp. 128 ff.; David Newsome, *Godliness and Good Learning* (London, 1961), p. 201.

4. Willoughby de Broke, *Sport,* p. 17.

5. Fletcher, *Edmond Warre,* p. 267. Over 70 percent of those diehards whose secondary schools are known attended Eton, while nearly 65 percent of the rest of the House of Lords did so (statistics from *Burke's Peerage* and *Complete Peerage*).

6. George F. M. Cornwallis-West, *Edwardian Hey-Days: Or, a Little about a Lot of Things* (London, 1930), p. 38.

7. Rosslyn, *Gamble,* pp. 20, 25, 29, 71.

8. Viscount Mahon to Stanhope, 2 January 1900, and "Monday," 1903, Stanhope Papers, U1590, 450 (2).

9. *Burke's Peerage* and *Complete Peerage.*

10. Sir Osbert Sitwell, *Great Morning!* (Boston, 1947), p. 13.

11. Baroness Raglan, *Memories of Three Reigns* (London, 1928), p. 169.

12. Packet of letters labeled "America, Lewis, 1873," Clifford of Chudleigh Papers.

13. *Burke's Peerage* and *Complete Peerage.*

14. For example, the Sheffield battalion of the Boys' Brigade listed as its honorary president in 1900-1901 the Earl Fitzwilliam, and its staff included the Earl of Scarbrough ("Sheffield Battalion of the Boy's Brigade, 12th Annual Report, 1900-1901," Wentworth Woodhouse Muniments, T73).

15. *Rugby Advertiser,* 1 May 1909.

16. Meath, *Nineteenth Century,* p. 338.

17. Winterton, *Pre-War,* p. 33.

18. Salisbury to Balfour, 5 September 1909, Balfour Papers, Add. MS. 49,758, f. 185.

19. *Complete Peerage* (1913), II, app. B, pp. 592-596. The diehards served in various military capacities during the Boer War. Lord Roberts was commander-in-chief after 1899. The Duke of Westminster was A.D.C. to Milner in 1899 and to Roberts, 1900-1901. The Duke of Marlborough served with the Imperial Yeomanry in South Africa, as did other diehards, and was assistant military secretary to Lord Roberts in 1902. A large number of diehards or members of their families served with the Guards or their territorial regiments as officers. Lord Bathurst, as colonel of his battalion of the Gloucestershire Regiment, went first to Ireland and then to St. Helena to guard Boer prisoners of war. Rosslyn went out to South Africa as a roving correspondent for the Harmsworth papers, got a commission after the Spion Kop disaster, and was twice captured by the Boers. Lord Lovat organized a troop of scouts, known as Lovat's Scouts, from among highland volunteers. He commanded and fought with the scouts in South Africa. Lord Sempill was one of his officers, and Lord Leith of Fyvie fitted out and maintained at his own expense two companies of the scouts. (See Reginald Lucas, *Lord Glenesk and the 'Morning Post'* [London, 1910], p. 380; Rosslyn, *Gamble,* pp. 180, 185; Lindley, *Lovat,* pp. 77 ff.; Stirling, *Fyvie Castle,* pp. 400-401.)

20. *Complete Peerage,* VIII, app. F, pp. 759-826.

21. 4 *Hansard* (Commons) 53: 65 (8 February 1898).

22. *Rugby Advertiser,* 7 October 1899.

23. 4 *Hansard* (Lords) 78: 8 (30 January 1900).

24. Earl Roberts, *Defence of the Empire* (London, 1905), pp. 25-26.

25. *Wilts and Gloucestershire Standard,* 3 March 1906.

26. Earl of Malmesbury, *The New Order* (London, 1908), pp. 7, 13 (a collection of conservative essays).

27. Somerset to Law, 26 March 1912, Andrew Bonar Law Papers, 26/1/59.

28. Milner to Roberts, 24 November 1909, Papers of Field Marshal Lord Roberts, 7101-23-45-115.

29. For the Fisher reforms, see Arthur J. Marder, *From the Dreadnought to Scapa Flow*, I, *The Road to War, 1904-1914* (London, 1961).

30. Ibid., pp. 21-22, 28-29; Archibald Hurd, *Who Goes There?* (London, 1942), pp. 77-79, 80.

31. Earl of Selborne, preface to Archibald Hurd, *Our Navy* (London, 1914), pp. v-vi.

32. 4 *Hansard* (Commons) 162: 86, 91 (27 July 1906).

33. 5 *Hansard* (Commons) 19: 638 (14 July 1910).

34. See preface to the catalogue of Arnold White Papers, National Maritime Museum.

35. H. W. Wilson and Arnold White, *When War Breaks Out* (London, 1898).

36. Bedford wrote White in December 1912, thanking him for his notes on Germany and stating that he was "glad to learn that German opinion is against a war with England and that they realize it would mean the loss of their fleet. This is indeed a proof of the peace preserving capacities of great armaments" (Bedford to White, 12 December 1912, Arnold White Papers, WHI/80, National Maritime Museum). For more on the tension between Germany and Great Britain before 1914, see William L. Langer, *The Diplomacy of Imperialism, 1890-1902*, 2nd ed. (New York, 1951), and Raymond J. Sontag, *Germany and England, Background of Conflict, 1848-1894* (New York, 1938). For further information on Arnold White, see introduction to Arnold White, *Efficiency and Empire*, ed. G. R. Searle (Brighton, Sussex, 1973).

37. 4 *Hansard* (Lords) 124: 1140 (2 July 1903); see also Meath, *Twentieth Century*, pp. 92-93.

38. 4 *Hansard* (Lords) 177: 1039 ff. (8 July 1907).

39. Sir Frederick Maurice, *Haldane, 1856-1915: The Life of Viscount Haldane of Cloan* (London, 1937), pp. 177-178, 181, 204.

40. Elie Halévy, *A History of the English People in the Nineteenth Century*, VI, *The Rule of Democracy, 1905-1914* (New York, 1961), p. 177; Maurice, *Haldane*, pp. 207-209.

41. Halévy, *History*, VI, 183; Maurice, *Haldane*, p. 206.

42. Maurice, *Haldane*, pp. 206-207; Sir John K. Dunlop, *The Development of the British Army, 1889-1914* (London, 1938), pp. 267-271, 274.

43. Hastings, Duke of Bedford, *The Years of Transition* (London, 1949), pp. 84-85.

44. 1904 *P.P.* 30, 31 (*Reports*, vol. 23, 24, Cd.2061-2064). Report of the Royal Commission on the Militia and the Volunteers.

45. Cyril Falls, "The Army," in Simon Nowell-Smith, ed., *Edwardian England, 1901-14* (London, 1964), p. 527.

46. Selborne to Arnold-Forster, 7 July 1904, Balfour Papers, B.L., Add. MS. 49,708, f. 7.

47. 4 *Hansard* (Lords) 141: 735 (21 February 1905); ibid. 148: 932 (4 July 1905).

48. It has been suggested that the militia colonels and other opponents of Haldane's plan idealized the current position of the militia and based their resistance to the secretary of War on a firm adherence to the status quo. As the statements by Bedford, Lovat, and Selborne illustrate, this was not in fact the case. The diehards and others recognized weaknesses in the auxiliary forces but maintained that the existing system could be made to work with less drastic alteration than Haldane demanded. (See Dunlop, *Development of the British Army*, p. 268.)

49. 4 *Hansard* (Lords) 138: 704-705 (21 July 1904).

50. Ibid. 171: 1221 (21 March 1907).

51. Earl of Erroll, "Mr. Haldane's Dream of a 'National' Army," *Nineteenth Century and After,* 61 (1907), 542; Lord Willoughby de Broke, "The Coming Campaign," *National Review,* 56 (1910), 70.

52. Bedford to White, 20 June 1906, Arnold White Papers, WHI/80.

53. 4 *Hansard* (Lords) 161: 938, 936, 994 (24 July 1906).

54. Ellis Ashmead Bartlett, "The Militia," *Nineteenth Century and After,* 62 (1907), 213-214.

55. 1904 *P.P.* 30 (*Reports,* vol. 23, Cd.2063), Royal Commission on the Militia and Volunteers, vol. II. *Minutes,* pp. 148, 152, 146.

56. 4 *Hansard* (Lords) 178: 831 (18 July 1907).

57. Viscount Wolmer (later Earl of Selborne), "A Militia Regiment," *Nineteenth Century,* 21 (1887), 569-570. For a study of the theme of the city and the country in English literature, see Raymond Williams, *The Country and the City* (New York, 1973).

58. 1904 *P.P.* 30 (*Reports,* vol. 23, Cd.2062), Royal Commission on the Militia and Volunteers, vol. I, *Minutes,* p. 161.

59. *Wilts and Gloucestershire Standard,* 22 February 1908.

60. 4 *Hansard* (Lords) 176: 1061 (25 June 1907).

61. Charles à Court Repington, *Vestigia: Reminiscences of Peace and War* (Boston and New York, 1919), pp. 274-275.

62. Erroll, "Mr. Haldane's Army," 544.

63. Willoughby de Broke paid tribute to the Marquess of Hertford at Stratford-upon-Avon: "It was men like him . . . that Mr. Lloyd-George and his friends were doing their best to destroy, notwithstanding that they were the very people whom Mr. Haldane relied upon for the formation of the territorial army, and it was through the influence, hard work, and patriotism of people like the Marquis of Hertford that the territorial army—such as it was—had been made possible at all" (*Stratford-upon-Avon Herald,* 22 October 1909).

64. Maurice, *Haldane,* pp. 289-291.

65. White to Maxse, 8 January 1911, L. J. Maxse Papers, 463, T4; Bedford to White, 8 October 1914, Arnold White Papers, WHI/185.

66. 4 *Hansard* (Lords) 53: 1017ff. (18 February 1898); ibid. 137: 1165 (11 July 1904).

67. Halévy, *History,* VI, 155; David James, *Lord Roberts* (London, 1954), pp. 416-417.

68. Samuel Hynes, *The Edwardian Turn of Mind* (Princeton, 1968), p. 39.

69. Raglan to Roberts, 12 August 1905, Roberts Papers, 7101-23-46-132.

70. Earl of Meath, "The Defence of the Empire, III, Universal Military Training for Lads," *Nineteenth Century and After,* 57 (1905), 739.

71. Malmesbury, *New Order,* p. 13.

72. Earl Roberts, "Imperial and National Safety," 458.

73. Lord Willoughby de Broke, "The Comfortable Classes and National Defence," *National Review,* 63 (1914), 428.

74. For instance, in 1904, Lord Lovat, who believed war with Germany was inevitable, formed a small, informal committee of himself, Lord Roberts, Sir Samuel Scott, and Colonel Repington. This group submitted a report to Balfour in 1907, and Balfour in turn handed it to Asquith. The prime minister set up a subcommittee of the defence committee to investigate Lovat's committee's findings. Roberts asked Lord Lansdowne to receive the group whose purpose was "to place before you the inade-

quacy of our military arrangements for the defence of this country . . . An invasion of
these islands by [Germany] is as possible (unless we take timely precautions to prevent
it) as it would be (were we unprepared) for the Russians to invade India." Not all of
those in this group favored compulsion. In fact, in 1906 those who favored voluntary
service, including Lovat and Repington, formed the National Defence Association, in
which they were joined by Lord Scarbrough, among other diehards who favored universal service but not compulsion. (See Lindley, *Lovat,* pp. 114-116; Roberts to Lansdowne, 12 May 1907, Roberts Papers, 7101-23-122-10; Repington, *Vestigia,* p. 266.)

75. Roberts, *Defence,* p. 42.
76. Milner to Roberts, 10 March 1908, Roberts Papers, 7101-23-45-93; Roberts to
Balfour, 7 April 1909, Balfour Papers, B.L., Add. MS. 49,725, ff. 286-290.
77. 5 *Hansard* (Lords) 2: 269ff. (12 July 1909); Lindley, *Lovat,* p. 126.
78. 5 *Hansard* (Lords) 2: 277-279; 285, 350 (12 July 1909).
79. Ibid.: 333, 327 (12 July 1909).
80. Willoughby de Broke, *Passing Years,* p. 252.
81. Stanhope to Maxse, 18 February 1910, Maxse Papers, 461, R. 579.
82. Roberts to Bathurst, 2 August 1913, vol. 7, Bathurst Papers, Cirencester.
83. Milner to St. Loe Strachey, 8 May 1909, St. Loe Strachey Papers, S/10/11/2.
84. Milner to Midleton, 27 July 1909, Midleton Papers, PRO 30/67/24, ff. 1235-
1242.
85. Roberts to Percy, 28 April 1911, Roberts Papers, 7101-23-125-1, letter book,
p. 81.
86. G. R. Searle, *The Quest for National Efficiency* (Oxford, 1971); see also
Robert J. Scally, *The Origins of the Lloyd George Coalition* (Princeton, 1975). Scally
greatly underestimates the commitment of many diehard peers, besides Milner, to the
cause of "efficiency" (p. 11 and *passim*).
87. Arnold White, *Efficiency and Empire* (London, 1901), pp. 1-3, 9, 71ff., 246.
88. A. M. Gollin, *Proconsul in Politics* (London, 1964), p. 45.
89. See Walter Nimcocks, *Milner's Young Men: the 'Kindergarten' in Edwardian
Imperial Affairs* (London, 1968); Searle, *National Efficiency,* p. 71.
90. Salisbury to Selborne, 20 May 1908, Selborne Papers, 5/208-209.
91. John Flint, *Cecil Rhodes* (Boston, 1974), pp. 100, 182; Gollin, *Proconsul,* p.
27; Nimcocks, *Milner's Young Men,* pp. 6-8.
92. Cecil Headlam, ed., *The Milner Papers* (2 vols., London, 1931-1933), II, 539.
93. Nimcocks, *Milner's Young Men,* p. 81.
94. Gollin, *Pronconsul,* p. 164.
95. 4 *Hansard* (Lords) 132: 184-186 (21 March 1904); Lindley, *Lovat,* p. 108.
96. 4 *Hansard* (Lords) 154: 1410-1411, 1419, 1421-1422, 1427-1428, 1451-1452,
1459, 1499-1504 (29 March 1906).
97. Gollin, *Proconsul,* p. 96.
98. Lindley, *Lovat,* pp. 108-114.
99. *Directory of Directors* (London, 1912).
100. Selborne to E. Pretyman, 19 September 1903, Selborne Papers, 73/5-6.
101. Maxse to Selborne, 5 March 1904, Selborne Papers, 73/232; Duke of Bedford,
"Some Reflections on the Fiscal Question," *National Review,* 43 (1904), 51-52.
102. *Wilts and Gloucestershire Standard,* 20 March 1909.
103. Fabian Ware to Lady Bathurst, 29 May and 17 March 1909, Bathurst Papers,
B(1).
104. Duke of Westminster, "Practical Imperialism," *Nineteenth Century and
After,* 72 (1912), 870, 872, 875.
105. Hynes, *Edwardian Mind,* pp. 22-27.

106. Meath, *Twentieth Century,* pp. 63-64; Earl of Meath, "Have We the 'Grit' of Our Forefathers?," *Nineteenth Century and After,* 64 (1908), 421-429.

107. Meath, *Twentieth Century,* pp. 76-77.

108. C. W. Saleeby, *Biology and History* [*The Creed of Eugenics*] (London, 1908), p. 5.

109. Arnold White, *The Views of 'Vanoc': An Englishman's Outlook* (London, 1910), pp. 284-285.

110. Lord Willoughby de Broke, "The Tory Tradition," *National Review,* 58 (1911), 211.

Chapter 6: The Politics of Unionist Discontent

1. Thus an observer commented in 1914 that "the so-called 'Die-Hard' campaign . . . really represented a stand, but not the last stand, by the most thoroughly English members of the Peerage" (J. M. Kennedy, "Toryism and the Election," *Nineteenth Century and After,* 75 [1914], 505). More recently, R. K. Webb has stated that "the Tory Revolt was the last important distillation of hatred of what the social and political changes of the past sixty years had done to the power and position of the upper classes" (*Modern England,* p. 470).

2. Viscount Halifax, "The Crisis in the Church," *Nineteenth Century and After,* 52 (1903), 553.

3. Viscount Milner's introduction to Christopher Turnor, *Land Problems and National Welfare* (London, 1911), p. v.

4. Malmesbury, *New Order,* p. 3.

5. Charles E. Wood [Viscount Halifax], *The Tendencies of the Age in Relation to the Development of Religion and Unbelief* (London, 1883), p. 1.

6. Willoughby de Broke to Maxse, 29 January 1911, Maxse Papers, 463, T9.

7. The Earl Percy [later Duke of Northumberland], "What is a Whig?," *National Review,* 1 (1883), 542.

8. Arthur Gordon [Lord Stanmore] to Selborne, 4 January 1890, Stanmore Papers, B.L., Add. MS. 49,220, f. 3; Gordon to Stanmore, 24 March 1890, ibid., ff. 28-29.

9. Earl of Meath, " 'A Thousand More Mouths Every Day,' " *Nineteenth Century,* 25 (1889), 60.

10. Gordon to Selborne, 29 January 1892, Stanmore Papers, B.L., Add. MS. 49,220, f. 87-88.

11. Northumberland to Strachey, 8 June 1908, St. Loe Strachey Papers, S/11/5/3.

12. Salisbury to Selborne, 3 October and 26 April 1907, Selborne Papers 5/201 and 5/155.

13. 4 *Hansard* (Lords) 34: 434-435 (28 May 1895).

14. Ibid. 42: 1091 (9 July 1896).

15. See Donald Southgate, *The Passing of the Whigs* (London, 1962), p. 409.

16. Collier, *Victorian Diarist,* p. 207.

17. 4 *Hansard* (Lords) 17: 638-640 (8 September 1893); ibid. 171: 784-793 (20 March 1907).

18. "The Ulster Unionist Convention" [pamphlet] (Belfast, 1892), p. 29.

19. 4 *Hansard* (Lords) 43: 1230 (31 July 1896).

20. Waldegrave to Salisbury, 1 September 1896, Salisbury Papers, CCC, Class E.

21. 4 *Hansard* (Lords) 127: 809-810 (11 August 1903).

22. Ibid. 85: 737 (6 July 1900).

23. Ashtown to Bonar Law, 21 April 1912, and 6 December 1913, A. Bonar Law Papers, 26/2/37 and 31/1/11.

24. See B. H. P. Turner, "Tariff Reform and the Conservative Party, 1895-1906," Ph.D. diss., University of London, pp. 10-62.

25. See Robert Blake, *The Unknown Prime Minister* (London, 1955), p. 44; Turner, "Tariff Reform," pp. 114-117.

26. See Alfred Gollin, *Balfour's Burden* (London, 1965).

27. R. B. Jones, "Balfour's Reform of Party Organization," *Bulletin of the Institute of Historical Research,* 38 (1965), 94.

28. Blake, *Unknown Prime Minister,* p. 43.

29. Neal Blewett, "Free Fooders, Balfourites, Whole Hoggers: Factionalism within the Unionist Party, 1906-10," *Historical Journal,* 11 (1968), 98-99.

30. Ibid., p. 121; Neal Blewett, *The Peers, the Parties and the People: The General Elections of 1910* (London, 1972), pp. 78-79.

31. As Richard Rempel has pointed out in *Unionists Divided* (p. 110), "the vague description of [the Unionist Free Traders] representing an 'older style of Conservatism' is an oversimplification. . . Many 'old Conservatives' were ardent Chamberlainites." They were also future diehards; in fact, they may have formed a substantial part of this component of the Chamberlainite movement.

32. L. S. Amery, *My Political Life,* I: *England before the Storm* (London, 1953), pp. 395-396.

33. 1894 *P.P.* 16 (*Reports,* vol. 1, C7400), Royal Commission on Agriculture, *Minutes of Evidence,* II, 382; 1895 *P.P.* 16 (*Reports,* vol. 3, C7671), Royal Commission on Agriculture, *Report on the County of Lincolnshire.*

34. Haggard, *Rural England,* I, 385.

35. A. Wilson-Fox, *The Earl of Halsbury* (London, 1929), p. 207.

36. Turner, "Tariff Reform," pp. 103-105; memorandum by Lord Cranborne to the Cabinet, May 1901, Hicks Beach Papers, PC/PP 76.

37. Salisbury to Balfour, 26 September 1903, Balfour Papers, B.L., Add. MS. 49,757, ff. 252-253.

38. Salisbury to Selborne, 10 August 1904, Selborne Papers, 5/90.

39. Gollin, *Balfour's Burden,* p. 73.

40. Joseph Chamberlain to Fitzwilliam, 8 June 1904, Wentworth Woodhouse Muniments, T74.

41. Amery, *Chamberlain,* pp. 603, 635.

42. Lockhart, *Halifax,* II, p. 197.

43. 4 *Hansard* (Lords) 124: 747 (29 June 1903).

44. Maxse to Lady Bathurst, 17 December 1906, Bathurst Papers, A(1), Cirencester.

45. *Wilts and Gloucestershire Standard,* 30 October 1909.

46. Milner to Stanhope, 16 May 1908 (pencil note by Stanhope), Stanhope Papers, U1590.

47. Leconfield to Maxse, 3 and 17 March 1907, Maxse Papers, 457, S492 and 497.

48. 4 *Hansard* (Lords) 189: 212 (20 May 1908).

49. Malmesbury, *New Order,* pp. 5-6.

50. Lord Ebury, "The Conservative Party, Its Councillors and Its Compromise," *National Review,* 61 (1913), 781.

51. Ivor Maxse to Lady Bathurst, 4 February 1906, Bathurst Papers, A(1), Cirencester.

52. Ebury to Maxse, 20 July 1906, Maxse Papers, 456, S328.

53. Lady Bathurst to Maxse, 8 February 1906, ibid., 455, S252.

54. Lord Robert Cecil to Lord Hugh Cecil, 22 August 1909, Quickswood Papers 12/53-55.

55. Salisbury to Selborne, 19 January 1906, Selborne Papers 5/115-116.

56. Amery, *Chamberlain,* pp. 818, 24.

57. Northumberland to Strachey, 22 September 1909, St. Loe Strachey Papers, S/11/5/8.

58. Alfred Gollin, *The Observer and J. L. Garvin* (London, 1960), p. 262.

59. Blewett, *Peers, Parties,* p. 82.

60. Jenkins, *Poodle,* p. 46; Klaus Epstein, "The British Constitutional Crisis," Ph.D. diss., Harvard University, 1953.

61. Epstein, "British Constitutional Crisis."

62. Blewett, *Peers, Parties,* pp. 76-77.

63. Sir Osbert Sitwell's father snapped: " 'The fact is that the grocer who has sanded one's sugar all these years has at last got his way, and introduced the principle of petty swindles into public legislation' " (Sitwell, *Morning,* p. 37).

64. Fabian Ware to Lady Bathurst, 2 May 1909, Bathurst Papers, B(1), Cirencester.

65. Wilson-Fox, *Halsbury,* p. 214.

66. Stanmore to Halifax, 23 June 1909, Stanmore Papers, B.L., Add. MS. 49,242, f. 292.

67. Milner to Midleton, 23 August 1909, Midleton Papers, PRO 30/67/24, ff. 1244-1250.

68. Northcote to Salisbury, 2 October 1909, Salisbury Papers, HH, S4/66/46.

69. 5 *Hansard* (Lords) 4: 775 (22 November 1909).

70. Stanhope to his mother, 25 November 1909, Stanhope Papers, U1590, 1217; 5 *Hansard* (Lords) 4: 777 (22 November 1909), and 785 (22 November 1909).

71. Ampthill to Curzon, 3 January 1909, Curzon Papers, Eur. F. 112/16, ff. 5-8.

72. For a summary of the results of the 1910 elections, see Blewett, *Peers, Parties,* pp. 377-415.

73. Stanhope to his mother, 8 December 1910, Stanhope Papers, U1590, 1217.

74. 5 *Hansard* (Lords) 8: 543 and 404 (17 and 14 May 1911).

75. Ibid., 543.

76. 4 *Hansard* (Lords) 173: 1260 (6 May 1907).

77. Wilson-Fox, *Halsbury,* p. 227.

78. 5 *Hansard* (Lords) 5:478 (22 March 1910).

79. Lord Willoughby de Broke, "A Plea for an Unreformed House of Lords," *National Review,* 49 (1907), 770-771.

80. 5 *Hansard* (Lords) 8: 471 (16 May 1911).

81. Ibid: 455 (15 May 1911).

82. Ibid: 657-658 (22 May 1911).

83. Ibid: 467 (16 May 1911).

84. Ibid., 5: 267 (15 March 1910).

85. 4 *Hansard* (Lords) 173: 1240-1241 (6 May 1907).

86. See Samuel Beer, *British Politics in the Collectivist Age* (New York, 1966).

87. Somerset to Halsbury, 8 May 1911, Halsbury Papers, Add. MS. 56,374, ff. 83-84.

88. 5 *Hansard* (Lords) 8: 405-406 (15 May 1911) and 563-564 (17 May 1911).

89. Earl of Meath, "How to 'Mend' the House of Lords," *Nineteenth Century,* 37 (1895), 196.

90. Selborne to Salisbury, 15 August 1907, Selborne Papers, 5/176-177; Salisbury to Selborne, 20 September 1907, ibid., 5/190.

91. Jenkins, *Balfour's Poodle,* p. 137.

92. 5 *Hansard* (Lords) 8: 543 and 800 (17 and 24 May 1911).

93. Memorandum by Selborne, 28 February 1910, Balfour Papers, B.L., Add. MS. 49,708, f. 196; memorandum by Selborne, February 1910, ibid., f. 192.

94. 5 *Hansard* (Lords) 8: 785 (24 May 1911).

95. Memorandum by Selborne, February 1910, Balfour Papers, B.L., Add. MS. 49,708, f. 192.

96. Lord Hugh Cecil to Selborne, April 1911, Selborne Papers, 74/84.

97. Fabian Ware to Lady Bathurst, Bathurst Papers, 29 March 1910, B(1), Cirencester.

98. Lord Robert Cecil to Lady Selborne, 29 April 1910, Selborne Papers, 75/15.

99. Selborne to Lady Selborne, 21 August 1910, Selborne Papers, 101/194.

100. Willoughby de Broke, *Passing Years,* p. 271.

101. L. J. Maxse, "Episodes of the Month: The Unionist Reveille," *National Review,* 56 (1910), 367-69.

102. Lansdowne to Willoughby de Broke, Willoughby de Broke Papers, H.L.R.O., Hist. Coll. 142, WB 1/8.

103. Jebb to Lady Bathurst, 19 January 1911, Bathurst Papers, B(1), Cirencester; Lady Bathurst to H. A. Gwynne, 26 July 1911, ibid., B(2); Gwynne to Lady Bathurst, 7 August 1911, ibid., B(2).

104. Jenkins, *Balfour's Poodle,* pp. 165-166.

105. Willoughby de Broke to Maxse, 19 June 1910, Maxse Papers, 461, R661.

106. Stanhope to his mother, 8 December 1910, Stanhope Papers, U1590, 1217.

107. Wyndham to Willoughby de Broke, 11 June 1911, Willoughby de Broke Papers, H.L.R.O., Hist. Coll. 142, WB 2/114.

108. Northcote to Willoughby de Broke, 14 June 1911, ibid., WB 2/10.

109. Willoughby de Broke, *Passing Years,* p. 289.

110. Northcote to Selborne, 1 August 1911, Selborne Papers, 74/168.

111. Plymouth to Halsbury, 9 July 1911, Halsbury Papers, B.L., Add. MS. 56,374, ff. 95-96.

112. Roberts to Curzon, 31 July 1911, and Roberts to Lansdowne, 11 August 1911, Roberts Papers 7101-23-125-1, pp. 105, 107.

113. Willoughby de Broke to Halsbury, 10 July 1911, Halsbury Papers, B.L., Add. MS. 56,374, f. 97.

114. Willoughby de Broke to Maxse, 19 July 1911, Maxse Papers, 463.

115. 5 *Hansard* (Lords) 9: 898 (9 August 1911), 974 (9 August 1911), 1041, 1060 (10 August 1911), 943 (9 August 1911), and 930 (9 August 1911).

116. Meath, "How to Mend the Lords," p. 199.

117. Wilson-Fox, *Halsbury,* p. 249.

118. Selborne to Chamberlain, 20 December 1909, Joseph Chamberlain Papers, JC 22/124; Joseph Chamberlain to Halsbury, 4 August 1911, ibid., JC 22/88.

119. 5 *Hansard* (Lords) 8: 810 (24 May 1911).

120. Willoughby de Broke, "The House of Lords and After," *National Review,* 57 (1911), 397.

121. 5 *Hansard* (Lords) 8: 730 (23 May 1911).

122. Cf. ibid., 735-736 (23 May 1911), 1204 (29 June 1911).

123. Stanmore to Lansdowne, 25 July 1911, Willoughby de Broke Papers, H.L.R.O., Hist. Coll. 142, WB 2/38.

124. Mowbray to Cecil, 3 August 1911, Quickswood Papers, 14/141.

125. 5 *Hansard* (Lords) 9: 978 (9 August 1911). See Selborne to Balfour, 24 December 1911, Selborne Papers, 1/143.

126. Roberts to editor of the *Times,* London, 8 August 1911, Roberts Papers 7101-23-125-1, p. 106.

127. Cf. Clarendon to Willoughby de Broke, 31 July 1911, Willoughby de Broke Papers, H.L.R.O., Hist. Coll. 142, WB 2/63.

128. See Jenkins, *Balfour's Poodle,* pp. 148-164, and Blake, *Unknown Prime Minister,* p. 69.

129. Selborne to Willoughby de Broke, 5 August 1911, Willoughby de Broke Papers, H.L.R.O., Hist. Coll. 142, WB 2/79; Rothes to Willoughby de Broke, n.d., ibid., WB 2/118; Ampthill to Willoughby de Broke, 26 June 1911, ibid., WB 2/17; Raglan to Willoughby de Broke, 17 June 1911, ibid., WB 2/15; Beaufort to Bathurst, 13 June 1911, ibid., WB 2/14; Ebury to Willoughby de Broke, 14 June 1911, ibid., WB 2/6; Scarbrough to Willoughby de Broke, 27 July 1911, ibid., WB 2/42.

130. See *Truth,* 16 August 1911.

131. Wyndham to Chamberlain, 3 August 1911, Austen Chamberlain Papers, AC 9/2/12.

132. Salisbury to Lord Hugh Cecil, 5 August 1911, Quickswood Papers, 14/143.

133. List of peers voting in Parliament Bill division, n.d. (probably 10 August 1911), Willoughby de Broke Papers, H.L.R.O., Hist. Coll. 142, WB 2/113. George Wyndham told his wife of the defeat: "Well—we are beaten. But I call the 114 Peers who voted like gentlemen 'The Beaten Gold' " (J. W. Mackail and Guy Wyndham, *Life and Letters of George Wyndham* [2 vols., London, n.d.], II, 699).

Chapter 7: The Diehards and the Tory Revolt

1. Gollin, *Observer,* p. 387.

2. Northumberland to Willoughby de Broke, 11 August 1911, Willoughby de Broke Papers, H.L.R.O., Hist. Coll. 142, WB 3/14.

3. Cf. Bedford to Willoughby de Broke, 12 August 1911, and Ampthill to Willoughby de Broke, 13 August 1911, ibid., WB 3/17 and WB 3/25.

4. Cf. Saltoun to Willoughby de Broke, 10 October 1911, ibid., WB 3/81.

5. Willoughby de Broke to Selborne, 12 August 1911, Selborne Papers, 74/176-177.

6. Lovat to Willoughby de Broke, 17 August 1911, Willoughby de Broke Papers (All references are to H.L.R.O., Hist. Coll. 142), WB 3/44.

7. Northumberland to Willoughby de Broke, 14 August 1911, ibid., WB 3/26.

8. Selborne to Wyndham, 22 August 1911, Selborne Papers, 74/191.

9. Willoughby de Broke to Selborne, 17 August 1911, ibid., 74/182.

10. Selborne to Willoughby de Broke, 18 August 1911, Willoughby de Broke Papers, WB 3/46.

11. Selborne to Chamberlain, 4 September 1911, Austen Chamberlain Papers, AC 9/3/56.

12. Willoughby de Broke to Halsbury and others, 7 October 1911, Halsbury Papers, Add. MS. 56,374.

13. Lovat to Willoughby de Broke, 11 October 1911, Willoughby de Broke Papers, WB 3/82.

14. "Brief Summary of Lord Milner's Views Given on Night of September 18th, 1911," initialled by Lord Milner, Austen Chamberlain Papers, AC 9/3/41.

15. Selborne to Chamberlain, 7 October 1911, ibid., AC 9/3/57.

16. Salisbury to Halsbury, 23 October 1911, Halsbury Papers, Add. MS. 56,372, ff. 158-160.

17. Note of resolution in Austen Chamberlain's handwriting, 6 November 1911, Selborne Papers, 75/1.

18. Announcement of the executive committee of the Halsbury Club, signed by Willoughby de Broke, 7 November 1911, Selborne Papers, 75/4; rules of the Halsbury Club, 17 November 1911, Halsbury Papers, Add. MS. 56,374, ff. 207-208.

19. Willoughby de Broke to Lord Robert Cecil, 30 November 1911, Cecil of Chelwood Papers, B.L., Add. MS. 51,160, ff. 31-32.

20. Cf. Blake, *Unknown Prime Minister,* p. 75.

21. Lord Robert Cecil to Salisbury, 17 October 1911, Salisbury Papers, HH, S(4), 71/69-60.

22. Scarbrough to Maxse, 31 October 1911, Maxse Papers, 464,P841.

23. Wyndham to Balfour, 8 November 1911, Balfour Papers, Add. MS. 49,806, ff. 102-104.

24. Northumberland to Willoughby de Broke, 14 August 1911, Willoughby de Broke Papers, WB 3/26.

25. Willoughby de Broke to Selborne, 17 August 1911, Selborne Papers, 74/181-182. A. Gwynne told Lady Bathurst that he hoped to forge the "Forwards" into a "bullet" for Balfour's destruction, 12 August 1911, Bathurst Papers, B(2) Cirencester.

26. Cf. Maxse Papers, 464, P838, 854, 853: Bathurst to Maxse, 30 October 1911; Somerset to Maxse, 11 November 1911; Leconfield to Maxse, 9 November 1911.

27. Stanhope to Maxse, 15 November 1911, ibid., 464, P859.

28. Midleton to Curzon, 15 October 1911, Curzon Papers, Eur. F112/18, ff. 119-120.

29. St. Aldwyn to Curzon, 19 October 1911, ibid., f. 1.

30. Steel-Maitland to Halsbury, four letters in September and early October, and a memorandum, Halsbury Papers, Add. MS. 56,374, ff. 186-192, 193-195.

31. Steel-Maitland to Balfour, 17 October 1911, Balfour Papers, Add. MS. 49,861, ff. 351-355.

32. It is interesting to note the much greater proportion of correspondence with the landed aristocracy in the papers of Austen Chamberlain than in those of his father, Joseph.

33. Plymouth to Chamberlain, 30 March 1910, Austen Chamberlain Papers, 9/3/49; Selborne to Chamberlain, 7 October 1911, ibid., AC 9/3/57; Malmesbury to Chamberlain, 11 October 1911, ibid., AC 9/3/4; Willoughby de Broke to Chamberlain, 12 November 1911, ibid., AC 9/4/9.

34. Gwynne to Lady Bathurst, 11 November 1911, Bathurst Papers, B(2), Cirencester.

35. Blake, *Unknown Prime Minister,* pp. 120-121; Gollin, *Observer,* pp. 393-394.

36. 5 *Hansard* (Lords) 8: 790 (24 May 1911).

37. Ibid. 14: 928 (14 July 1913).

38. Willoughby de Broke to Maxse, 18 October 1912, Maxse Papers, 467, P917.

39. Blake, *Unknown Prime Minister,* p. 159.

40. 5 *Hansard* (Lords) 14: 924 (14 July 1913).

41. Willoughby de Broke to Lord Robert Cecil, 21 September 1913, Cecil of Chelwood Papers, Add. MS. 51,161, ff. 24-25.

42. Ampthill to Willoughby de Broke, 4 January 1914, Willoughby de Broke Papers, WB 7/1; Leconfield to Willoughby de Broke, 12 January 1914, ibid., WB 7/6.

43. Stewart, *Ulster,* p. 72.

44. 5 *Hansard* (Lords) 9: 155-156 (4 July 1911).

45. Ibid., 13: 574 (28 January 1912).

46. Bedford to Willoughby de Broke, 7 September 1912, Willoughby de Broke Papers, WB 5/4.

47. Bedford to Willoughby de Broke, 5 March 1914, ibid., WB 9/9.

48. Stewart, *Ulster,* p. 73; T. C. Platt to White, 4 December 1913, Arnold White Papers, WHI/82.

49. 5 *Hansard* (Lords) 14: 921 (14 July 1913); Willoughby de Broke to Cecil, 21 September 1913, Cecil of Chelwood Papers, Add. MS. 51,161, f. 24. Lord Robert told Willoughby de Broke on September 18, 1913, that he had a "profound horror of civil war. . . . I dare say you will think this point of view very chicken hearted. I can't help it. Civil war if it failed would be disastrous to Ulster, if it succeeded it would be probably fatal to the United Kingdom. That seems to me the teaching of History" (Willoughby de Broke Papers, WB 6/1).

50. *Rugby and Kineton Advertiser,* 11 July 1914. Lord Denbigh told an audience at Southam that the Liberals had put themselves in a difficult position by refusing to believe in the reality of resistance: "you cannot very well tell a man he is shamming, and then arrest him the next moment for doing something."

51. *Morning Post,* 18 November 1913.

52. Roberts to Bonar Law, 2 August 1912, Roberts Papers, 7101-23-125-2, p. 103.

53. Stanhope to Willoughby de Broke, 3 November 1913, Willoughby de Broke Papers, WB 6/6.

54. Letter to newspapers with list of signatories, 2 March 1914, Milner Papers, Add. 689-136.

55. Milner to Selborne, 18 February 1914, ibid., 689-16-18.

56. Milner to Roberts, 30 October 1913, Roberts Papers, 7101-23-45-126.

57. Gollin, *Observer,* pp. 416-423; Blake, *Unknown Prime Minister,* pp. 174-182.

58. Saltoun to Willoughby de Broke, 16 January 1914, Willoughby de Broke Papers, WB 7/10; letter circulated to peers by Willoughby de Broke, Arran, Stanhope and Ampthill, 4 February 1914, ibid., WB 8/5; numerous letters to Willoughby de Broke, February 1914, ibid., WB 8/1-ff.

59. Northumberland to Willoughby de Broke, 7 February 1914, ibid., WB 8/36; Ampthill to Willoughby de Broke, 29 June 1914, and Stanhope to Willoughby de Broke, n.d., ibid., WB/10/14, 17; Lindley, *Lovat,* pp. 132-133.

60. Willoughby de Broke to Halsbury, 5 July 1914, Halsbury Papers, Add. MS. 56,375, ff. 53-54.

61. Draft letter, Bathurst to Norfolk, 21 March 1914, and Norfolk to Bathurst, 1 April 1914, Bathurst Papers, vol. 7, Cirencester.

62. Milner to Willoughby de Broke, 1 October 1915, Willoughby de Broke Papers, WB 11/12.

63. "National Party Meeting at the Offices of the Tariff Reform League" [pamphlet], 27 July 1917, Petworth House Archives, uncatalogued; National Party pamphlets, ibid.; National Party pamphlet, 1918, and "A National Party to Promote Reform, Union, and Defence," ibid. For a fuller discussion, see W. D. Rubenstein,

"Henry Page Croft and the National Party," *Journal of Contemporary History,* 9 (1974), 129-148.

64. Pamphlet issued by the National Party, "How are we going to vote next time?" 1918, Petworth House Archives, uncatalogued.

65. Willoughby de Broke to Law, 19 November 1912, Andrew Bonar Law Papers, 27/4/74.

66. Willoughby de Broke, "Tory Tradition," p. 208, and "The Unionist Position," *National Review,* 62 (1913), 214.

67. Willoughby de Broke, "Tory Tradition," p. 211, and "National Toryism," *National Review,* 59 (1912), 419.

68. Willoughby de Broke to Saleeby, 6 November 1912, Willoughby de Broke Papers, DR 14511, Stratford-upon-Avon.

69. Paul Smith, *Lord Salisbury on Politics* (Cambridge, 1972), p. 2.

70. Willoughby de Broke in Sir William R. Anson, et al., *Rights of Citizenship: A Survey of Safeguards for the People* [an anthology of essays] (London, 1912), p. 54; Willoughby de Broke, "National Toryism," p. 415.

71. Seymour Martin Lipset, "The Sources of the 'Radical Right,' " in Daniel Bell, ed., *The Radical Right* (New York, 1964), p. 307.

Bibliography

Primary Sources

Manuscripts

Allerton Park Papers, Sheepscar Library, Leeds.
Arundel Castle Manuscripts, Sheffield Central Library, Sheffield.
Ashbourne Papers, House of Lords Record Office, London.
A. J. Balfour Papers, British Library, Additional Manuscripts.
Bathurst Papers, British Library, London.
Bathurst Papers, Cirencester Park, Cirencester.
Bathurst Papers, Gloucestershire Record Office, Gloucester.
Bedford Papers, Bedford Estate Office, London.
Bedford Papers, Trustees of the Bedford Estates (Tavistock Deposit), Devon Record Office, Exeter.
Andrew Bonar Law Papers, House of Lords Record Office, London.
Cecil of Chelwood Papers, British Library, Additional Manuscripts.
Austen Chamberlain Papers, University of Birmingham, Birmingham.
Joseph Chamberlain Papers, University of Birmingham, Birmingham.
Clanricarde Papers, Earl of Harewood's Archives, Sheepscar Library, Leeds.
Clifford of Chudleigh Papers, Ugbrooke Park, Chudleigh, Devon.
Courtenay of Powderham Papers, Devon Record Office, Exeter.
Curzon Collection: British Political Papers, India Office Library, London.
Dynevor Muniments, Carmarthen Record Office, Carmarthen.
Gladstone Papers, British Library, Additional Manuscripts.
Halsbury Papers, British Library, Additional Manuscripts.
Harewood Accounts, Earl of Harewood's Archives, Sheepscar Library, Leeds.
Hervey Papers, Bury St. Edmunds and West Suffolk Record Office, Bury St. Edmunds.
Iddesleigh Papers, British Library, London.
Kilmaine Papers, The Mount House, Brasted, Kent.
Lloyd George Papers, House of Lords Record Office, London.
Londonderry Papers, Durham Record Office, Durham.
Malton Estate Office Papers of the Earl Fitzwilliam, North Riding Record Office, Northallerton.
L. J. Maxse Papers, West Sussex Record Office, Chichester.
Michelmore, Loveys & Carter, Totnes, Papers, Devon Record Office, Exeter.
Midleton Papers, Public Record Office, London.
Additional Milner Papers, Bodleian Library, Oxford.
Morley Papers, British Library, Additional Manuscripts.
Northcote Papers, Public Record Office, London.
The Onslow Archive, Guildford Muniment Room, Surrey Record Office, Guildford.
Petworth House Archives, Petworth House, Petworth.
Petworth Rural District Council Minute Book, No. 6 (March, 1905-January, 1911), West Sussex Record Office, Chichester.

Plymouth Estate Papers, Glamorgan Record Office, Cardiff.
Quickswood Papers, Hatfield House, Hatfield.
Roberts Papers, National Army Museum, London.
Russell Papers, Bedfordshire Record Office, Bedford.
Papers of the 3rd Marquess of Salisbury, Christ Church College Library, Oxford.
Papers of the 4th Marquess of Salisbury, Hatfield House, Hatfield.
Scarbrough Papers, Sandbeck Park, Rotherham.
Papers of Roundell Palmer, First Earl of Selborne, Lambeth Palace, London.
Selborne Papers, Bodleian Library, Oxford.
Seymour of Berry Pomeroy Papers, Devon Record Office, Exeter.
Sondes Papers, Kent Record Office, Maidstone.
Stanhope Papers, Kent Record Office, Maidstone.
Stanmore Papers, British Library, Additional Manuscripts.
St. Loe Strachey Papers, House of Lords Record Office, London.
Wentworth Woodhouse Muniments, Sheffield Central Library, Sheffield.
Arnold White Papers, National Maritime Museum, London.
Willoughby de Broke Papers, House of Lords Record Office, London.
Willoughby de Broke Papers, Shakespeare Birthplace Trust, Stratford-upon-Avon.
Wood End Records, North Riding Record Office, Northallerton.
Yarburgh Muniments, Borthwick Institute, University of York, York.

Public Documents: Parliament

Hansard's Parliamentary Debates, ser. 3, 4, 5 (1880-1914).
Journals of the House of Lords (1900-1914).

Parliamentary Papers (Commons)

A. Accounts and Papers

Board of Agriculture, Returns as to the Number and Size of Agricultural Holdings in
    Great Britain in the Year 1895. *1896*, vol. 67 (*Accounts and Papers*, 19), C.-8243.
Board of Agriculture and Fisheries, Report on the Decline in the Agricultural Popula-
    tion of Great Britain, 1881-1906. *1906*, vol. 96 (*Accounts and Papers*, 32), Cd.
    3273.
Local Government: "County Council Elections, 1889 (Cost)." *1889*, vol. 65 (*Accounts
    and Papers*, 19), no. 247.
Local Government: "County Council Elections, 1892 (Cost)." *1892*, vol. 68 (*Accounts
    and Papers*, 21), no. 268.
Return of Market Rights and Tolls. *1886*, vol. 56 (*Accounts and Papers*, 19), no. 221.
Return to Owners of Land, 1872-73. *1874*, vol. 72, parts I, II (*Accounts and Papers*,
    38, parts I, II), C.-1097 (England and Wales); *1874*, vol. 72, part III (*Accounts and
    Papers*, 38, part III), C.-899 (Scotland); *1876*, vol. 80 (*Accounts and Papers*, 39),
    C.-1492 (Ireland).
Returns of Advances under the Irish Land Act of 1891. *1892*, vol. 65 (*Accounts and
    Papers*, 18), no. 18; *1893-94*, vol. 75 (*Accounts and Papers*, 26), no. 235; *1894*, vol.
    72 (*Accounts and Papers*, 22), no. 155; *1895*, vol. 82 (*Accounts and Papers*, 22), no.
    278; *1896*, vol. 69 (*Accounts and Papers*, 21), no. 259; *1898*, vol. 74 (*Accounts and
    Papers*, 23), no. 42; *1899*, vol. 79 (*Accounts and Papers*, 29), no. 11, no. 354; *1900*,
    vol. 69 (*Accounts and Papers*, 23), no. 302; *1901*, vol. 61 (*Accounts and Papers*,

25), no. 308; *1902,* vol. 84 (*Accounts and Papers,* 30), no. 334; *1903,* vol. 57 (*Accounts and Papers,* 22), no. 335; *1904,* vol. 80 (*Accounts and Papers,* 32), no. 329; *1905,* vol. 65 (*Accounts and Papers,* 22), no. 308.

Returns of Advances under the Irish Land Act, 1903. *1906,* vol. 100 (*Accounts and Papers,* 36), Cd. 2988, etc.; *1907,* vol. 70 (*Accounts and Papers,* 24), Cd. 3447, etc.; *1908,* vol. 90 (*Accounts and Papers,* 29), Cd. 3815, etc.; *1909,* vol. 73 (*Accounts and Papers,* 24), Cd. 4453, etc.; *1910,* vol. 76 (*Accounts and Papers,* 18), Cd. 5059, etc.; *1911,* vol. 66 (*Accounts and Papers,* 22), Cd. 5488, etc.; *1912-13,* vols. 69, 70, 71 (*Accounts and Papers,* 21, 22, 23), Cd. 6028, etc.; *1913,* vol. 53 (*Accounts and Papers,* 13), Cd. 6728, etc; *1914,* vol. 66 (*Accounts and Papers,* 17), Cd. 7114, etc.; *1914-16,* vol. 53 (*Accounts and Papers,* 16), Cd. 7664, etc.; *1916,* vol. 22 (*Accounts and Papers,* 6), Cd. 8231; *1917-18,* vol. 25 (*Accounts and Papers,* 7), Cd. 8562, etc.; *1918,* vol. 20 (*Accounts and Papers,* 6), Cd. 9063, etc.; *1919,* vol. 42 (*Accounts and Papers,* 11), Cmd. 57, etc.; *1920,* vol. 40 (*Accounts and Papers,* 14), Cmd. 582, etc.; *1921,* vol. 28 (*Accounts and Papers,* 10), Cmd. 1142, etc.

B. Reports of Commissioners

On Agricultural Depression. *1894,* vol. 16 (*Reports,* 1), C.-7334, etc.; *1895,* vols. 16, 17, (*Reports,* 3, 4), C.-7624, etc.; *1896,* vol. 16 (*Reports,* 2). C.-7981, etc.; *1897,* vol. 15 (*Reports,* 1), C.-8540.

On Agricultural Interests. *1881,* vols. 15, 16, 17, (*Reports,* 1, 2, 3), C.-2778, etc.; *1882,* vol. 14 (*Reports,* 1), C.-3309, C.-3309-I.

On the Coal Industry. *1919,* vols. 11, 12, 13 (*Reports,* 4, 5, 6), Cmd. 84, etc.

On the Housing of the Working Classes. *1884-85,* vols. 30, 31 (*Reports,* 17, 18), C.-4402, etc.

On Land in Wales and Monmouthshire. *1894,* vol. 36 (*Reports,* 21), C.-7439-I; *1895,* vol. 41 (*Reports,* 28), C.-7757.

On the Land Law (Ireland) Act, 1881, and the Purchase of Land (Ireland) Act, 1885. *1887,* vol. 26 (*Reports,* 13), C.-4969.

Local Government Act. *1892,* vol. 37 (*Reports,* 19), C.-6839, C.-6839-I.

On the Militia and Volunteers. *1904,* vols. 30, 31 (*Reports,* 23, 24), Cd. 2061-64.

On Mining Royalties. *1890,* vol. 25 (*Reports,* 18), C.-6195; *1890-1,* vol. 41 (*Reports,* 23), C.-331, C.-6529; *1893-4,* vol. 41 (*Reports,* 26), C.-6979-6980.

On Secondary Education, VI, Reports of the Assistant Commissioners. *1895,* vol. 48 (*Reports,* 35), C.-7862-V.

On the Selection of Justices of the Peace. *1910,* vol. 37 (*Reports,* 31), Cd. 5250, Cd. 5358.

On Tenant Farmers and Sales of Estates. *1912-13,* vol. 47 (*Reports,* 38), Cd. 6030, Cd. 6031.

Parliamentary Papers (Lords)

"Temporal Peers." Session 1910, no. 13.

Directories, Reference Works, Political Party Year Books, Programmes, etc.

Burke's Peerage and Baronetage. London, 1911, 1949, etc.
Bute County Directory. Rothesay: Higgie, 1909-1910.

Cokayne, G. E., *The Complete Peerage*. London: St. Catherine Press, 1910-1959.
Constitutional Year Book. London: Conservative Central Office, 1888-1914.
County Almanac and Directory and Year Book of Useful Information. Cirencester:
    W. H. Smith & Son, 1914.
County Directory of Scotland. Edinburgh: A. Giles, 1912.
Debrett's Peerage, Baronetage, Knightage and Companionage. London: Dean & Son,
    1912.
Diary and Directory for the Use of Surveyors, Auctioneers, Land and Estate Agents.
    London: F. P. Wilson, 1900.
Directory of Directors. London: Thomas Skinner, 1911, 1920.
Dod's Parliamentary Companion. London: Whitaker, 1909.
Dod's Peerage, Baronetage and Knightage of Great Britain and Ireland. London:
    Simpkin, Marshall, Hamilton, Kent, 1912.
House of Lords in 1907: An Unconventional Handbook. London: "Pall Mall" Press,
    1907.
Inverness County Directory. Inverness: 1904, 1906, 1907.
Kelly's Directory of Bedfordshire, Hunts and Northants. London: 1910.
_____ *Berkshire, Bucks and Oxon*. London: 1907.
_____ *Birmingham and the Counties of Stafford, Warwick and Worcester*. London:
    1908.
_____ *Cambridgeshire, Norfolk and Suffolk*. London: 1912.
_____ *Cheshire*. London: 1912.
_____ *Cumberland and Westmorland*. London: 1910.
_____ *Derby, Nottingham, Leicester and Rutland*. London: 1908.
_____ *Devon and Cornwall*. London: 1910.
_____ *Durham and Northumberland*. London: 1910.
_____ *Essex, Herts and Middlesex*. London: 1910.
_____ *Hampshire, Wiltshire and Dorsetshire*. London: 1907.
_____ *Herefordshire and Shropshire*. London: 1913.
_____ *Ireland*. London: 1905.
_____ *Kent, Surrey and Sussex*. London: 1909.
_____ *Lancashire*. London: 1909.
_____ *Lincolnshire*. London: 1909.
_____ *Monmouthshire and South Wales*. London: 1910.
_____ *Sussex*. London: 1909.
_____ *the West Riding of Yorkshire*. London: 1908.
Liberal Unionist Association, *Memoranda*. London: 1893-1912.
Liberal Year Book. London: Liberal Publication Dept., 1912.
Macdonald's Scottish Directory and Gazetteer. Edinburgh: William Macdonald,
    1909-1910.
National Union of Conservative and Constitutional Associations, Home Counties Divi-
    sion. *Book of Reference, Rules, etc.* London, 1899.
_____. *Annual Conference Programs*. London, 1893-1913.
National Union of Conservative Associations for Scotland. *Annual Conference Pro-
    gramme*. Edinburgh, 1899.
Royal National Directory of Scotland. London: Kelly's Directories, 1907.
Steer, Francis W., and Noel H. Osborne, eds., *The Petworth House Archives*, I, *A
    Catalogue*. Chichester: West Sussex County Council, 1968.
Stock Exchange Year Book. London: Thomas Skinner, 1911.
Walford's County Families of the United Kingdom. London: Spottiswoode, 1911.

Newspapers and Serial Publications

Agricultural Record (London).
Alnwick and County Gazette.
Andover Advertiser and Northern Hants Gazette.
Atlantic Monthly.
Bedale and Northallerton Times.
Bedfordshire Mercury (Bedford).
Bedfordshire Times and Independent (Bedford).
Belfast News-Letter.
Beverley Recorder and General Advertiser.
Blackwood's Edinburgh Magazine.
Bray and South Dublin Herald.
Bury Free Press (Bury St. Edmunds).
Bury and Norwich Post, Suffolk Standard and Advertiser.
Chichester Observer and West Sussex Recorder.
Contemporary Review.
Country Gentleman's Estate Book.
County Companion (London).
County Council and Agricultural Record (London).
County Council Gazette (London).
County Council Magazine.
County Council Times (London).
County Council Year Book.
County Councils and Municipal Corporations Companion.
County and Local Government Magazine.
Crediton Chronicle.
Dorset and Somerset Standard (Sherborne).
Economic Review.
Edinburgh Review.
Estate Magazine.
Estates Gazette (London).
Fortnightly Review.
Fraserburgh Advertiser.
Hampshire Observer and Basingstoke News (Winchester).
Local Government Directory, Almanac and Guide.
Local Government Gazette (London).
Local Government Review.
Longman's Magazine.
Morning Post (London).
National Review.
Newark Advertiser.
Nineteenth Century and *The Nineteenth Century and After.*
Northern Chronicle and General Advertiser for the North of Scotland (Inverness).
Oswestry and Border Counties Advertiser.
Primrose League Gazette (London).
Quarterly Review.
Roscommon Herald (Boyle).
Rugby Advertiser.
Rugby and Kineton Advertiser.

Salisbury Times and South Wilts Gazette.
Scarborough Post.
South Devon Weekly Express (Chudleigh).
Staffordshire Chronicle (Stafford).
Stratford-upon-Avon Herald and South Warwickshire Advertiser.
Times (London).
Truth.
Tyrone Courier (Dungannon).
Wellington Journal and Shrewsbury News.
West Sussex Gazette (Arundel).
Western Times (Exeter).
Western Weekly Mercury (Plymouth).
Wilts and Goucestershire Standard (Cirencester).
Worcestershire Advertiser and Agricultural Gazette (Worcester).
World.

Memoirs, Diaries, and Letters

Amery, L. S. *My Political Life,* I: *England before the Storm, 1896-1914.* London: Hutchinson, 1953.
Balsan, Consuelo Vanderbilt. *The Glitter and the Gold.* New York: Harper & Brothers, 1952.
Barrington, Charlotte, Viscountess. *Through Eighty Years (1855-1935).* London: John Murray, 1936.
Bedford, Hastings, 12th Duke of. *The Years of Transition.* London: Andrew Dakers, 1949.
Bedford, John, 13th Duke of, ed.. *The Flying Duchess: The Diaries and Letters of Mary, Duchess of Bedford.* London: Macdonald, 1968.
_____. *A Silver-Plated Spoon.* London: Cassell, 1959.
Blunt, Wilfred Scawen. *The Land War in Ireland: Being a Personal Narrative of Events,* 2nd ed. London: Herbert & Daniel, 1913.
_____, *My Diaries: Being a Personal Narrative of Events, 1888-1914,* 2 vols. New York: Knopf, 1921.
Chamberlain, Sir Austen. *Politics from Inside: An Epistolary Chronicle, 1906-1914.* London: Cassell, 1936.
Churchill, Viscount. *All My Sins Remembered.* London: William Heinemann, 1964.
Collier, E. C. F., ed.. *A Victorian Diarist: Extracts from the Journals of Mary, Lady Monkswell, 1873-1895.* London: John Murray, 1944.
Cornwallis-West, George F. M. *Edwardian Hey-Days: or, a Little about a Lot of Things.* London: Putnam, 1930.
Cripps, F. H. *Life's a Gamble.* London: Odhams Press, 1957.
Croft, Henry Page. *My Life of Strife.* London: Hutchinson, 1948.
Dugdale, Blanche E. C. *Family Homespun.* London: John Murray, 1940.
Dunraven, Earl of. *Past Times and Pastimes,* 2 vols. London: Hodder & Stoughton, 1922.
Dynevor, Lord. *My Reminiscences.* Carmarthen: W. Sperrell & Son, 1937.
Elwes, Winefride. *The Feilding Album.* London: Geoffrey Bles, 1950.
Ernle, Lord (Rowland Prothero). *Whippingham to Westminster.* London: John Murray, 1938.
Fingall, Elizabeth, Countess of. *Seventy Years Young.* London: Collins, 1937.

Gathorne-Hardy, Robert, ed. *Memoirs of Lady Ottoline Morrell: A Study in Friend-ship, 1873-1915.* New York: Knopf, 1964.

Headlam, Cecil, ed. *The Milner Papers,* 2 vols. London: Cassell, 1931-1933.

Hewins, W. A. S. *The Apologia of an Imperialist,* 2 vols. London: Constable, 1929.

Hurd, Sir Archibald. *Who Goes There?* London: Hutchinson, 1942.

Jones, L. E. *An Edwardian Youth.* London: Macmillan, 1956.

_____. *A Victorian Boyhood.* London, Macmillan, 1965.

Keppel, Sonia. *Edwardian Daughter.* London: Hamish Hamilton, 1958.

Londonderry, Marchioness of. *Henry Chaplin: A Memoir.* London: Macmillan, 1926.

_____. *Retrospect.* London: Frederick Muller, 1938.

Lovelace, Mary, Countess of. *Ralph Earl of Lovelace: A Memoir.* London: Chris-tophers, 1920.

Lucas, Reginald. *Lord Glenesk and the 'Morning Post.'* London: Alston Rivers, 1910.

Meath, Earl of, ed. *The Diaries of Mary Countess of Meath,* 2 vols. London: Hutchin-son, 1928-1929.

_____. *Memories of the Nineteenth Century.* London: John Murray, 1923.

_____. *Memories of the Twentieth Century.* London: John Murray, 1924.

Midleton, Earl of. *Records and Reactions, 1856-1939.* London: John Murray, 1939.

Nevill, Lady Dorothy. *My Own Times.* London: Methuen, 1912.

_____. *The Reminiscences of Lady Dorothy Nevill,* ed. Ralph Nevill. London: Edward Arnold, 1906.

_____, *Under Five Reigns,* ed. Ralph Nevill. London: Methuen, 1910.

Norfolk, Gwendolen, Duchess of. *Henry Fitzalan-Howard, Fifteenth Duke of Norfolk.* London: Frederick Hall, 1917.

Onslow, Earl of. *Sixty-Three Years.* London: Hutchinson, 1944.

Percy, Eustace. *Some Memories.* London: Eyre & Spottiswoode, 1958.

Portland, Duke of. *Men, Women and Things.* London: Faber & Faber, 1937.

Radnor, Helen, Countess-Dowager of. *From a Great-Grandmother's Armchair.* Lon-don: The Marshall Press, 1928.

Raglan, Ethel, Baroness. *Memories of Three Reigns,* ed. Erica Beale. London: E. Nash & Grayson, 1928.

Repington, Charles à Court. *Vestigia: Reminiscences of Peace and War.* Boston and New York: Houghton Mifflin, 1919.

Rosslyn, Earl of. *My Gamble With Life.* London: Cassell, 1928.

Selborne, Earl of. *Memorials,* II, *Personal and Political, 1865-1895.* London: Macmil-lan, 1898.

Sitwell, Sir Osbert. *Great Morning!* Boston: Little, Brown, 1947.

_____. *Left Hand, Right Hand!* Boston: Little, Brown, 1944.

_____. *The Scarlet Tree.* Boston: Little, Brown, 1946.

Warwick, Frances, Countess of. *Discretions.* New York: Charles Scribner's Sons, 1931.

_____. *Life's Ebb and Flow.* New York: William Morrow, 1929.

Warwick and Brooke, Earl of. *Memories of Sixty Years.* London: Cassell, 1917.

Webb, Beatrice. *My Apprenticeship.* London: Longmans, Green, 1926.

Williams, W. P. *A Monograph of the Windsor Family.* Cardiff: Daniel Owen, 1879.

Willoughby de Broke, Lord. *The Passing Years.* London: Constable, 1924.

Winterton, Earl. *Pre-War.* London: Macmillan, 1932.

Other Contemporary Printed Material

Adeane, Charles, and Edwin Savill. *The Land Retort.* London: John Murray, 1914.

Alderson, E. A. H.. *Pink and Scarlet, or Hunting as a School for Soldiering.* London: Hodder & Stoughton, 1913.

Ampthill, Lord. "State Registration of Nurses: A Rejoinder," *Nineteenth Century and After,* 68 (1910), 303-306.

Anson, Sir William, et al. *Rights of Citizenship: A Survey of Safeguards for the People.* London: Frederick Warne, 1912.

Aronson, Hugh. *The Land and the Labourer.* London: Andrew Melrose, 1914.

Ashtown, Lord, ed. *The Unknown Power Behind the Irish Nationalist Party.* London: Swan, Sonnenschein, 1908.

Badeau, Adam. *Aristocracy in England.* London, 1886.

Banfield, Frank. *The Great Landlords of London.* London, 1888.

Barker, Charles E. "The New Councils," *County Council Magazine,* 1 (1889), 1-4.

Barrington, Viscountess. "The Servant Problem," *National Review,* 44 (1905), 1025-1036.

Bartlett, Ellis Ashmead, "The Militia," *Nineteenth Century and After,* 62 (1907), 206-219.

Bateman, John. *The Great Landowners of Great Britain and Ireland,* 4th ed. London, 1883.

Bathurst, Earl. *A History of the V.W.H. Country.* London: Constable, 1936.

Bedford, Duke of. "The Collapse of the Special Infantry Reserve," *Nineteenth Century and After,* 73 (1913), 1-18.

———. *A Great Agricultural Estate,* 3rd ed. London, 1897.

———. "How to Restore Our Military Efficiency," *Nineteenth Century and After,* 64 (1913), 38-67.

———. "Our Special Infantry Reserve: The Case for Inquiry," *Nineteenth Century and After,* 73 (1913), 258-277.

———. "Some Reflections on the Fiscal Question," *National Review,* 43 (1904), 50-62.

———. "The Territorial Force Fiasco," *Nineteenth Century and After,* 73 (1913), 1376-1398.

Belloc, Hilaire. *Emmanuel Burden.* London: Methuen, 1904.

———. *Mr. Clutterbuck's Election.* London: T. Nelson and Sons, 1908.

———, and Cecil Chesterton. *The Party System.* London: Stephen Swift, 1911.

Bennett, E. N. *Problems of Village Life.* London: Williams & Norgate, 1912.

Bowles, Thomas Gibson. *The Lords of the Land as Lords of Parliament and Lords of the Kingdom.* London: John Heywood, 1907.

Bowley, A. L. "The Economics of a Small Village," *Economic Review,* 14 (1904), 202-206.

Brodrick, George C. *English Land and English Landlords.* London: Cassell, Potter & Galpin, 1881.

Cairnes, W. E. "Fox-Hunting in Ireland," *National Review,* 40 (1902), 430-442.

Carpenter, Edward. *British Aristocracy and the House of Lords.* London: A.C. Fifield, 1908.

Carrington, Earl of. "The Land and the Labourers," *Nineteenth Century,* 45 (1899), 368-377.

Cecil, Lord Hugh. "The Unionist Party and Its Fiscal Sore," *Nineteenth Century and After,* 65 (1909), 584-598.

Chesterton, Cecil. *Party and People.* London: Alston Rivers, 1910.

Clayton, Joseph. *The Truth about the Lords: Fifty Years of the New Nobility, 1857-1907.* London: A. C. Fifield, 1907.

Colchester, Lord. *The Endowed Schools' Acts and Their Administration.* London, 1885.

_____. "The Evil of Ignoring Minorities," *Nineteenth Century and After,* 61 (1907), 548-558.

Cox, Harold. "Changes in Landownership in England," *Atlantic Monthly,* 129 (1922), 556-562.

Cranworth, Lord. "The Decay of the English Village," *National Review,* 53 (1909), 584-591.

Cust, Lionel. *A History of Eton College.* New York, 1899.

Dun, Finlay. *Landlords and Tenants in Ireland.* London, 1881.

Ebury, Lord. "A Commentary on 'The Case for Woman's Suffrage,' " *National Review,* 57 (1911), 431-435.

_____. "The Conservative Party, Its Councillors and Its Compromise," *National Review,* 61 (1913), 779-789.

_____. "The Parliament Bill, A Sketch of Its Origin, Progress, and Adoption," *National Review,* 58 (1911), 55-65.

Erroll, Earl of. "The Defence of the Empire, IV. — The Dearth of Officers," *Nineteenth Century and After,* 57 (1905), 745-750.

_____. "Mr. Haldane between the Devil and the Deep Sea," *Nineteenth Century and After,* 60 (1906), 679-688.

_____. "Mr. Haldane's Dream of a 'National' Army," *Nineteenth Century and After,* 61 (1907), 542-547.

_____. "The Nation and the Army: The Responsibility of the Individual Citizen," *Nineteenth Century and After,* 58 (1905), 173-177.

_____. "Our Military Weakness," *Nineteenth Century and After,* 65 (1909), 11-15.

_____. "Parliament and the Army," *Nineteenth Century and After,* 59 (1906), 866-870.

_____. "A Rude Awakening," *Nineteenth Century and After,* 65 (1909), 565-569.

_____. "The Scotch Land Bill," *National Review,* 49 (1907), 466-471.

Escott, T. H. S. *England: Its People, Polity, and Pursuits.* London, 1881.

_____. *Social Transformations of the Victorian Age.* London, 1897.

_____. *Society in the Country House.* Philadelphia: George W. Jacobs, 1906.

"Foreign Resident." *Society in London.* New York, 1885.

_____. *Society in the New Reign.* London, 1904.

"Foxhunting, Old and New." *Quarterly Review,* 206 (1907), 197-215.

Galsworthy, John. *The Country House.* New York: Charles Scribner's & Sons, 1907.

_____. *The Island Pharisees.* New York and London: G. P. Putnam's Sons, 1908.

Gaskell, Charles Milnes. "The Country Gentleman," *Nineteenth Century,* 12 (1882), 460-473.

Gilbert, Sir W. S. *The Savoy Operas.* London: Macmillan, 1926.

Graham, P. Anderson. *The Rural Exodus.* London: Methuen, 1892.

Green, F. E. *The Tyranny of the Countryside.* London: T. Fisher Unwin, 1913.

Haggard, H. Rider. *Rural England,* 2 vols. London: Longmans, Green, 1906.

Halifax, Viscount. "The Crisis in the Church," *Nineteenth Century and After,* 3 (1903), 533-554.

_____. "The Education Bill," *Nineteenth Century and After,* 59 (1906), 724-732.

_____. "The Present Crisis in the Church of England," *Nineteenth Century,* 45 (1899), 173-187.

_____. *The Relations of Church and State.* London: English Church Union, 1913.

_____. "The Reunion of Christendom," *Nineteenth Century,* 39 (1896), 850-870.

———. *The Tendencies of the Age in Relation to the Development of Religion and Unbelief.* London, 1883.

Hall, A. D. *A Pilgrimage of British Farming.* London: John Murray, 1914.

Harcourt, A. F. P. "Where the Village Gentry Are," *Nineteenth Century and After,* 51 (1902), 417-420.

Heath, Francis George. *British Rural Life and Labour.* London: P. S. King & Son, 1911.

Heath, Richard. "The Rural Revolution," *Contemporary Review,* 67 (1895), 182-200.

Howard, James. "Landowning as a Business: A Reply," *Nineteenth Century,* 11 (1882), 555-571.

Hughes, T. J. '*Cymru Fydd*': *Landlordism in Wales.* Cardiff, 1887.

Hurd, Archibald. *Our Navy.* London: Frederick Warne, 1914.

"Ireland From Within." *Quarterly Review,* 197 (1903), 1-40.

James, Henry. "The Velvet Glove," in *The Finer Grain.* London: Methuen, 1910.

Jones, Harry. *Liberalism and the House of Lords: The Story of the Veto Battle.* London: Methuen, 1912.

Jones, W. Bence. "Landowning as a Business," *Nineteenth Century,* 11 (1882), 346-368.

Kebbel, T. E. "Conservative Organisation and the Agricultural Labourers," *Nineteenth Century and After,* 60 (1906), 126-135.

Kennedy, J. M. "Toryism and the Next Election," *Nineteenth Century and After,* 75 (1914), 499-513.

Land Enquiry Committee. *The Land: The Report of the Land Enquiry Committee,* I, *Rural.* London: Hodder & Stoughton, 1913.

Lefevre, George Shaw. *Agrarian Tenures.* London: Cassell, 1893.

"Local Government," *Quarterly Review,* 208 (1908), 322-332.

M., W.D. "The Peasants' Charter," *Local Government Review,* 1 (1910), 286-292.

Maitland, F. W. *Justice and Police.* London, 1885.

———. "The Shallows and Silences of Real Life," in H. A. L. Fisher, ed., *The Collected Papers of Frederic William Maitland.* Cambridge: Cambridge University Press, 1911.

Mallock, W. H. "The Highlanders and their Landlords," *Quarterly Review,* 159 (1885), 113-146.

———. "The House of Lords," *Quarterly Review,* 167 (1888), 217-248.

———. *The Old Order Changes.* London, 1887.

Malmesbury, Countess of. "The Primrose League," *National Review,* 7 (1886), 413-418.

Malmesbury, Earl of, ed. *The New Order: Studies in Unionist Policy.* London: Francis Griffiths, 1908.

Marlborough, Duke of. "The New Tories," *Nineteenth Century,* 26 (1889), 733-745.

Martineau, John. "A Plea for Landlords," *Blackwood's Edinburgh Magazine,* 143 (1888), 193-202.

Masterman, C. F. G. *The Condition of England.* London: Methuen, 1909.

Maxwell, Sir Herbert. "Country Gentlemen," *National Review,* 20 (1892), 10-24.

Maxse, L. J. "Episodes of the Month: The Unionist Reveille," *National Review,* 56 (1910), 367-369.

Meath, Earl of. "The Cultivation of Patriotism," ed. William Harbutt Dawson. *After-War Problems.* New York: Macmillan, 1917.

———. "The Defence of the Empire, III. Universal Military Training for Lads," *Nineteenth Century and After,* 57 (1905), 734-744.

‗‗‗‗‗. "Have we the 'Grit' of our Forefathers?" *Nineteenth Century and After*, 64 (1908), 421-429.

‗‗‗‗‗. "How to 'Mend' the House of Lords," *Nineteenth Century*, 37 (1895), 195-205.

‗‗‗‗‗. "Reasonable Patriotism," *Nineteenth Century*, 39 (1896), 295-315.

‗‗‗‗‗. " 'A Thousand More Mouths to Feed Every Day,' " *Nineteenth Century*, 25 (1889), 57-72.

Mordaunt, Sir Charles, and W. R. Verney. *Annals of the Warwickshire Hunt, 1795-1895*, 2 vols. London, 1896.

"The Needs of Rural England," *Quarterly Review*, 197 (1903), 540-568.

Northumberland, Duke of. "Religion and the Physical Sciences," *Nineteenth Century and After*, 52 (1902), 951-956.

‗‗‗‗‗. "What is a Whig?" *National Review*, 1 (1883), 540-547.

Onslow, Earl of. *Landlords and Allotments*. London, 1886.

"The Past and Future of Rural England," *Quarterly Review*, 218 (1913), 490-512.

Pedder, D. C. "Farmers' Villages," *Contemporary Review*, 79 (1901), 57-68.

‗‗‗‗‗. "Where are the Village Gentry?" *Nineteenth Century and After*, 51 (1902), 149-159.

‗‗‗‗‗. "Where are the Village Gentry? A Rejoinder," *Nineteenth Century and After*, 51 (1902), 644-648.

‗‗‗‗‗. *Where Men Decay: A Survey of Present Rural Conditions*. London: A. C. Fifield, 1908.

"The Political Education of the Country Voter," *Fortnightly Review*, 46 (1886), 36-48.

Ponsonby, Arthur. *The Decline of Aristocracy*. London: T. Fisher Unwin, 1912.

Prothero, Rowland E. (Lord Ernle). *English Farming Past and Present*. London: Longmans, Green, 1912.

Purchas, F. H. "The Earl of Loudoun's Ayrshire Estate," *Estate Magazine*, 8 (1908), 49-57.

‗‗‗‗‗. "Lord Denbigh's Experiments in Sugar-beet Growing and Fish Culture," *Estate Magazine*, 7 (1907), 161-170.

‗‗‗‗‗. "Lord Radnor's Wiltshire Estate," *Estate Magazine*, 12 (1913), 57-64.

‗‗‗‗‗. "Lord Rayleigh's Farm Organisation," *Estate Magazine*, 18 (1918), 337-342.

‗‗‗‗‗. "The Rt. Hon. the Baron Hothfield's Northern Estates," *Estate Magazine*, 7 (1907), 449-456.

‗‗‗‗‗. "A Visit to the Duke of Westminster's Eaton and Chester Estates," *Estate Magazine*, 5 (1905), 1-12.

Redlich, Josef, and Francis W. Hirst. *Local Government in England*, 2 vols. London: Macmillan, 1903.

Report of the Proceedings at the Great Aggregate Meeting of the Irish Landlords held in Dublin on Tuesday, 3rd January, 1882. Dublin, 1882.

Roberts, Earl. *Defence of the Empire*. London: Spottiswoode, 1905.

‗‗‗‗‗. "Imperial and National Safety, I. How to Restore our Military Efficiency: A Reply to the Duke of Bedford," *Nineteenth Century and After*, 64 (1913), 453-461.

Round, J. Horace. *Studies in Peerage and Family History*. London: Archibald Constable, 1901.

Russell, George W. E. "Land and Lodging-Houses (A colloquy with the Duke of Bedford)," *Nineteenth Century*, 42 (1897), 383-392.

‗‗‗‗‗. *An Onlooker's Note-Book*. London: Harper & Brothers, 1902.

‗‗‗‗‗. *Seeing and Hearing*. London: E. Grant Richards, 1907.

_____. *Sketches and Snapshots.* London: Smith, Elder, 1910.

_____. *Social Silhouettes.* New York: E. P. Dutton, 1906.

Sackville-West, Victoria. *The Edwardians.* New York: Doubleday, Doran, 1930.

Saleeby, Caleb Williams. *Biology and History (The Creed of Eugenics).* London: Eugenics Education Society, 1908.

_____. *The Methods of Race-Regeneration.* New York: New Tracts for the Times, 1911.

_____. *Parenthood and Race Culture: An Outline of Eugenics.* London: Cassell, 1909.

Saltoun, Lady. "What Shall we do with our Land," *Nineteenth Century and After,* 61 (1907), 419-428.

Sclater-Booth, G. "Local Government in the Rural Districts," *Nineteenth Century,* 21 (1887), 253-261.

Selborne, Earl of. "The Case for Woman's Suffrage," *National Review,* 57 (1911), 251-257.

_____. "A Militia Regiment," *Nineteenth Century,* 21 (1887), 566-575.

_____. and F. S. Oliver, *A Method of Constitutional Cooperation.* London, private circulation, 1918.

Simpson, John. *British Woods and their Owners.* London: Simpkin, Marshall, Hamilton, Kent, 1909.

Traill, Anthony. "The Irish Landowners' Convention," *National Review,* 10 (1888), 757-767.

Trollope, Anthony. *The Duke's Children.* New York: Dodd, Mead, 1909.

_____. *The Way We Live Now.* New York: Knopf, 1950.

Tuckwell, Rev. W. "Village Life and Politics in France and England, II. — England," *Contemporary Review,* 61 (1892), 397-407.

Turnor, Christopher. *Land Problems and National Welfare.* London: John Lane, 1911.

"The Two Land Campaigns," *Quarterly Review,* 219 (1913), 582-614.

Ulster Unionist Convention held at Belfast, 17th June, 1892, *Report of the Great Meeting of 12,000 Delegates From all the Counties of Ulster.* Belfast, 1892.

Underhill, George F., et al. *The Master of Hounds.* London: Grant Richards, 1903.

Unionist Convention for Provinces of Leinster, Munster and Connaught (June, 1892): *Report of the Proceedings, Lists of Committees, Delegates, etc.* Dublin, 1892.

Upton, H. M. (later 4th Viscount Templetown). *Profitable Dairy Farming.* London: Sampson Low, Marston, Searle & Rivington, 1888.

Vernon, Lord. "Over-Mortgaging the Land," *Nineteenth Century,* 29 (1891), 415-422.

Vincent, Edmund. *Tenancy in Wales: A Reply to 'Landlordism in Wales.'* Carnarvon, 1889.

Ward, Mrs. Humphry. *Marcella.* New York and London: 1894.

Waters, W. G. "Where the Village Gentry Are," *Nineteenth Century and After,* 51 (1902), 411-416.

West, Sir Algernon. "Some Changes in Social Life during the Queen's Reign," *Nineteenth Century,* 41 (1897), 639-655.

West, Leonard H. "A Year Under County Councils," *National Review,* 15 (1890), 341-347.

Westminster, Duke of. "Practical Imperialism," *Nineteenth Century and After,* 72 (1912), 869-878.

White, Arnold. *Efficiency and Empire.* London: Methuen, 1901; reprint, edited with introduction by G. R. Searle. Brighton: Harvester, 1973.

_____. *The Views of 'Vanoc': An Englishman's Outlook.* London: Kegan Paul, Trench, Trübner, 1910.
Willoughby de Broke, Lady. "The Pros and Cons of Domestic Service," *National Review,* 60 (1912), 452-460.
Willoughby de Broke, Lord. "The Comfortable Classes and the National Defence," *National Review,* 63 (1914), 419-442.
_____. "The Coming Campaign," *National Review,* 56 (1910), 59-70.
_____. "The House of Lords and After," *National Review,* 57 (1911), 394-404.
_____. *Hunting the Fox.* Boston and New York: Houghton Mifflin, 1921.
_____. "National Toryism," *National Review,* 59 (1912), 413-427.
_____. "A Plea for an Unreformed House of Lords," *National Review,* 49 (1907), 770-777.
_____. "The Restoration of the Constitution," *National Review,* 58 (1912), 857-869.
_____. "The Tory Tradition," *National Review,* 58 (1911), 201-13.
_____. "The Unionist Party and the General Election," *National Review,* 63 (1914), 775-86.
_____. "The Unionist Position," *National Review,* 62 (1913), 213-24.
_____, and George Peel. "Correspondence: Lord Willoughby de Broke and the Hon. George Peel (Radical candidate for the Rugby Division)," *National Review,* 62 (1913), 697-98.
_____, ed. *The Sport of our Ancestors.* London: Constable, 1921.
Wilson, H. W. and Arnold White. *When War Breaks Out.* London and New York, 1898.

Secondary Materials

Amery, Julian. *The Life of Joseph Chamberlain, VI: Joseph Chamberlain and the Tariff Reform Campaign, 1903-1968.* London: Macmillan, 1969.
Ashby, M. K. *Joseph Ashby of Tysoe, 1859-1919.* Cambridge: Cambridge University Press, 1961.
Beer, Samuel H. *British Politics in the Collectivist Age.* New York: Knopf, 1966.
Beerbohm, Max. "London Revisted," in *Mainly on the Air.* New York: Knopf, 1947.
Blair, Right Rev. Sir David Hunter. *John Patrick, Third Marquess of Bute, K. T. (1847-1900).* London: John Murray, 1921.
Blake, Robert. *The Conservative Party from Peel to Churchill.* New York: St. Martin's Press, 1970.
_____. *The Unknown Prime Minister: The Life and Times of Andrew Bonar Law.* London: Eyre & Spottiswoode, 1955.
Blewett, Neal. "The Franchise in the United Kingdom, 1885-1918," *Past and Present,* 11 (1965), 27-56.
_____. "Free Fooders, Balfourites, Whole Hoggers. Factionalism Within the Unionist Party, 1906-10," *Historical Journal,* 11 (1968), 95-124.
_____. *The Peers, the Parties and the People: The General Election of 1910.* London: Macmillan, 1972.
Bristow, Edward Jay. "The Defence of Liberty and Property in Britain, 1880-1914." Ph.D. dissertation, Yale University, 1970.
Bromhead, P. A. *The House of Lords and Contemporary Politics, 1911-1957.* London: Routledge & Kegan Paul, 1958.
Buckland, P. J. *Irish Unionism: One, The Anglo-Irish and the New Ireland, 1885-1922.* Dublin: Gill & Macmillan, 1972.
_____. *Irish Unionism: Two, Ulster Unionism and the Origins of Northern Ireland,*

1886-1922. Dublin: Gill & Macmillan, 1973.

―――. "The Southern Irish Unionists, the Irish Question, and British Politics, 1906-14," *Irish Historical Studies,* 15 (1967), 228-255.

Cecil, Lord David. *Melbourne*. London: Constable, 1965.

Chapman, J. K. *The Career of Arthur Hamilton Gordon, First Lord Stanmore*. Toronto: U. of Toronto Press, 1964.

Churchill, Winston S., and C. C. Martindale. *Charles, IXth Duke of Marlborough, K.G.* London: Burns, Oates & Washbourne, 1964.

Coleman, D. C. "Gentlemen and Players," *Economic History Review,* n.s. 26 (1973), 92-116.

Cornford, James. "The Transformation of Conservatism in the Late Nineteenth Century," *Victorian Studies,* 7 (1963-1964), 35-66.

Crankshaw, Edward. *The Forsaken Idea: A Study of Viscount Milner*. London: Longmans, Green, 1952.

Curtis, L. P., Jr. "The Anglo-Irish Predicament," *Twentieth Century Studies,* 4 (1970), 37-63.

―――. *Coercion and Conciliation in Ireland, 1880-1892*. Princeton: Princeton University Press, 1963.

Dangerfield, George. *The Strange Death of Liberal England, 1910-1914*. New York: R. Smith & R. Haas, [1935]; reprint, Capricorn Books, [1961].

Davis, Richard W. *Political Change and Continuity, 1760-1885: A Buckinghamshire Study*. Newton Abbot: David & Charles, 1972.

Digby, Margaret. *Horace Plunkett*. Oxford: Basil Blackwell, 1949.

Dixon, William Scarth. *Fox-Hunting in the Twentieth Century*. London: Hurst & Blackett, 1925.

Dugdale, Blanche E. C. *Arthur James Balfour, First Earl of Balfour,* 2 vols. New York: G. P. Putnam's Sons, 1937.

Dunbabin, J. P. D. "Expectations of the New County Councils and Their Realization," *Historical Journal,* 8 (1965), 353-379.

―――. *Rural Discontent in Nineteenth Century Britain*. London: Faber & Faber, 1974.

Dunlop, Sir John Kennenmont. *The Development of the British Army, 1899-1914*. London: Methuen, 1938.

Ensor, R. C. K. *England, 1870-1914*. London: Oxford University Press, 1936.

Epstein, Klaus Werner. "The British Constitutional Crisis." Ph.D. dissertation, Harvard University, 1953.

Fanning, Ronan. "The Unionist Party and Ireland, 1906-1910," *Irish Historical Studies,* 15 (1966), 147-171.

Fergusson, Sir James. *The Curragh Incident*. London: Faber & Faber, 1964.

Fletcher, C. R. L. *Edmond Warre*. London: John Murray, 1922.

Fletcher, T. W. "The Great Depression of English Agriculture," *Economic History Review,* 2nd ser., 13 (1960-1961), 417-432.

Flint, John. *Cecil Rhodes*. Boston: Little, Brown, 1974.

Fraser, Peter. *Joseph Chamberlain: Radicalism and Empire, 1868-1914*. London: Cassell, 1966.

―――. "Unionism and Tariff Reform: The Crisis of 1906," *Historical Journal,* 5 (1962), 149-166.

―――. "The Unionist Debacle of 1911 and Balfour's Retirement," *Journal of Modern History,* 35 (1963), 354-365.

Frederick Sir Charles, et al. *Fox-Hunting*. London: Seeley, Service, 1930.

Garvin, J. L. *The Life of Joseph Chamberlain,* II, *Disruption and Combat, 1885-1895.* London: Macmillan, 1933.

Gavin, Sir William. *Ninety Years of Family Farming.* London: Hutchinson, 1967.

Ginsberg, Morris, ed. *Law and Opinion in England in the Twentieth Century.* Berkeley and Los Angeles: University of California Press, 1959.

Gollin, Alfred M. *Balfour's Burden: Arthur Balfour and Imperial Preference.* London: Anthony Blond, 1965.

————. *The Observer and J. L. Garvin, 1908-1914.* London: Oxford University Press, 1960.

————. *Proconsul in Politics: A Study of Lord Milner in Opposition and in Power.* London: Anthony Blond, 1964.

Guttsman, W. L. *The British Political Elite.* New York: Basic Books, 1963.

Halévy, Elie. *A History of the English People in the Nineteenth Century,* I, *England in 1815.* New York: Barnes & Noble, 1961.

————. *A History of the English People in the Nineteenth Century,* V, *Imperialism and the Rise of Labour.* New York: Barnes & Noble, 1961.

————. *A History of the English People in the Nineteenth Century,* VI, *The Rule of Democracy, 1905-1914.* New York: Barnes & Noble, 1961.

Hanham, H. J. *Elections and Party Management.* London: Longmans, Green, 1959.

————. "The Sale of Honours in Late Victorian England," *Victorian Studies,* 3 (1960), 277-289.

Harbinson, John F. *The Ulster Unionist Party, 1882-1973.* Belfast: Blackstaff Press, 1973.

Harrison, Michael. *Lord of London: A Biography of the 2nd Duke of Westminster.* London: W. H. Allen, 1966.

Haxey, Simon. *Tory M.P.* London: Victor Gollancz, 1939.

Ho, Ping-Ti. "Land and State in Great Britain, 1873-1910; A Study of Land Reform Movements and Land Policies." Ph.D. dissertation, Columbia University, 1952.

Hogg, Spencer. "Landed Society and the Conservative Party in the Late Nineteenth and Early Twentieth Centuries." B. Litt. thesis, University of Oxford, 1972.

Howard, Michael. *Studies in War and Peace.* New York: Viking Press, 1972.

Howarth, Janet. "The Liberal Revival in Northamptonshire, 1880-1895: A Case Study in Late Nineteenth Century Elections," *Historical Journal,* 12 (1969), 78-118.

Hutchinson, Keith. *The Decline and Fall of British Capitalism.* New York: Scribner & Sons, 1950.

Huxley, Gervas. *Victorian Duke: The Life of Hugh Lupus Grosvenor, First Duke of Westminster.* London: Oxford University Press, 1967.

Hynes, Samuel. *The Edwardian Turn of Mind.* Princeton: Princeton University Press, 1968.

James, David. *Lord Roberts.* London: Holles & Carter, 1954.

Jenkins, Roy. *Asquith.* New York: Chilmark Press, 1966.

————. *Mr. Balfour's Poodle.* London: Heinemann, 1954.

Jones, R. B. "Balfour's Reform of Party Organization," *Bulletin of the Institute of Historical Research,* 38 (1965), 94-101.

Kendle, J. E. "The Round Table Movement and 'Home Rule All Round,' " *Historical Journal,* 11 (1968), 332-353.

Kinnear, Michael. *The British Voter: An Atlas and Survey since 1885.* London: B. T. Batsford, 1968.

Kitson Clark, George. *The Making of Victorian England.* New York: Atheneum, 1969.

Langer, William. *The Diplomacy of Imperialism,* 2nd ed. New York: Knopf, 1951.

Laver, James. *Edwardian Promenade.* London: Houghton Mifflin, 1958.

Lee, J. M. "Parliament and the Appointment of Magistrates: The Origin of Advisory Committees," *Parliamentary Affairs,* 7 (1959), 85-94.

_____. *Social Leaders and Public Persons: A Study of County Government in Cheshire since 1888.* Oxford: Oxford University Press, 1963.

Lindley, Sir Francis. *Lord Lovat.* London: Hutchinson, 1935.

Lipset, Seymour Martin. "The Sources of the 'Radical Right,' " in Daniel Bell, ed., *The Radical Right,* pp. 259-312. New York: Doubleday, 1963.

Lloyd, Trevor. "Uncontested Seats in British General Elections, 1852-1910," *Historical Journal,* 8 (1965), 260-265.

Lockhart, J. G. *Charles Lindley, Viscount Halifax,* 2 parts. London: Geoffrey Bles, 1935.

Mack, Edward C. *Public Schools and British Opinion since 1860.* New York: Columbia University Press, 1941.

Mackail, J. W., and Guy Wyndham. *Life and Letters of George Wyndham,* 2 vols. London: Hutchinson, n.d.

Magnus, Philip. *King Edward the Seventh.* London: John Murray, 1964.

Marder, Arthur J. *From the Dreadnought to Scapa Flow, The Royal Navy in the Fisher Era, 1904-1919,* I, *The Road to War, 1904-1914.* London: Oxford University Press, 1961.

Marsh, David C. *The Changing Social Structure of England and Wales.* London: Routledge & Kegan Paul, 1958.

Matthew, H. C. G. *The Liberal Imperialists.* London: Oxford University Press, 1973.

Matthews, A. H. H. *Fifty Years of Agricultural Politics, Being the History of the Central Chamber of Agriculture, 1865-1915.* London: P. S. King & Son, 1915.

Maurice, Sir Frederick. *Haldane, 1856-1915: The Life of Viscount Haldane of Cloan, K.T., O.M.* London: Faber & Faber, 1937.

McCreedy, H. W. "The Revolt of the Unionist Free Traders," *Parliamentary Affairs,* 16 (1963), 188-206.

McGregor, O. R. "Introduction" to Lord Ernle, *English Farming Past and Present,* 6th ed. London: Heinemann, 1961.

Morris, Anthony. "Haldane's Army Reforms, 1906-08," *History,* 56 (1971), 17-34.

Newman, Aubrey. *The Stanhopes of Chevening: A Family Biography.* London: Macmillan, 1969.

Newsome, David. *Godliness and Good Learning.* London: John Murray, 1961.

Newton, Lord. *Lord Lansdowne.* London: Macmillan, 1929.

Nicolson, Nigel. *Portrait of a Marriage.* New York: Atheneum, 1973.

Nimcocks, Walter. *Milner's Young Men: The 'Kindergarten' in Edwardian Imperial Affairs.* Durham, North Carolina: Duke University Press, 1968.

Nowell-Smith, Simon, ed. *Edwardian England, 1901-14.* London: Oxford University Press, 1964.

Orwin, Christabel S., and W. R. Peel. *The Tenure of Agricultural Land,* 2nd ed. Cambridge: Cambridge University Press, 1926.

_____, and Edith H. Whetham. *History of British Agriculture, 1846-1914.* London: Longmans, 1964.

Pelling, Henry. *Social Geography of British Elections, 1885-1910.* London: Macmillan, 1967.

Perry, P. J., ed. *British Agriculture, 1875-1914.* London: Methuen, 1973.

Pumphrey, Ralph. "The Introduction of Industrialists into the British Peerage: A

Study in Adaptation of a Social Institution," *American Historical Review,* 65 (1959), 1-16.

Rayleigh, Robert John Strutt, 4th Baron. *Life of John William Strutt, Third Baron Rayleigh,* new ed. Madison, Milwaukee and London: University of Wisconsin, 1968.

Rempel, Richard A. *Unionists Divided: Arthur Balfour, Joseph Chamberlain and the Unionist Free Traders.* New York: David & Charles, 1972.

Rhee, H. A. *The Rent of Agricultural Land in England and Wales.* London: Central Landowners' Association, 1949.

Robb, Janet Henderson. *The Primrose League, 1883-1906.* New York: Columbia University Press, 1942.

Robson, Robert, ed. *Ideas and Institutions of Victorian Britain: Essays in Honour of George Kitson Clark.* London: G. Bill & Sons, 1967.

Rogger, Hans, and Eugen Weber, eds. *The European Right.* Berkeley and Los Angeles: University of California Press, 1965.

Ronaldshay, Earl of. *The Life of Lord Curzon,* 3 vols. London: Ernest Benn, 1928.

Rose, Kenneth. *The Later Cecils.* New York: Harper & Row, 1975.

———. *Superior Person: A Portrait of Curzon and His Circle in Late Victorian England.* London: Weidenfield & Nicolson, 1969.

Rose, Richard. *Studies in British Politics.* New York: St. Martin's Press, 1966.

Ross, Alan, S. C., et al. *Noblesse Oblige.* London: Hamish Hamilton, 1956.

Rowland, Peter. *The Last Liberal Governments: The Promised Land, 1905-1910.* London: Barrie & Rockliff, 1968.

———. *The Last Liberal Governments: Unfinished Business, 1911-1914.* London: Barrie & Jenkins, 1971.

Rubenstein, William D. "Henry Page Croft and the National Party," *Journal of Contemporary History,* 9 (1974), 129-148.

Russell, A. K. *Liberal Landslide: The General Election of 1906.* Newton Abbot: David & Charles, 1975.

Saville, John. *Rural Depopulation in England and Wales, 1851-1951.* London: Routledge & Kegan Paul, 1951.

Scally, Robert J. *The Origins of the Lloyd George Coalition: The Politics of Social-Imperialism, 1900-1918.* Princeton: Princeton University Press, 1975.

Searle, G. R. *The Quest for National Efficiency.* Oxford: Oxford University Press, 1971.

Semmel, Bernard. *Imperialism and Social Reform.* New York: Doubleday, 1960.

Shannon, Catherine B. "The Ulster Liberal Unionists and Local Government Reform, 1885-98," *Irish Historical Studies,* 18 (1973), 407-423.

Sheppard, F. H. W., ed. *Survey of London, XXXVI: The Parish of St. Paul, Covent Garden.* London: University of London Athlone Press, 1970.

Smith, Paul, ed. *Lord Salisbury on Politics: A Selection from His Articles in the Quarterly Review, 1860-1883.* Cambridge: Cambridge University Press, 1972.

Solow, Barbara Lewis. *The Land Question and the Irish Economy, 1870-1903.* Cambridge, Mass.: Harvard University Press, 1971.

Sontag, Raymond James. *Germany and England: Background of Conflict, 1848-1924.* New York: W. W. Norton, 1938.

Southgate, Donald. *The Passing of the Whigs, 1832-1886.* London: Macmillan, 1962.

Spring, David. "The English Landed Estate in the Age of Coal and Iron, 1830-1880," *Journal of Economic History,* 11 (1951), 3-24.

———. *The English Landed Estate in the Nineteenth Century: Its Administration.* Baltimore: Johns Hopkins Press, 1965.

————. "English Landed Society in the Eighteenth and Nineteenth Centuries," *Economic History Review,* 2nd ser., 16 (1964), 146-153.

————. "English Landownership in the Nineteenth Century: A Critical Note," *Economic History Review,* 2nd ser., 9 (1957) 472-484.

————. "The Gentlemen's Revolution: A Study in the English Ruling Class, 1880-1914." Ph.D. dissertation, Harvard University, 1948.

————. "Some Reflections on Social History in the Nineteenth Century," *Victorian Studies,* 4 (1960), 55-64.

Stansky, Peter, "The Unbought Grace of Life," *Victorian Studies,* 10 (1967), 268-272.

Stanworth, Philip, and Anthony Giddens, eds. *Elites and Power in British Society.* London: Cambridge University Press, 1974.

Stewart, A.T.Q. *The Ulster Crisis.* London, Faber & Faber, 1967.

Stirling, A. M. W. *Fyvie Castle: Its Lairds and Their Times.* London: John Murray, 1928.

Thompson, F. M. L. "The End of a Great Estate," *Economic History Review,* 2nd ser., 8 (1955), 36-52.

————. "English Great Estates in the Nineteenth Century, 1790-1914," in *First International Conference of Economic History Contributions.* Paris and The Hague, 1960.

————. *English Landed Society in the Nineteenth Century.* London: Routledge & Kegan Paul, 1963.

————. "The Land Market in the Nineteenth Century," in *Essays in Agrarian History,* vol. 2, ed. W. E. Minchinton. Newton Abbot: David & Charles, 1968.

————. "Land and Politics in England in the Nineteenth Century," *Transactions of the Royal Historical Society,* ser. 5, 15 (1965), 23-44.

Thornton, A. P. *The Habit of Authority: Paternalism in British History.* London: George Allen & Unwin, 1966.

————. *The Imperial Idea and Its Enemies: A Study in British Power.* London: Macmillan, 1959.

Tucker, Albert. "The Issue of Army Reform in the Unionist Government, 1903-5," *Historical Journal,* 9 (1966), 90-100.

Turberville, A. S. "The House of Lords and Finance." Unpublished paper in the House of Lords Library.

Turner, B. H. P. "Tariff Reform and the Conservative Party, 1895-1906." Ph.D. dissertation, University of London, 1967.

Walker, Brian. "The Irish Electorate, 1868-1915," *Irish Historical Studies,* 18 (1973), 359-406.

Ward, J. T. "The Earls Fitzwilliam and the Wentworth Woodhouse Estate in the Nineteenth Century," *Yorkshire Bulletin of Economic and Social Research,* 12 (1960), 19-27.

————. "West Riding Landowners and Mining in the Nineteenth Century," *Yorkshire Bulletin of Economic and Social Research,* 15 (1963), 61-74.

————, and R. G. Wilson, eds. *Land and Industry: The Landed Estate and the Industrial Revolution.* Newton Abbot: David & Charles, 1971.

Webb, R. K. *Modern England.* New York: Dodd, Mead, 1971.

Wedgwood, Josiah. *The Economics of Inheritance.* London: George Routledge & Sons, 1929.

Weston, Corinne Comstock. "The Liberal Leadership and the Lords' Veto, 1907-1910," *Historical Journal,* 11 (1968), 508-537.

Whyte, J. H. "Landlord Influence at Elections in Ireland, 1760-1885," *English Historical Review,* 80 (1965), 740-760.

Williams, J. E. "Paternalism in Local Government in the Nineteenth Century," *Public Administration,* 33 (1955), 439-446.

Williams, Raymond. *The Country and the City.* New York: Oxford University Press, 1973.

Wilson-Fox, A. *The Earl of Halsbury.* London: Chapman & Hall, 1929.

Zangerl, C. H. E. "The Social Composition of the County Magistracy in England and Wales, 1831-1887," *Journal of British Studies,* 11 (1971), 113-125.

Index

Abingdon, 7th Earl of, 33, 36, 47, 162
Abinger, 5th Baron, 88, 93, 162
Agricultural depression, 25-29 passim; effects of, 32, 50, 58, 76, 118
Allotments, 67-71
Amherst, 4th Earl, 5n, 162
Ampthill, 2nd Baron, 7, 70, 91, 106, 140, 162; and tariff reform, 73, 121; and military service, 101-102; and House of Lords reform, 128, 129; and Home Rule, 150, 153, 155
Anderson, Robert, 75
Armed services, 8-9, 82, 85-91, 93-103
Ashtown, 3rd Baron, 10, 49, 118, 162
Atkinson, Baron, 7n, 10, 116, 162

"Backwoodsmen," 2-3, 55
Bagot, 4th Baron, 36, 162
Balfour, Arthur J., 78, 99, 103-105, 118, 156; tariff reform and, 119, 123-124; budget of, 126; hostility to, 132-139; and Halsbury Club, 144-148
Barrington, 9th Viscount, 162
Bateman, John, 26
Bathurst, Countess, 60, 121, 134
Bathurst, 6th Earl, 69-70
Bathurst, 7th Earl, 23, 36, 72, 94, 98, 102-103, 140, 155, 162; investments of, 34, 42-43; in local government, 70, 75; and defense spending, 90; and tariff reform, 107, 121, 132; and House of Lords reform, 128, 130; and Irish crisis, 154
Bedford, 11th Duke of, 9, 60, 101, 162; investments of, 34-35, 42, 47-49; author of *A Great Agricultural Estate*, 44; in local government, 70-74; and Arnold White, 92, 109; and naval affairs, 92-93; and Haldane reforms, 93-96, 98-99; and tariff reform, 107, 121; and House of Lords reform, 128, 131; and Home Rule, 151
Belloc, Hilaire, 13, 38, 50

Bills: Amending (1914), 154; Divorce Amendment, 114; Education (1906), 115; Irish Land (1909), 115-116; Marriage with a Deceased Wife's Sister (1907), 114-115; National Service (Training and Home Defence), 101, 115; Reconstitution of the Lords, 7, 130; Reference to the People (1911), 131; Territorial and Reserve Forces, 93. *See also* Home Rule; Parliament Bill
Birth dates of peers, 84
Boer War, 88-89, 103-106
Bonar Law, Andrew, 99, 118, 148, 152
Brabourne, 3rd Baron, 5n, 88, 163
Bristol, 3rd Marquess of, 54
Bristol, 4th Marquess of, 29, 36-37, 54-55, 78, 92, 163
British Empire, fears for, 82, 89, 92, 103-108
British League for the Support of Ulster, 151-152
Budget (1909), 3n, 120-127. *See also* Tariff reform
Business interests of peers, 32-43 passim, 51, 55, 56, 125
Bute, 4th Marquess of, 32-33, 35, 74, 163

Cabinet, criticism of, 127, 130
Cathcart, 4th Earl, 52-53, 163
Cecil, Lord Hugh, 120, 132, 138
Cecil, Lord Robert, 120, 146, 150-152 passim
Chamberlain, Austen, 121, 144, 147-148
Chamberlain, Joseph, 78, 148; and tariff reform, 106, 118-122; and Parliament Bill, 137-138
"Chinese slavery," 106
Churchill, 1st Viscount, 8, 11, 39, 47, 163
Clanricarde, 2nd Marquess of, 10, 43, 49, 50, 163
Clanwilliam, 5th Earl, 163

Clarendon, 5th Earl of, 7n, 63, 72-73, 163
Clifford of Chudleigh, 9th Baron, 11, 16, 36, 64-66, 87, 115, 155, 163
Clonbrock, 4th Baron, 7n, 10, 43, 49, 117, 163
Coal Industry Commission (1919), 33, 74
Colchester, 3rd Baron, 8, 131, 164
Coleridge, 2nd Baron, 66
Combermere, 4th Viscount, 164
Commons, House of, 78, 92; members of, 9, 76; opposition to, 129, 131
Conservative party, *see* Unionist party
Conservatives, policies of, 66, 72, 89-90, 108, 142, 156-157
Cornwall, 28
Cornwallis-West, George, 85
Councils (county, district, parish), 57, 61-62, 66-76 passim
County society, 21-22, 67, 88, 94, 97-98. *See also* Councils; Fox-hunting; Landed aristocracy; Society
Coventry, 9th Earl of, 7n, 29, 120, 164
Cranborne, Lord, *see* Salisbury, 4th Marquess of
Crawford and Balcarres, 26th Earl of, 33-34, 164
Creation dates of peers, 21
Croft, Henry Page, 79, 133
Crouch, James, 70, 73
Curtis, Lionel, 105

Death duties, 42, 45-48, 80, 124
DeFreyne, 4th Baron, 9, 49, 88-89, 164
Democracy, diehard views of, 108, 113, 129-130
Denbigh, 9th Earl of, 8, 16, 69, 77, 80, 83, 87, 89, 91; and tariff reform, 164
Deramore, 3rd Baron, 49, 164
Derbyshire, 60
Devon, 14th Earl of, 43, 49, 53, 64, 164
Devonshire, 28, 66
Dicey, A. V., 153
Diehards: definition of, 1, 2-3, 55; political activities of, 7-9; agricultural income of, 28-30, 32; economic status of, 43; education of, 83-86; and Liberal defense policy, 89-90; and physical fitness, 108; attitudes of, toward political change, 111-113; as a political faction, 114; and Unionist leadership, 130,

132-134, 148; organization of, 142-147, 155-156; and Home Rule, 149-155
Dymond, Robert, 64
Dynevor, 7th Baron, 5, 9, 45, 92, 162; properties of, 11, 32, 42

Ebury, 2nd Baron, 34, 35, 83, 122-123, 140, 155, 165
Elgar, Sir Edward, 153
Erne, 4th Earl of, 7n, 9, 10, 49, 116, 117, 165
Erroll, 20th Earl of, 86-87, 96, 98, 101, 165
Essex, lands in, 31, 41
Estates, size of, 26-27. *See also* Landed aristocracy
Eton College, 15, 84-85
Eugenics, 82, 109

Falkland, 12th Viscount, 36, 165
Farnham, 11th Baron, 5n, 10, 150, 165
Farrer, A. R., 53-54
Fingall, 11th Earl of, 7n, 10, 37, 140, 165; properties of, 41, 44, 49, 52-53
Fitzwilliam, 7th Earl, 11, 77-78, 89, 91; properties of, 33, 35, 48, 50
Forester, 5th Baron, 166
Forrest, Robert, 74
"Fourth Party," 156
Fox-hunting, 22-23
Franchise reform, 112
Free-traders, 79, 118-120, 123

Garrioch, J. T., 75
Germany, fear of, 87, 89, 92-93, 100-101, 104, 107, 118, 152
Gladstone, W. E., 77, 113
Glamorganshire, 33, 65, 74
Gloucestershire, 69-70, 75
Goodenough, Rev. L., 75
Gormanston, 15th Viscount, 49, 165
Great War, casualties in, 88-89
Gwynne, H. A., 134, 148

Haldane, R. B., army reforms of, 93-99
Halifax, 2nd Viscount, 8, 16, 51, 53, 121, 166; supports Milner, 106; and religious issues, 111, 112, 114-115; and referendum, 131
Hall, Charles, 70, 72, 74

Halsbury, 1st Earl of, 7, 106, 120, 123, 128, 153, 166; and budget, 125, 127; and Parliament Bill, 136, 139
Halsbury Club, 145-148
Hardwicke, 8th Earl of, 5n, 40, 166
Harlech, 3rd Baron, 47, 48, 49, 166
Hervey, F. W. F., *see* Bristol, 4th Marquess of
Hervey, Lord Francis, 78
Holmpatrick, 2nd Baron, 166
Home Rule: diehards' opposition to, 9-10, 49, 137, 142; 1886 bill for, 62, 67, 77, 112; resistance to bills for, 116, 138; crisis over, 149-155
Hood, 5th Viscount, 166
Hothfield, 1st Baron, 166
Hutton, William, 75

Income, sources of, 32, 39, 41-44. *See also* Business interests of peers; Landed aristocracy; Mineral properties; South Africa
Ireland, 28-29, 152; diehard properties in, 8-10, 35-36, 43, 48-49, 117-118; local government of, 75-76; Unionist leadership in, 115-118. *See also* Home Rule; Land: purchase acts
Irish nationalists, 10, 75-76, 138

Jebb, Richard, 134
Jenkins, Roy, 134
Justices of the peace, *see* Magistrates

Kensington, 6th Baron, 34, 166
Kesteven, 2nd Baron, 88, 167
Kilmaine, 5th Baron, 5n, 43, 49, 167
"Kindergarten," Milner's, 104-106
Kinnoul, 13th Earl of, 87, 167
Kipling, Rudyard, 153

Lambert, Lionel F., 74
Lancashire, 34, 79
Land: purchase acts (Ireland), 41, 43, 48, 117-118; sales of, 44-50, 53; agents for, in local government, 73-76. *See also* Budget (1909); Wyndham Act
Landed aristocracy, 22, 25, 38; estates of, 26-27, 28-29, 44-50 passim, 52-53; and local government, 57ff, 66-67; and tariff reform, 119
Landsdowne, 5th Marquess of, 1, 23,

133, 139, 150; hostility to, 103, 104, 124, 126, 130, 132, 137; diehard support for, 114-116, 136, 145
Lauderdale, 13th Earl of, 167
Leconfield, 3rd Baron, 11, 122, 150, 155, 167; properties of, 29, 34, 42, 49
Leeds, 10th Duke of, 33, 69, 167
LeFanu, Victor, 75
Leith of Fyvie, 1st Baron, 36, 40, 139, 167
Leitrim, 5th Earl of, 10, 36, 40, 52, 167
Liberal government: diehard opposition to, 24, 48, 55, 110, 114, 116, 123, 139, 142; and landed aristocracy, 34, 98; imperial and defense policies of, 82, 89-93, 101, 103, 105, 106; and *Morning Post*, 132
Liberal party, 1, 123; and local councils, 72
Liberal Unionists, 11, 117, 119
Limerick, 3rd Earl of, 77
Limerick, 4th Earl of, 36, 49, 167
Llandaff of Hereford, Viscount, 7, 167
Lloyd George, David, 1, 124-125
Local government, diehards in, 58, 60-61, 63, 66-69.
Local Government Acts (1888, 1894), 66-67
Londesborough, 2nd Earl of, 11, 47, 51, 167
London, properties in, 34-35, 47
Long, Walter, 125, 148
Lords, House of: Unionist majority in, 1; reform of, 3, 128-132, 145; attendance at, 3-5; committees of, 5-6; members of, 6, 26, 28, 36-37, 39, 55, 58, 60, 85, 86, 87; and Local Government Acts, 66-67; and Haldane reforms, 93; and Milner, 106; voting patterns in, 114-116; veto power of, 124, 133, 135-137, 140, 142
Loudoun, 11th Earl of, 34, 167
Lovat, 14th Baron, 9, 51, 75, 106, 139, 145, 168; and Haldane's proposals, 94-95, 99; and Roberts' proposals, 101; and Parliament Bill, 139, 143
Lovelace, 3rd Earl of, 168

Magistrates, 57, 60-68 passim, 74-76
Mallock, W. H., 38
Malmesbury, 5th Earl of, 47, 91, 148,

168; *New Order* by, 90, 113, 133
Mar, 33rd Earl of, 168
Market rights, 32-35
Marlborough, 9th Duke of, 7n, 8, 36,
    47, 106, 145, 168; and tariff reform,
    122; and Parliament Bill, 137
Marriage patterns, 32, 36-37
Massy, 6th Baron, 49, 168
Maxse, Ivor, 123
Maxse, L. J., 73, 99, 102, 122, 146
Mayo, 7th Earl of, 139
Meath, Countess of, 16-17, 37
Meath, 12th Earl of, 7n, 10, 16, 30, 75,
    91, 93, 168; properties of, 35-36, 49;
    public service of, 69, 88; policies of,
    102, 108-109, 113, 131, 137
Merthyr, 1st Baron, 5n, 40, 168
Military service, *see* Armed services; Mi-
    litia; Navy; Territorial Force Associa-
    tions; Volunteers
Militia, 9, 85, 87-88, 93-99
Milner, Viscount, 7, 45, 121, 123, 155,
    169; and national policy, 101, 103-
    105, 112, 155; support for, 106; and
    tariff reform, 126, 144-145; and Home
    Rule, 152-153. *See also* "Kindergar-
    ten"
Mineral properties, 32-34
Money, Sir Leo Chiozza, 33
Monkswell, Lady, 16, 116
Monkswell, 3rd Baron, 5n, 169
Morley, 3rd Earl of, 52, 65
Morley, 4th Earl of, 169
Morning Post, 107, 132-134. *See also*
    Bathhurst, Countess; Bathurst, 7th
    Earl; Gwynne, H. A.; Ware, Fabian
Mortgages, 50, 54
Mowbray, Segrave, and Stourton, 24th
    Baron, 29, 33, 138, 169
Muskerry, 4th Baron, 7, 49, 93, 117, 121,
    169
Mutiny Act, 153
Mynors, Walter, 74-75

National defense, 83, 90, 107
National efficiency, 12, 103-104, 112
National party, 155-156
National Review, 7, 83, 99, 138, 146, 156
National Service League, 8, 82, 93, 109,
    111, 115; diehard role in, 99-103, 141

National Union of Conservative and Con-
    stitutional Associations, 11, 144, 146
Navy, 8-9, 40, 82, 86, 91-92, 101, 107
Nevill, Lady Dorothy, 20
Newcastle, 7th Duke of, 16, 34, 35, 51,
    121, 169
Nineteenth Century, 6-7
Nobility, new, 40
Norfolk, 15th Duke of, 7-8, 10, 11, 101,
    127, 169; properties of, 33, 34, 35; and
    militia reform, 95, 97, 99; diehards
    seek support of, 140; and Home Rule,
    154
Northcote, Baron, 7-8, 11, 36, 126, 135,
    169
Northcote, Lady, 136
Northesk, 10th Earl of, 43, 155, 170
Northumberland, 7th Duke of, 7n, 10-
    11, 15, 45, 143, 170; properties of, 33,
    35; and military service, 97, 101-102;
    and socialism, 112-123, 124; and de-
    mocracy, 129-130, 138; and Halsbury
    Club, 145, 146; and Home Rule, 154

Parliament: elections to, 66, 74, 76-81,
    127, 149; diehard members of, 76
Parliament Bill (Act), 1, 2, 23-24, 46-47,
    55, 58, 64, 81-83, 93, 102-103; crisis
    over, 111, 112, 114-115; division on,
    132; resistance to, 134-142 passim
Party system, 127, 129-130
Peers' Campaign, 127
Pensions, 50, 77
"People's Budget," *see* Budget (1909)
Percy, Earl, *see* Northumberland, 7th
    Duke of
Philanthropies, 58-60
Plymouth, 1st Earl of, 7, 8, 10-11, 59,
    145, 148, 170; investments of, 32, 35,
    42; and local government, 65, 74; and
    Parliament Bill, 136
Portsmouth, 6th Earl of, 8, 36, 43, 93,
    106, 170; land sales of, 47, 49
Primrose League, 76
Privy Council, diehards in, 7
Protectionism, 118-124
Prothero, Rowland, 70, 74
Public schools, 15, 83, 85

Quarter sessions, *see* Magistrates

"Radical right," 112, 114, 157

Radnor, 6th Earl of, 35, 51, 170

Raglan, 3rd Baron, 7-8, 87, 94, 100, 130, 140, 170

Ralston, Andrew, 75

Ranfurly, 5th Earl of, 7n, 8, 10, 49, 91, 121, 170

Religion, 8, 16, 111, 112, 114. *See also* Roman Catholicism

Repington, Col. Charles à Court, 98

Reserve forces, 87-88, 93-99

"Return of Owners of Land," 26

Reveille Movement, 133

Roberts, Earl, 7-8, 86, 88, 171; and military service, 90-91, 93, 94-95, 100-103, 115; supports Milner, 106; and Parliament Bill, 135-136; and Home Rule, 152

Roman Catholicism, 16, 115

Rosmead, 2nd Baron, 105, 106, 171

Rosslyn, 5th Earl of, 14, 26, 34, 43, 171

Rothes, 19th Earl of, 140, 171

Round Table, 105, 106

Russell, George W. E., 19, 21, 45

St. Levan, 2nd Baron, 3, 35, 47, 86-87, 89, 171

Salisbury, 3rd Marquess of, 42, 66, 67, 157

Salisbury, 4th Marquess of, 7, 11, 34-35, 69, 101, 105, 139, 146, 171; and local government, 62-64, 79-80; and protectionism, 120, 123; and House of Lords reform, 131-132

Saltoun, 18th Baron, 35, 43-44, 46, 53, 140, 153, 171

Sandys, 5th Baron, 39-40, 74, 171

Scarbrough, 10th Earl of, 10, 33, 35, 52, 59, 172

Scotland, lands in, 28, 32, 75-76

Second Chamber, 129, 137. *See also* Lords, House of; Upper Chamber

Selborne, 1st Earl of, 15, 67, 113

Selborne, 2nd Earl of, 7, 8-9, 11, 17, 20-21, 113, 121, 153, 172; on women's suffrage, 83; and navy, 91-93; and militia, 95, 97; high commissioner for South Africa, 105; and tariff reform, 107; and protectionism, 123; and House of Lords reform, 131-132, 137;

and Halsbury Club, 143-148 passim

Sempill, 18th Baron, 5n, 172

Shadow Cabinet, 139, 147

Shrewsbury, 20th Earl of, 16, 34, 39, 47, 52, 75, 172

Sinclair, 15th Baron, 172

Smith, Abel Henry, 80

Smith, F. E., 139

Social reform, 109, 138

Socialism, 90, 113, 118, 122

Society: "Season" of, 19, 86; new members of, 19-21, 38, 104. *See also* County society; Nobility

Somerset, 12th Duke of, 64

Somerset, 15th Duke of, 8, 41, 59, 106, 155, 172; and armed forces, 89-91; and tariff reform, 121; opposes House of Lords reform, 128-130

Sondes, 3rd Earl, 42-43, 46-47, 53, 172

South Africa, 89, 104-106. *See also* Boer War

South Wales, 28, 32, 35, 40

Southampton, 4th Baron, 34, 47, 172

Stanhope, 6th Earl, 51-52, 60, 76

Stanhope, 7th Earl, 16, 18, 29, 46, 69, 102, 135, 172; land sales of, 48-49; subscriptions of, 60; and Primrose League, 76; military service of, 85; and tariff reform, 121-122, 127; and Parliament Bill, 139; and Home Rule, 152-153

Stanmore, 1st Baron, 7, 66-67, 106, 112-113, 126, 138, 173

Steel-Maitland, Arthur, 147

Strathmore and Kinghorne, 14th Earl of, 75, 120, 173

Strutt, Edward, 31

Tariff reform, 79-80, 88, 103-108, 118-126, 132-134, 155

Taxation, 33, 67

Templetown, 4th Viscount, 10, 40, 49, 117, 173

Territorial Force Associations, 74, 87, 94, 96, 98-99

Third Reform Act, 57, 80, 112

Tollemache, 3rd Baron, 173

Tory party, 23, 123. *See also* Conservatives; Unionist party

Trollope, Anthony, 25, 32

Ulster, 49, 76, 149, 150
Ulster Unionists, 10, 116
Unionist party, 1, 10-11, 55, 62, 78, 139; diehards' opposition to policies of, 12, 24, 110-112, 114-120 passim, 122-124, 132-133, 135-136, 141, 156; peers among, 67, 117; and military reforms, 95, 101, 103-104; diehards and leadership of, 130-131, 146, 148-149, 156-157; policies of, 134, 140
Universal service, 99-100, 102. *See also* National Service League
Universities, 84-86
Upper Chamber, 128, 139
Urban land, 32, 34-35

Van Raalte, Charles, 79
Vanderbilt, Consuelo, 18, 36
"Vanoc" (A. White), 92
Vaux of Harrowden, 7th Baron, 173
Verney, Hon. Richard Greville, *see* Willoughby de Broke, 19th Baron
Vivian, 4th Baron, 173
Volunteers, 87-88, 93-94

Waldegrave, 9th Earl, 7n, 8, 173
Wales, 28, 75-76
Walford's County Families, 61
Ward, Mrs. Humphry, 57
Ware, Fabian, 107, 125, 132
Warre, Edmond, 84
Wells, Lionel, 78

Welsh disestablishment, 138, 142
Wentworth, B. C. V., 78
Westminster, 1st Duke of, 77
Westminster, 2nd Duke of, 11, 34-35, 47-48, 91, 107-108, 121, 139, 173
White, Arnold, 92, 96, 99, 104, 109
Wicklow, 7th Earl of, 173
Wicklow, 48-49, 75
Wilkinson, Spencer, 107
Willoughby de Broke, 18th Baron, 71-73, 75, 80
Willoughby de Broke, 19th Baron, 8-9, 13-14, 17-18, 22, 84, 91, 148, 155-157, 173; lands of, 47, 52-53; and local government, 69, 72-73, 75; elected M. P., 80-81; and Haldane reforms, 96; and national service, 100-102; on eugenics, 109; and tariff reform, 112, 126-128; and House of Lords reform, 131, 133; and Parliament Bill crisis, 135-136, 138-140; and Halsbury Club, 142-147; opposes Home Rule, 149-155
Winchester, 16th Marquess of, 11, 106, 174
Women's suffrage, 83, 109
Worcestershire, 29, 74
Wyndham Act (1903), 48-49, 117-118, 135, 140, 146-147
Wynford, 6th Baron, 174

Yeomanry, 87-88, 93-94
Yorkshire, 28-29, 33, 59, 77

Harvard Historical Studies

Out of Print Titles are Omitted

33. *Lewis George Vander Velde.* The Presbyterian Churches and the Federal Union, 1861-1869. 1932.
35. *Donald C. McKay.* The National Workshops: A Study in the French Revolution of 1848. 1933.
38. *Dwight Erwin Lee.* Great Britain and the Cyprus Convention Policy of 1878. 1934.
48. *J. H. Hexter.* The Reign of King Pym. 1941.
58. *Charles C. Gillispie.* Genesis and Geology: A Study in the Relations of Scientific Thought, Natural Theology, and Social Opinion in Great Britain, 1790-1850. 1951
60. *Robert G. L. Waite.* Vanguard of Nazism: The Free Corps Movement in Post-war Germany, 1918-1923. 1952.
62, 63. *John King Fairbank.* Trade and Diplomacy on the China Coast: The Opening of the Treaty Ports, 1842-1854. One-volume edition. 1953.
64. *Franklin L. Ford.* Robe and Sword: The Regrouping of the French Aristocracy after Louis XIV. 1953.
66. *Wallace Evan Davies.* Patriotism on Parade: The Story of Veterans' and Hereditary Organizations in America, 1783-1900. 1955.
67. *Harold Schwartz.* Samuel Gridley Howe: Social Reformer, 1801-1876. 1956.
69. *Stanley J. Stein.* Vassouras: A Brazilian Coffee Country, 1850-1900. 1957.
72. *John B. Blake.* Public Health in the Town of Boston, 1630-1822. 1959.
74. *Alexander Sedgwick.* The Ralliement in French Politics, 1890-1898. 1965.
75. *E. Ann Pottinger.* Napoleon III and the German Crisis, 1865-1866. 1966.
76. *Walter Goffart.* The Le Mans Forgeries: A Chapter from the History of Church Property in the Ninth Century. 1966.
77. *Daniel P. Resnick.* The White Terror and the Political Reaction after Waterloo, 1966.
78. *Giles Constable.* The Letters of Peter the Venerable. 1967.
79. *Lloyd E. Eastman.* Throne and Mandarins: China's Search for a Policy during the Sino-French Controversy, 1880-1885. 1967.
80. *Allen J. Matusow.* Farm Policies and Politics in the Truman Years. 1967.
81. *Philip Charles Farwell Bankwitz.* Maxime Weygand and Civil-Military Relations in Modern France. 1967.
82. *Donald J. Wilcox.* The Development of Florentine Humanist Historiography in the Fifteenth Century. 1969.
83. *John W. Padberg, S.J.* Colleges in Controversy: The Jesuit Schools in France from Revival to Suppression, 1813-1880. 1969.

84. *Marvin Arthur Breslow*. A Mirror of England: English Puritan Views of Foreign Nations, 1618-1640. 1970.

85. *Patrice L. R. Higonnet*. Pont-de-Montvert: Social Structure and Politics in a French Village, 1700-1914. 1971.

86. *Paul G. Halpern*. The Mediterranean Naval Situation, 1908-1914. 1971.

87. *Robert E. Ruigh*. The Parliament of 1624: Politics and Foreign Policy. 1971.

88. *Angeliki E. Laiou*. Constantinople and the Latins: The Foreign Policy of Andronicus, 1282-1328. 1972.

89. *Donald Nugent*. Ecumenism in the Age of the Reformation: The Colloquy of Poissy. 1974.

90. *Robert A. McCaughey*. Josiah Quincy, 1772-1864: The Last Federalist. 1974.

91. *Sherman Kent*. The Election of 1827 in France. 1975.

92. *A. N. Galpern*. The Religions of the People in Sixteenth-Century Champagne. 1976.

93. *Robert G. Keith*. Conquest and Agrarian Change: The Emergence of the Hacienda System on the Peruvian Coast. 1976.

94. *Keith Hitchins,* Orthodoxy and Nationality: Andreiu Şaguna and the Rumanians of Transylvania, 1846-1873. 1977.

95. *A. R. Disney*. Twilight of the Pepper Empire: Portuguese Trade in Southwest India in the Early Seventeenth Century. 1978.

96. *Gregory D. Phillips*. The Diehards: Aristocratic Society and Politics in Edwardian England. 1979.

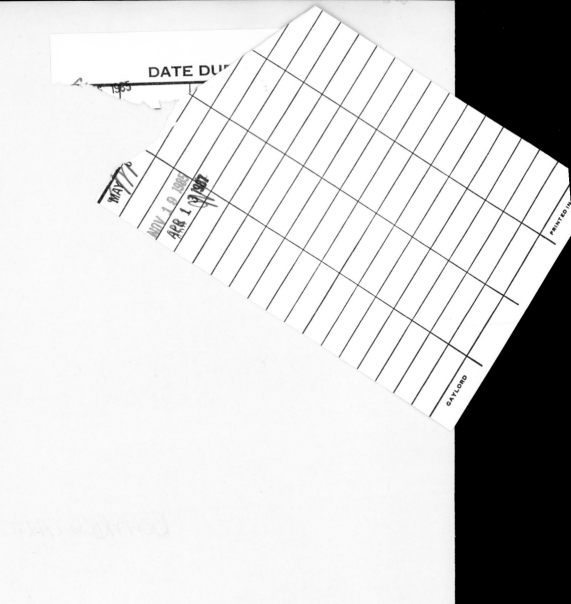